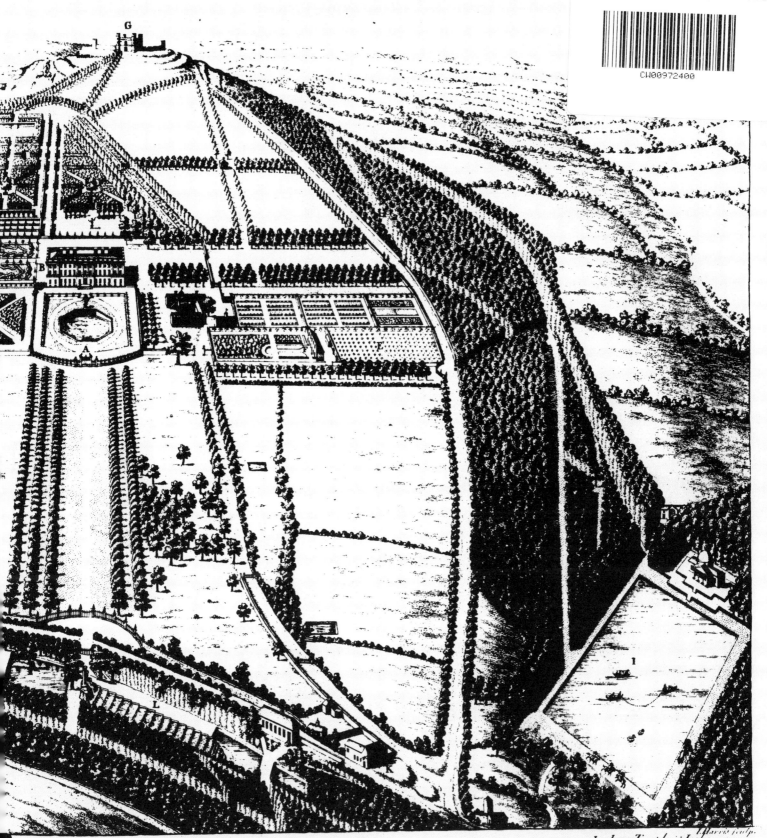

J. Harris Sculp.

WENTWORTH CASTLE, *in the County*
Honourable Thomas Earl of Strafford,
Woodhouse, and of Stainborough, Baron of
of the most Noble Order of the Garter.

I . *Law-Temple & Lake.*
K. *The Inn.*
L. *Menagerie house & Cascade.*
M. *Fish-ponds & stews.*
N. *Ivas-wood 50 Acres.*
O. *Bromroyd-wood 80 Acres.*
P. *Park.*
Q. *Rockly Lake.*

TOUT

May A Woods
29 Ranelagh Avenue
London SW6 3PJ.
0171 736 3210

Text and photographs by May Woods

VISIONS OF ARCADIA

European Gardens from Renaissance to Rococo

Aurum

For my mother,
Frances May Laird,
and in memory of my sister,
Jinty Blanckenhagen,
and for her husband Michael

First published in Great Britain 1996 by Aurum Press Ltd,
25 Bedford Avenue, London WC1B 3AT

A catalogue record for this book is available from the British Library.

ISBN 1 85410 429 2

10 9 8 7 6 5 4 3 2 1
1999   1998   1997   1996

Designed by Derek Birdsall RDI

Printed and bound in Singapore by CS Graphics

Contents

Foreword

I first visited the Villa d'Este 30 years ago, to be entranced, as travellers have been since the 16th century, by the drama of its cascades and fountains. Reading *Visions of Arcadia* has reawakened inspiring memories and made me long to return to this garden, and to many others: Isola Bella, the Villa Lante, Fontainebleau. Some of the gardens described here I have not seen, but with the help of the author's expressive prose and the lavish illustrations I can visualise them clearly.

What comes across most vividly is the passion, the flair, the intelligence and the wit that went into the creation of these early surviving gardens. The span of May Woods' book is 350 years – a long time in gardening – and it is fascinating to discover how one style yielded to the next, and how the major European countries shaped these styles to suit their differing natural circumstances and national characteristics.

Do these grand landscaped gardens hold any message for gardeners today, other than to command our admiration? I think they do, for in their ingenuity in making a vision fit the reality of the site, their passion for craftsmanship, their forging of an alliance between house and garden, architecture and nature, their delight in the unexpected *jeu d'esprit*, their use of light and shade and water, these landscape gardeners and their patrons are saying something universal to gardeners today, no matter how small their plot or restricted their budget. And new gardens like the late Gervase Jackson-Stops' in Northamptonshire show that, as May Woods writes, *Each age has its own Arcadia.*

One of the cardinal principles behind the creation of these great gardens was expressed by the first truly Arcadian designer, Leon Battista Alberti, in 1452: *Let all things smile and seem to welcome the arrival of your Guests.* It is a precept that gardeners and garden designers should ever bear in mind.

Rosemary Verey

Acknowledgements

This book was first suggested by Michael Alcock, at that time managing director of Aurum Press, soon after the publication of *Glass Houses* in 1988, and the contract was signed in February 1990.

Condensing the history of gardens over five and a half centuries into a single affordable and portable volume proved an impossible task, so it has been cut into two parts, this first book finishing with the last of the 18th-century formal gardens and the final throes of Rococo. It also covers only Western Europe because my husband wisely drew a line between Germany and Eastern Europe, knowing that the project would never be finished if Poland, Czechoslovakia, the Austro-Hungarian Empire and Russia were to be included. Thank goodness for his realism!

In weary moments, though, when the list of books to read and gardens to visit kept increasing instead of diminishing, it seemed that only a fool would have attempted to integrate such a vast range of material. But it seemed even more foolish to give up, especially when provocative, thoughtful opinions of bygone tourists breathed life into old engravings, and the gardens themselves revealed the subtlety of the design.

Accuracy has been a major goal, even if, as no doubt, it is not always achieved. Without *The Oxford Companion to Gardens* by Jellicoe, Goode and Lancaster, the search for truth would have been even longer, but even though many efforts have been made to find the most accurate source of information, there are bound to be errors in the text. Any corrections, therefore, will be gratefully received.

The garden history fraternity, as generous with information as gardeners are with roots and cuttings, has been an invaluable source of encouragement and enlightenment. Rosemary Verey's offer at an early stage to write a foreword was a welcome boost to confidence, and helped to concentrate my mind.

Several experts on foreign gardens have kindly read my text. I am particularly grateful, for their comments on sections of the book, to Angela Delaforce on Portugal, to Ana Luengro on Spain, and to the late Harry Jorissen and to Wim Meulenkamp on the Netherlands.

Concerning France, much useful information has come from Monsieur Claude Baudet, Monsieur Olivier Choppin de Janvry, Madame Lilibeth Dewavrin, Monsieur Jean Feray, Dr Giroux, Madame Amélie Lefébure, Madame Mary Mallet, Monsieur and

Madame Robert Poujois, and Madame Charles de Yturbe. The staff in the library of the Société Nationale d'Horticulture de France were also very helpful.

Queries on Portuguese gardens have been generously answered by Patrick Bowe, the late John Delaforce, Gerald Luckhurst and Clare Pinsent, and those on Spanish gardens by Carmen Anon and Consuelo Martinez Correcher. The Contessa Cigogna Mozzoni, Signora Jean Salvadore, Dott. Luigi Sartori, Dott. Giovanni Bettini and the Viscount Lambton were welcoming or informative about Italy, while Dr Ing. Modrow, Prinz Franz zu Sayn Wittgenstein, Dr Schmid, Erika Vogt and Dr and Mrs Peter Zier shed light on gardens in Germany. Baron Gösta Adelswärd kindly shared his expertise on Swedish gardens.

In Britain, I am indebted in varying degrees to a host of experts and owners, including Jane Anderson, Viscount Cobham, Mavis Collier, Fiona Cowell, Caroline Dalton, Sir Francis Dashwood, Lord Dickinson, Brian Dix, Althea Dundas-Bekker, Edward Fawcett, Daphne Ford, the Duchess of Hamilton, R.H. Harcourt Williams, John Harris, Dr Dorothy Johnston, Lord Ralph Kerr, Nicholas Mander, Pamela Marshall, Col. D.G. McCord, Christine McGeoch, Nancy McLaren, Charles Quest-Ritson, Dr M.S. Spurr, Dr Simon Thurley, Martin Tyson, Peter Vasey, David Walker, Basil Williams, Kamal Surya of The Print Room and to many staff of the National Trust.

The research would have been impossible without the resources of the British Library, the London Library, and the RIBA library, whose staff have all been unfailingly helpful. In particular, Chrissie Ronalds and her colleagues in British Library Reproductions have handled my complicated photographic orders with much good humour.

This book has been a long time a-writing. This is partly, it must be said, due to the irresistible distractions of family, friends, gardening and the like. Jack Osbourn's scepticism about its completion was a blessing in poetic disguise. Sheila Murphy of Aurum Press has been remarkably tolerant about missed deadlines, and I am extremely grateful for her patience and encouragement, and for the meticulous care she has taken with detail.

I am also indebted to Sheila for asking Derek Birdsall to design the book, for Derek's unrivalled skill in selecting and arranging illustrations adds greatly to the text, as well as producing a handsome volume. Working with Derek and his wife Shirley was the fun part of *Glass Houses*, as it has been of this book.

Friends and family have played a vital support role, and their regular 'how's the book?' question, however perfunctory on their part, has been more cheering than perhaps they suspected. Some have helped considerably, including Ellen Warner, who took my photograph, and Mary Murphy, both in New York. Renate Baillieu has been an indispensable consultant on the German language, and Maria La Roche has answered frequent, urgent faxes about the Italian language. Renate, Maria, Judy Chetwood and Mary Wilson, were all excellent travelling companions on European trips, as were my mother-in-law, Aileen Dodds-Parker, my husband and my sisters, Ruth Wither and Jinty Blanckenhagen. Jinty, who died of cancer in 1992, shared my delight in gardens and in the characters involved, and collected snippets of fact and cuttings and books for me. My cousin, John McKinlay, read Chapter 4 in its early, muddled state, and his perceptive remarks made me reorganise the text. My mother gave me endless encouragement and a new word processor, and made the most astute of comments on the title of the book and the section on Versailles. My father-in-law, Douglas Dodds-Parker, is the most loyal of supporters.

To one and all, I express my heartfelt thanks.

But my greatest thanks go to my kind, tolerant, immediate family, who have groaned but quietly as we have run round yet another garden, and survived the frustrations of getting lost, from the byways of Scotland to the back streets of Florence. I am forever indebted to James, for making me laugh; to Hattie, for advice on art history; to Simon, for research into Arcadia; and to Gil, my husband, not only for cooking dinner and watering the conservatory in moments of crisis, but, more significantly, for reading every word and making many wise suggestions. On my own, it would have been impossible.

May A. Woods
March 1996

Introduction

The word Arcadia conjures up a vision of an idyllic place suffused with beauty and tranquillity, poetry and music. It is a heaven on earth, visually and intellectually perfect, with comfort enough to dispel the irritations of everyday living. It is nature's Utopia, irresistibly attractive, impossible to capture in total, yet inspiring infinite attempts at recreation.

What was the source of this enchanting vision? It came from an area still known as Arcadia, a plateau in the centre of the Peloponnese in Greece. It is surrounded by mountains crossed only with difficulty; in spring, the rivers flow and the vegetation is lush, but in summer the earth bakes hard and dry and the rivers dwindle to a trickle, only to turn into rushing torrents when the winter rains return. It is a challenging environment, not a perfect pastoral landscape in which life is easy. The early inhabitants of this bleak isolated setting are said to have led a simple life enriched by piety and kindness.

Writing in *Eclogues* in the 1st century BC, Virgil turned their way of life into an idyllic existence, where youthful Arcadian shepherds were both poets and musicians, and roamed through an exquisite pastoral landscape. This was the vision that inspired Renaissance scholars, and which they attempted to create in their gardens.

In *Eclogue* X, one of Virgil's characters, a romantic musician, addresses the inhabitants thus: *Arcadians, you will be singing the tale of my love to your mountains, whatever befall. You are masters of music, you Arcadians. How tranquil my bones would rest, if over them your reed-pipes were making my love immortal.*[1] A few lines later, there are references to soft meads, cool streams and woodlands. The only threat to this paradise came occasionally from Pan, the wild god of Arcadia, who made his own music and pursued his earthy passions.

This was the vision that Renaissance scholars chose to emphasise, and which, mistakenly, they thought was an accurate portrayal of the real Arcadia. They saw in Virgil's sunlit Arcadia man and nature in harmony, a harmony that brought harvests from the land, with time to spare for both contemplation and entertainment, while the mischievous Pan played his pipes in the shadows. The concept was profoundly appealing.

In the early days of the Renaissance, this vision inspired the great architect Leon Battista Alberti to formulate the setting in which man could live this ideal life, the perfect combination of house and garden in a benign, productive and tranquil landscape. In this composition, the garden was as important as the house, in a climate in which, for half the year, much time was spent out of doors. It was a place of escape from the cares of the world. Following the Roman perception that beauty lay in formality, Alberti's ideal garden was laid out in precise geometric patterns with carefully calculated angles, and, whenever possible, in perfect symmetry. Trees were planted to provide essential shade and pools of water added for refreshment.

As tastes changed, Alberti's principles of design were copied and expanded, and his concept was distorted with Mannerist sophistication or loaded with Baroque extravagance. Yet shade and water remained integral elements, and despite their embellishments, a geometric groundplan underpinned all these gardens until, later, the whimsical element of Rococo design introduced a measure of asymmetry. In the age of Rococo, the concept of Arcadian shepherds inspired a new generation of artists and sculptors, and peopled gardens with statues of winsome figures harkening back to Theocritus and Virgil.

Then in England, in the early 18th century, the concept of a garden created out of the landscape was born. Straight lines were banished, as gardens and parks were remodelled into natural contours enhanced with trees and features to catch the eye. Scholars, forever searching the classical writers for sources to consolidate the latest taste, rediscovered Virgil's *Arcadia*, and imagined it as the English countryside tamed into a garden, enlivened by lakes and islands, twisting streams, bridges, Greek temples, obelisks and majestic trees. This, too, bore little resemblance to the true Arcadia; it was yet another version of the idea, far cooler and greener than Virgil's concept, and with important architectural additions.

All these gardens, from the early Renaissance gardens of Alberti to the landscaped gardens of the 18th century, share the common aim of providing the setting for the ideal life, in which beauty is allied with tranquillity to encourage contemplation and enjoyment. In this sense, they are all Arcadian. Each age generates new ideals of beauty and perfection, in art, architecture, interior design, and in gardens too. Each age has its own Arcadia.

Arcadia is a grand term befitting great gardens. Of course, the smaller gardens imitated the greater examples, but the former are generally hidden from us by lack of evidence. This book focuses on the great gardens, for these were praised, described and illustrated in their own time, and some have survived through the centuries until today. Those examined here are but a fragment of the whole, but they are the gardens where change is first detected, those which achieved the ideal of perfection in their day, or which had the greatest influence.

Gardens are a sensitive barometer of economic activity, for in times of hardship there are no resources for new creations, and sums available for maintenance are reduced. Just as they reflect the financial climate, so too are they an expression of the artistic and social pursuits of their times. They can never be seen in isolation for they are as much a part of the cultural fabric as interior decoration or music. Their history covers the relationship between architecture and design applied to topography, with the addition of trees, shrubs and flowers.

This book concentrates, however, on architecture and design, not on cultivation. Over the centuries, trees and plants have become an increasingly important element in garden design, and for much of the last two centuries they have become its focus. But in Renaissance times, and later, although the height, shape and colour of plants were components of the plan, nature was subservient to design.

A constant theme of this book is that gardens have always been created for people, for the individual who seeks comfort in nature, for the owner who longs to impress, and for the merry band that loves to dine in style under the stars. Gardens were made primarily for pleasure, so a study of them must include accounts of those who enjoyed them.

Another theme is the way new ideas were spread from one country to another by professional designers, by books, by engravings and by the accounts – both verbal and written – of travellers. New ideas were sometimes carried from one country to another with surprising speed, while, at other times, they sometimes failed to travel at all.

Descriptions of gardens are a vital source of information, and are usually reliable. Travel journals and guidebooks bring old gardens back to life with their impressions and opinions as well as detailed observations. Drawings, paintings and engravings are invaluable, although sometimes less dependable than the written word, since a

little artistic licence may have been taken to improve the picture. Or, artists may draw a completed building or garden plan, when in reality the project was never finished. The motives for this innocent deception may be justifiable, but the result is often inconsistencies that may be pitfalls for historians. Plans, maps and account books, however, add to the picture, and archaeology, too, can also fill important gaps in understanding.

In academic terms, garden history is a young subject. Plentiful are the writings, engravings, sketches and plans that have been studied, but there are countless more in European archives whose analysis could consolidate or question some details of conventional wisdom. There is still much to discover.

Some aspects of garden history are confusing; terminology, for instance – names, like concepts of beauty, have changed throughout the ages. There is a name for every garden building, describing its significance or its function, or giving it a pretence to a function, but each building may come in a variety of forms. The banqueting house changes its appearance with developments in architectural styles; the garden hermitage may be made from dressed stone or rough branches or may be hewn from rocks; in Roman times an exedra was an open structure with seating; in the High Renaissance, it was a gigantic architectural niche; in early 18th-century Italy, the term described an elegant Baroque pavilion or, in England, a semicircle of statues backed by a yew hedge.

The history of gardens tells of many creations, ordered and tranquil, vast and spectacular, intimate and whimsical, but it also emphasises both that constant maintenance is essential and that changing tastes have brought much destruction. As the eminent garden historian Edward Fawcett has said, *Gardens are a form of art, and great gardens are great art; of all forms of art, gardens are the most fragile.* In the current climate of enthusiasm for heritage protection, these most fragile forms of art are, at last, attracting some funds for restoration. May this enthusiasm continue, for the challenge is immense.

I *The Renaissance: 1450–1600*

Medieval Gardens

It was the morning of the sixth of May,
And May had painted with her soft showers
A garden full of leaves and flowers.
And man's hand had arrayed it with such craft
There never was a garden of such price
But if it were the very Paradise.

Chaucer (1340–1400) 'The Franklin's Tale', *The Canterbury Tales*

A view of a medieval garden from a manuscript
of Renaud de Montaubon, Bruges, 1462–70.
(Ms. 5072.) The scene shows several features
typical of the time, including a gothic fountain
on one side, a tiered tree also known as an estrade,
a turfed seat and an enclosing fence.

To look back at gardens of five centuries ago, as depicted in medieval manuscripts, is to enter the world of chivalry. The brilliant costume and flowers, the slender ladies and elegant young men, the dogs and falcons, the feasts, the flowers and trees, all contribute to an idyllic picture of medieval life. People converse, read, play chess, make music, keep trysts, and look after the garden. If illustrations of life in medieval gardens are to be relied on as social history, they must also be regarded as records of garden history. There is certainly enough consistency in old manuscript illustrations to draw some firm conclusions about late medieval gardens.

The gardens of medieval Europe were small in size, adjoined the house, villa or castle, and were usually surrounded by a high wall for shelter and defence. Some of their features had a symbolic significance, or iconography, beyond that of their physical presence, a significance just as relevant to the medieval mind as their physical appearance. Perimeter walls and fences not only kept out animals, but symbolised protection from a harsh world. Flowers were associated with saints or virtues – lilies, for instance, symbolised purity.

Water in the garden was vital, for not only was it aesthetic and soothing, it was also a symbol of life, or an allegory of the Virgin Mary's endless love. A fountain was, therefore, one of the most important garden features. Sometimes it was in the centre, an obvious parallel with the well in a cloister garden, but more often than not it was built at one side. At Hesdin, in northern France, the fountains were renowned for their sophistication; they had been enhanced by the addition of 'automata', the term given to figures of men and beasts designed to move mechanically. Still water also played an important role in most properties, protective as in a moat and functional as in a fish-pond, but it was usually located outside the garden.

Other features were less loaded with meaning or more practical, such as the pergola or carpentry tunnel. Usually these were arched to make covered walks, perhaps just a metre or two long in the middle of the garden, but frequently they edged the perimeter of the garden – again in imitation of monastic cloisters. They provided shade, important in gardens rarely planted with tall trees, as well as the means for supporting roses, honeysuckle and vines.

Many gardens had a fixed stone table, rectangular or hexagonal, used for meals or playing games. Topiary enjoyed some popularity, with trees neatly clipped into simple shapes, or trained in Burgundian fashion to form estrades, tiers of two or three discs of foliage, sometimes encircled by a metal ring to accentuate the form. These could vary between one and four metres high, and would be a dramatic feature. Flowery meads, where the grass is thick with wild and cultivated blooms, are often shown surrounding the fountains and clipped trees, and also as separate meadows beyond the private garden, fenced with palisades or wattle to keep out livestock.

A few illustrations show rare instances of garden buildings: loggias or a summer-house, roofed and open sided, or a free-standing pavilion with a roof supported by columns and gothic cresting along the ridge. Occasionally there were mounts, conical grassy mounds that relieved the flatness of the garden and allowed a view into the countryside beyond. They may have originated by turning the spoil from digging out a moat into a positive feature, or they may have been purpose built, their origins lying as far back as the Druidic times.

Fountains, summer-houses, pergolas, mounts and topiary are still built and clipped today, but a turf seat was a popular feature of medieval gardens that has since disappeared. Sited against a wall or free-standing, it was built of brick or wattle, filled in with soil and covered with grass. Sometimes it was circular, with a tree in the middle, but the preferred shape was that of a wide U, like a bench with two narrow projections at either end between which a table could be placed for refreshments. In a damp climate, a turf seat is obviously not ideal, yet it was the principal permanent place of repose in the medieval garden, and Flemish, French and English manuscripts all picture ladies resting on turfed seats, sometimes accompanied by a troubadour.

Apart from the private garden, the other important area of the medieval garden was the Hortus Conclusus or enclosed garden, an inner garden surrounded by a low fence. Again its origins are steeped in allegory, for it is associated with the purity of the Virgin Mary, its fruit symbolising the flowers of virtue.

Inside the fence, which also served the practical purpose of excluding rabbits, was a chequerboard of sparsely planted beds where crocus, daffodils, primroses, foxgloves, iris, lavender, lilies, roses and scabious, as well as herbs and the all-important medicinal plants were carefully tended. A Hortus Conclusus along these lines was incorporated into most gardens until at least the end of the 16th century, and occasionally appeared after that date.

This painting of a Hortus Conclusus is taken from the Grimani Breviary, 1485. Also known as a 'Mary' Garden, it had a significance beyond its horticultural components; the important features were all labelled with biblical references, and the gothic fountain was surmounted with a dove of peace.

If medieval gardens were limited in size and choice of plants, they were also limited in structure and design. Illustrations show areas of the garden where small squared flowerbeds were fixed in rigid lines, while other component parts were generally arranged at random, being more significant for their iconography than for their position. Rarely were the several parts integrated into an overall axial plan, with the result that the garden remained a separate entity, visually unrelated to its adjoining house, villa or castle. Only the Hortus Conclusus was arranged on a strict geometric plan within its own boundaries.

When in the 1400s the learned men of Italy started to study the literature, philosophy and architecture of ancient Greece and Rome, they discovered, amongst many other truths, the classical approach to garden design. They found that the ideal garden had been profoundly architectural, and that its designs therefore had to be the responsibility of the architect, who designed it while designing the house. They looked at their pleasant but haphazard gardens, and decided to copy the ancients in uniting house and garden in one whole composition. This unity of structural elements was the great Renaissance contribution to the art of garden design.

Against the backdrop of the late medieval Old Palace at Hatfield House, holly trees have been shaped into tiered estrades. The knot garden beside the Old Palace was laid out in the 1980s by Lady Salisbury in the spirit of Tudor design, and filled with plants available in the 15th, 16th and 17th centuries.

The Birth of the Renaissance

While medieval gardeners treasured their flowers, clipped the turf seats and swept the paths of the Hortus Conclusus, the Renaissance was slowly gathering momentum in 15th-century Italy. Anxious to understand the harmonies of ancient architecture and its decoration, draughtsmen studied the crumbling ruins of Rome and other relics of the Empire. There followed a glorious intellectual fusion of purpose and genius, a crescendo of creativity that still dazzles five centuries later.

This overpowering desire to promote the study of classical antiquity, known as humanism, spread gradually through the city-states of Florence, Rome and Venice, discharging them from the darkness of medieval days into the sunlight of new learning. Of the many advocates of humanism, one of the shining stars of the time was the architect Leon Battista Alberti. His observations of the remains of ancient Roman gardens, a synthesis of designs from Persia and Arabia as well as Greece and Rome, furnished him with practical ideas on geometry and proportion. He, amongst all the architects of the period, had the greatest influence on gardens.

A leading figure of the early Renaissance, painter, poet, philosopher and musician as well as architect, Alberti joined the recurring debate on the ideal life, the conflict between bustling activity in town and peaceful contemplation in the countryside, between *urbs* and *rus*. It was *rus* that appealed to Alberti, not just for its fresh air and birdsong, but for tranquillity and the ordered pattern

A view of Rome from I Vestigi dell' Antichita di Roma *by du Pérac, published in 1575. Amongst the many ruins that survived till the 16th century, the Temple of Antoninus and Faustina, on the left of this picture, is one of the more significant remains in the Roman Forum today. From Alberti onwards, architects searched through documents and ruins to identify the features of Roman buildings and gardens so that they could recreate them with authenticity.*

of villa life. A garden was a place in which family and friends could think, play music, relax and be happy, where they could live like the shepherds in Arcadia, the idealised pastoral world of the ancient Greeks.

In his *Eclogues*, Virgil had described the idyllic life and landscape of Arcadia. As a concept, it was gloriously romantic, even if unattainable. Alberti wanted to approach this vision of perfection by first setting the scene. His ideal country villa had a harmonious relationship with the garden and with nature; nothing jarred the senses, nothing spoilt the peace. And the very beauty and tranquillity of the place would then encourage thoughts of philosophy and poetry. What better place to talk of Plato, Aristotle and Virgil than in a pleasant, peaceful garden?

In 1452, Alberti wrote *De Re Aedificatoria*. Although not fully published until 1485, the book was to have a profound impact on garden design. He was inspired by an intimate knowledge of classical literature, and referred, among others, to the works of

A supposed reconstruction of ancient Rome from Antiquae Urbis Splendor, *published by Lauro in 1612–14. Amongst the buildings in this view still extant are the Arch of Septimus Severus and a fragment of the circular Temple of Vesta, 27 and 21 below.*

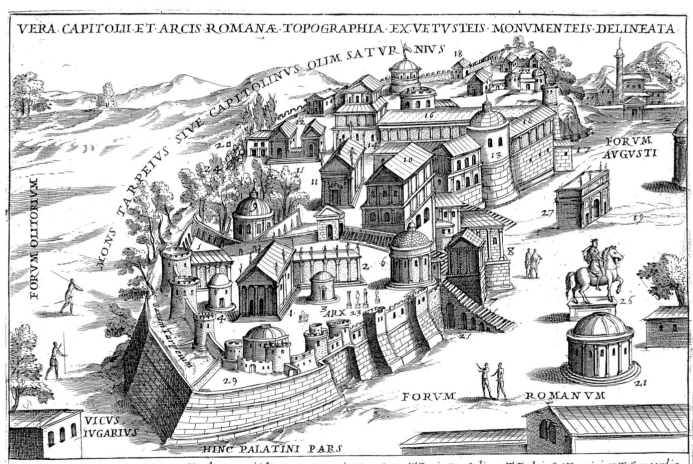

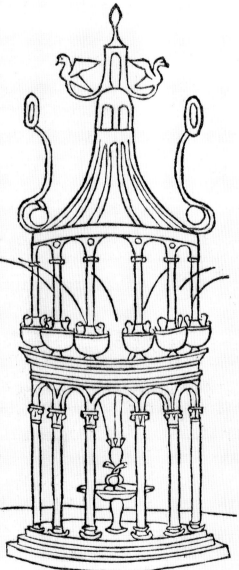

A fountain from Hypnerotomachia Poliphili *by Francesco Colonna, 1499. As is evident from the text surrounding the fountain, the text in* Visions of Arcadia *is set in monotype Poliphilus and is derived from this edition of* Hypnerotomachia Poliphili.

o dilla coæqua-
a dil periſtylio e
:ro una rotúda-
mente lacuna-
ſe attolleua uno
:.Sopra aſſideua
iptione hauea p
el meditullo dil
e di tre auree hy
namente trifarie
odulo ſtrictaṁ
:um il uentre in
a,cum repanda
e anguineamé-
trifaria diſpar-
:oncha odoriſſi
tiniuano erecte
iramento ouo-
:ato erano infi-
lequale tenuiſſi
a. Et p gli hiati
:ree colúne uſſi-
aṁte humectã-
iale ſpecula, era
itura lapidea,tuta era di diaſpro finiſſimo rubéte
ttatamente dinfinite macole ,di multiplice colo

Xenophon, Plato, Aristotle, Vitruvius, Virgil, Ovid, Columella and Pliny the Younger. And it was from his reading of these texts that many of Alberti's own ideas sprang.

In Book v, he wrote about the country gentleman and his country house: *We should build in the Middle of an open Champain* [gently undulating country], *under the Shelter of some Hill, where there is plenty of Water, and pleasant Prospects, and in the healthiest part of a healthy Country.*[1] The country gentleman should have the delights of gardens in order to pursue an active life: *Let there not be wanting open Places for Walking, Swimming, and other Diversions, Court-yards, Grass-plots and Porticoes* [loggias], *where the old men may chat together in the kindly Warmth of the sun in Winter, and where the Family may divert themselves and enjoy the Shade in Summer.*[2] In Book IX he proposed that the villa be on rising ground so that it looked outwards to the countryside: *Nor should there be any Want of pleasant Landskips, flowery Meads* [a medieval feature he wished to retain], *open Champains, shady Groves or limpid Brooks, or clear Streams and Lakes.*[3] The garden must be a cheerful place too, free from melancholy corners and dark shadows: *Let all things smile and seem to welcome the arrival of your Guests.*[4]

Alberti's garden was bonded to the villa by means of a ground-plan that echoed the ground-plan of the villa, with a central axis and a layout of straight lines, circles and semicircles. It did not include a Hortus Conclusus. Trees were to be planted in avenues, evenly spaced, and box was to be trimmed into elaborate shapes. He also proposed vine-clad pergolas for shady walks, and liked the grand way the ancients had made their pergolas with marble columns and Corinthian capitals.

Within this controlled plan, the garden should be enriched with rare plants and specimens for medicinal use. But Alberti also wished to amuse the ... *Grotto* ... of active leisure and the rural life, *rus in the* ... would be ... ne sophisticated additions. Sta ... place: *Nor am I displeased with* ... *provided they have nothing in them* ...

But Alberti's favourite feature was the grotto, built as a cool retreat and decorated with tufa stone after the manner of the ancients. Grottoes were clearly popular in mid-15th-century Italy, and Alberti described how a newly constructed grotto could be aged instantly by pouring green wax on the stone, imitating the mossy slime that develops over the years: *I was extremely pleased with an artificial Grotto which I have seen of this Sort, with a clear spring of Water falling from it; the Walls were composed of various Sorts of Sea-Shells, lying roughly together, some reversed, some with their Mouths outwards, their Colours being so artfully blended as to form a very beautiful variety.*[6]

Alberti was not the only architect who espoused the classical cause. Francesco di Giorgio Martini of Siena, the most celebrated architect in Italy in the 1480s and 1490s, also described the principles of garden design in *Trattato di architettura civile e militare*, written *c.* 1482. Not only did he advise a formal groundplan with straight paths crossed by others at right angles, but he filled it with fountains and watercourses, lawns and glades, seats and loggias, labyrinths and temples. He delighted in variety, and this may explain his inclusion of temples of classical design; in doing so, he was perhaps the first to use the aesthetic appeal of a temple in a garden setting.

Here is the first reference to temples, built not for religious reasons but purely to enhance the garden.

Both Alberti and Francesco di Giorgio Martini describe gardens that are inviting and full of interest, and contain features that seem very familiar today. The principles they defined held good with minor changes until the landscape movement overtook them in the 18th century, and have since been revived by more recent garden designers – Martini's formula might describe the gardens of Sir Edwin Lutyens and others throughout the 20th century. Alberti's enthusiasm for a harmonious relationship between villa, garden and nature is his vital contribution to garden design, and one that has lasted down the centuries.

Alberti is thought to have put some of his plans into practice at the Villa Quaracchi, a villa and garden built for Giovanni Rucellai, a rich Florentine merchant. In Rucellai's own description of his country retreat in 1459, the garden still retained some medieval features, such as a mount with spiral paths. Alberti's influence is seen in the siting of the villa on an eminence and the extension of the main axis over the immediate garden, across the road to Pistoia and continuing to the River Arno, marked by a line of trees. His delight in artifice can be found in the astonishing collection of topiary: men and women, popes and cardinals, galleys and temples, and mythical creatures.

There is no proof of Alberti's association with Villa Quaracchi, nor are there any illustrations of his ideal villa and garden in *De Re Aedificatoria*. However, in 1499 a book appeared showing signs of classical influence, and with illustrations relating to gardens. *Hypnerotomachia Poliphili*, attributed to Francesco Colonna, translates as *The Dream of Polyphilius*, and the aim of the author was to portray an exotic dream-land in which the hero, Polyphilo, searches for his love, Polia.

Hypnerotomachia Poliphili has about 160 woodcut illustrations, many of which are architectural, though there is an element of confusion about the proportions and rules of classical architecture in many of the buildings. Some portray extraordinary architectural hybrids; for example, a gigantic Egyptian pyramid has a pedimented porch flanked by Corinthian columns, at its peak an obelisk topped by a winged Mercury. Others show a freedom in adapting classical elements, such as columns and capitals, that was later restricted by the systematic analysis of 16th-century writers like Serlio, Vignola and Palladio. Yet other illustrations depict ruined classical cities, antique trophies, tablets of stone inscribed in Greek and in hieroglyphics together with elephants and lions and many strange beasts. Of the illustrations relating specifically to gardens, there are

Also from Colonna's book is this garden temple, a hybrid invention with classical columns and entablature below a bulbous ogee dome in the gothic tradition.

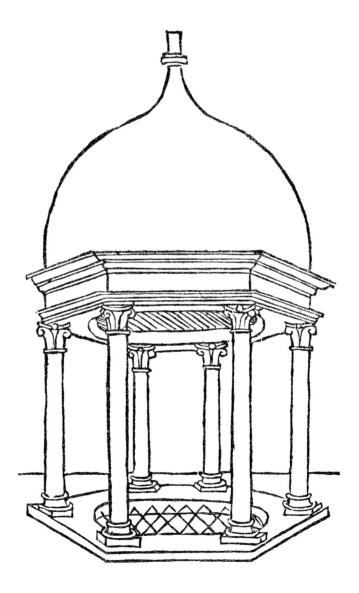

no images showing complete designs of villa and garden, but glimpses here and there of parts of gardens, as well as topiary and constructed features.

Signs of classicism are evident in some of the garden illustrations in *Hypnerotomachia Poliphili*. One has a fountain flowing from a curious structure with classical forms and motifs, while another is of a pergola or carpentry tunnel. Perhaps Alberti's praise of Roman pergolas was the impetus behind this design. Its proportions may be a little clumsy, but its significance lies not in its imperfect style but in the fact that it and many other illustrations in the book promoted the new taste for classical architecture.

With the advent of printing, books became the prime source for the dissemination of classical knowledge, in architecture as in all other spheres, and following demand for the text in a readable form *De Re Aedificario* was translated from Latin into Italian, and then into French in several editions from 1553, although it was not translated into English until 1755 when the architect James Leoni produced an English version.

Hypnerotomachia Poliphili was reprinted several times in Italy in the 16th century. It appeared in French in 1546, and in this edition, although the substance of the illustrations is unchanged, they have all been re-cut by a hand well versed in classical detail and proportion. The passage of time had resulted in more mature and sophisticated draughtsmanship. An English edition appeared in 1592, a much abridged version with only a dozen or so illustrations, none of which concerned the garden. Tudor England, so distant from the flourishing world of Italian art and architecture, carried on with its own traditions.

The creative frenzy of the Renaissance infected not only artists, architects and scholars but also the rich, educated rulers of the city states of Italy, and none more so than the Medici family in Florence. In the composition and position of their new country villa at Fiesole near Florence, designed by Michelozzo Michelozzi and built between 1458 and 1461, Cosimo de' Medici the Elder commissioned the first true Renaissance villa for his son, Giovanni. It was built on a steeply sloping hillside, close enough to afford views across the plain to the terracotta roofs of the city and the mighty Duomo. Two wide terraces were shaped out of the hillside to form the main feature of the gardens, on the upper of which the villa was constructed. This terrace itself became an extension of the house, an outside room for entertaining guests, refreshed in summer evenings by a slight breeze. Below, the lower terrace was probably planted with vines, fruit trees and vegetables. These two terraces, and the intimate *giardino segreto* to the west, remain in outline today, with only superficial alteration.

An arbour or pergola from Hypnerotomachia Poliphili, *1499, showing seats provided inside for shade. Details of classical decoration have been applied to the sturdy wooden frame, although with an imperfect understanding of classical conventions.*

Lauro also included in Antiquae Urbis
Splendor, *1612–14, a hypothetical version of
a Roman garden, complete with a central pergola
similar to the version by Colonna. In details such
as the architectural treatment of the pergola
that surrounds the garden, Lauro's view owes
more to contemporary taste than to authentic
Roman detail.*

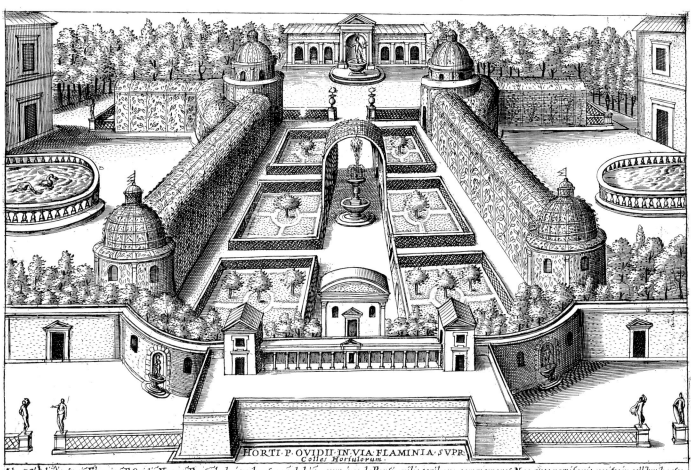

HORTI·P·OVIDII·IN·VIA·FLAMINIA·SVPR
Colles Hortulorum.

Ad uiā Claudiā iuxta uia Flaminiā P. Ouidiū Nasonē Poeta habuisse hortos nõ dubiū: cum ipse de Ponti exilio scribens comme̅moret. Nec quos pomiferis positos in collibus hortos,
Spectat Flaminiæ Claudia iuncta uiæ: quemadmodu ef in t̅. de tristib. domu nõ longe a Capitolio sibi fuisse dicit; hanc ego suspicient et̅ db̅ hac Capitolia cernens quanostrõ
frustra iuncta fuere lari. Neque etiam dubium quin hortī istī delitijs et amænitate alijs, quos hucusque descripsimus ādæquārint quid eos a māioribus suis qui equestri
erant ordinis, acceperat. enimuero crediderim ibi Nympharum inter fontes colludia, et Satyrorum crebras inter nemora imagines non defuisse per effigiem, nec cætera,
quæ uir tantus ingenio studioq̅ poesios suis carminibus adumbrauit: Fuit Ouidius patria Sulmonensis genere clarus patrimonij, diues ut diximus, Retor et orator mirabilis, quã
artem non coluit ex promore in Musas obsequio atque ingenio profluente quo omnes sui temporis poetas, qui et apud nos māximi iudicantur, omni in genere imitandos proposuit:
acre ipsa perfecit. nam tersus et fæcundus eloquio, iudicio excusus, sensus clarus, et acutus, ordine, stylog̅ rarissimus fuit, ut omnia quæ ipsius extant in Rep̅. literaria monumenta testan-
tur. Tandem quo, nescio iure miser exulauit, et in Ponso per octo fere annos usq̅. ad mortem detinuit: cũ nullus sit qui causas exilij asseuerare audeat, præsertim cũ ipse duas innuens, unamq̅ ex-
primens alteram sub est̅ uel si intelligi, et aliquando amice rogat occultari, dicens: ut quid præterea peccarim, quærere noli, ut pateat tola culpa sub arte mea: 1 dest̅ arte amãdi,
quam coposuerat; cuius prætextu Augustus, ne se traduceret, poētam amandauit in exilium: suspicor tamen fuisse, quod Cæsaris quid arcani aliunde sibi notu detexerit ut ex 3º de tristib. Inscia quod crimen uiderit lumina, plector, q̅ errorem merito appellat, quippe qui maximus esse solet, Regis aperire sacramentu, ut diuinis docemur oraculis.

The gardens of the Villa di Cafaggiolo probably date from the mid-15th century, as do two other villas built for Cosimo de' Medici about this time, Il Trebbio near Cafaggiolo and the Villa Medici at Careggi. It was Cosimo's pleasure to discuss philosophy with the members of the Platonic Academy in the garden at Careggi, just as Alberti would have wished.

Another leading architect, Michelozzi, built a palace and a *giardino segreto* behind it for the Pope, Pius II, in 1462 at Pienza. This is one of the few gardens from the early Renaissance to have survived, and, although altered over the centuries, it has been restored to the likely original design.

Apart from the Medici gardens, two important gardens near Naples, in the new taste – La Duquesa and Poggio Reale – were created for Alfonso II, King of Naples. Compared with restricted medieval gardens, La Duquesa was infinitely spacious, with wide avenues, marble fountains, pools of water, and a hippodrome for horse races.

Poggio Reale was even more striking, since it had been designed, *c.* 1488, by the Florentine architect Guiliano da Maiano, principally for court entertainments. No expense had been spared. With a panoramic view of the bay of Naples, its precise layout has been obscured by time since there are no contemporary illustrations and the garden was destroyed long ago. A late 17th-century engraving by Bastiaen Stoopendael, completed after outbuildings had covered part of the garden and the canals had been filled in, still shows a symmetric plan on two levels, with square and rectangular beds, a protective wall and a large handsome loggia.

From two descriptions of Poggio Reale, one by Sebastiano Serlio and another in a French poem, *Le Vergiez d'Honneur*, it is also clear that there were pavilions, aviaries, ornamental fishponds, canals, fountains, streams, statues and grottoes, and an amphitheatre that could be flooded for water spectacles, as had happened at the Colosseum in Rome in the days of the Empire.

If secular rulers like the Medici and Alfonso II were enjoying their new pleasure gardens, the Papacy had no wish to be outshone. The papal garden created from 1503 at the Vatican was an architectural marvel and the first of the High Renaissance gardens.

CAFAGIOLO

The magnificent medieval castle, Villa Cafaggiolo, one of the Medici properties in the hills above Florence, was painted by Giusto Utens, c. 1599. The garden behind shows Renaissance influence in the geometrical arrangement of a central axis terminating in a small pavilion, and crossed at right angles by a pergola draped with vines for shade.

Italian Gardens of the High Renaissance

The Circus Aurelius was one of many hippodromes for chariot races in ancient Rome. From the Renaissance onwards, the U-shape has appealed to garden designers who, abandoning the racing circuit, have repeated the design with modifications. It was illustrated by Lauro in Antiquae Urbis Splendor, *1612–14.*

A view of the Belvedere Court at the Vatican, engraved by Mario Cartaro in 1574 and published in I Vestigi dell' Antichita di Roma, *1575. Bramante aimed to emulate the villas of imperial Rome, and his design surpassed in grandeur any other garden composition of its time, influencing many that followed.*

By the turn of the century, the artistic centre of Italy was Rome, where the arrival in 1499 of the first of a new group of architects ushered in the era of the High Renaissance. Attracted by commissions from the city's important families and from the Pope, the richest source of all, they included Donato Bramante and Baldassare Peruzzi, followed by Raphael and many other great artists. These three had all trained initially as painters, but they turned their hands to architecture with alacrity. All readily absorbed the classical vocabulary of ancient Rome, and learned to experiment with the orders of architecture to suit their own inventive designs. They were not constrained into reproducing Roman buildings but adapted their principles to create new forms within classical ground rules.

After Julius II's election to the Papacy in 1503, he commissioned Bramante to draw up plans for the papal palaces in the Vatican and for St Peter's. While his design for St Peter's was only partly realised, his plan for linking the papal palace with the older Villa Belvedere was adopted in the Belvedere Court, from either side of which arcaded loggias stretched from the Vatican all the way to the villa, enclosing the new garden.

Several outstanding features made the Belvedere Court quite remarkable. This highly architectural plan displayed a unity of

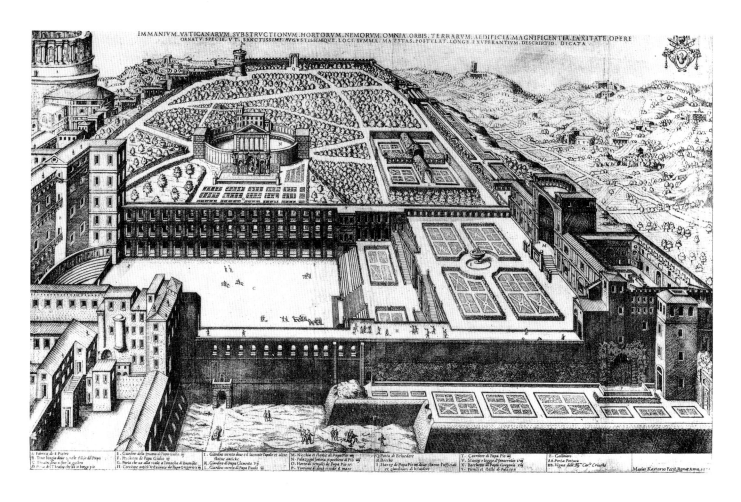

IMMANIVM.VATICANARVM.SVBSTRVCTIONVM.HORTORVM.NEMORVM.OMNIA.ORBIS.TERRARVM.AEDIFICIA.MAGNIFICENTIÆ.LAXITATE.OPERE
ORNATV.SPECIE.VT.SANCTISSIMI.AVGVSTISSIMIQVE.LOCI.SVMMA.MAIESTAS.POSTVLAT.LONGE.EXVPERANTIVM.DESCRIPTIO.DICATA

concept and an understanding of scale and proportion that had not previously been developed to such a sophisticated degree. Identification with ancient Rome was deliberate, not only in the exedra and in the mock façade of a Roman triumphal arch stretching across the centre of the garden, but also in the display of ancient sculptures that Julius was busy acquiring from excavation sites all over the city of Rome. All these elements rekindled the glory and power of the Roman Empire, and might, by association, enhance the image of Julius and the Catholic Church.

The Belvedere Court was designed to impress; it certainly achieved that aim, and it also influenced gardens in Rome and the surrounding countryside for many decades. However, it was effectively wrecked in 1580 by a later Pope, Sixtus V, when he built the Vatican Library across the middle terrace, cutting the garden in two and destroying the perspective. But in its early days, the design principles of the Belvedere Court inspired Raphael's 1517 plan for the Villa Madama.

Like Leonardo da Vinci and Michelangelo, Raphael turned his eclectic mind from art to architecture with ease. Commissioned by Cardinal Giulio de' Medici to build a villa on the sloping hillside of Monte Mario overlooking Rome, his plan for the design of villa and

garden was based on the description of Pliny the Younger's 1st-century AD garden at Laurentium, in which the interplay between house and nature was the key to the design. Raphael's version was closer to classical plans than any other that had been built by that time.

The core of the plan was a great round courtyard enclosed by a square villa, and each side of the villa was treated as a separate space. The approach was through a courtyard and up a monumental stair on the south-east side; an amphitheatre in the Roman style was to have been carved out of the hillside to the south-west, positioned for shade during afternoon and evening performances. Opposite, to the north-east, the sloping ground was to have been terraced to capitalise on the glorious view of the city of Rome, and make space for a hippodrome and stabling for 400 horses; to the north-west was, and is, the Giardino della Fontana, a parterre with box-edged beds and a splendid elephant's head fountain by Giovanni da Udine. Two of the four areas were planned to be largely architectural, with virtually no planting, while in the remaining two areas planting was contained within the framework of balustrades and perimeter walls.

In a letter to Cardinal de' Medici, Raphael described the plans to his client, drawing particular attention to the use of sun and shade for

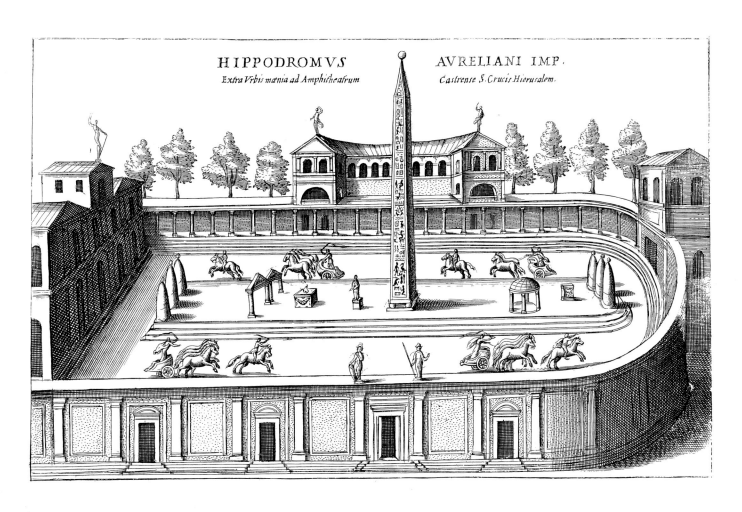

HIPPODROMVS
Extra Vrbis mœnia ad Amphitheatrum

AVRELIANI IMP.
Castrense S. Crucis Hierusalem.

The Elephant Fountain at the Villa Madama is by Giovanni da Udine (1487–1561) and was modelled on an elephant given by the King of Portugal to Pope Leo X in 1514. It is in a niche in a wall of the Giardino della Fontana, an integral part of Raphael's plan for the villa.

enjoyment and comfort. On top of one of the towers flanking the main entrance, he incorporated a *diaeta*, a circular room entirely walled with glass. *This place will be most charming*, he wrote, *not only because of the continuous sunshine but also because of the views of Rome and the countryside … It will really be a most pleasant place in winter for civilised discussions – the customary function of the diaeta.*[8] This winter room, a belvedere in the perimeter wall, accorded with Alberti's recommendation for the building of lofty towers from which to enjoy prospects of the countryside.

The principal summer apartments were on the shady north-east and north-west sides, beside the decorated loggia overlooking the fountain garden, the Giardino della Fontana. *This is the summer* diaeta, Raphael wrote, *which would be quite delightful both because it will never receive the sun and because the water and greenery will make it beautiful.*[9]

As a plan, it was profoundly civilised, satisfying the intellect and the eye at every angle. It was created for a man of refined tastes yet uncivilised behaviour, for the Cardinal was as scheming and treacherous as any of his contemporaries, at a time when competition in villainy was stiff.

Work at the villa had started in 1517, and, after Raphael's death in 1520, Antonio da Sangallo took over, influencing the development of the garden as well as of the house. The Cardinal became Pope Clement VII in 1523, but before he could enjoy the property, political events resulted in the devastating sack of Rome in 1527, and the villa was destroyed. Thereafter, it was partly rebuilt for the supposed son of Clement, Alessandro de' Medici, and his wife Margaret, illegitimate daughter of the Hapsburg Emperor Charles V, thereafter being known as the Villa Madama.

Of the four sides of the villa, only two were rebuilt after the destruction of 1527, so Raphael's courtyard is only a semicircle. The elegant north-west loggia that he designed has been glazed between the arches to protect the exquisite frescoes of Giovanni da Udine, Giulio Romano and Baldassare Peruzzi, but the north-east loggia still offers its view of the Eternal City. The gardens have been sorely neglected over the centuries, although the Giardino della Fontana was restored at the beginning of the 20th century according to Sangallo's plans.

Even though much of the garden was never made, the plans for the Villa Madama were well known, and had a major impact on the architects of the next generation. But it was not until the 1550s that the direct influence of Bramante's Belvedere Court and Raphael's Villa Madama could be seen in the gardens of Frascati and Tivoli outside Rome. The causes of the delay were political and economic, for Italy was in turmoil in the 1520s, as François I of France and Charles V of Spain fought over the riches of the Italian city states. After the sack of Rome by the armies of the Emperor Charles V, the city was impoverished and the artists fled.

In Florence, the Medici were expelled, a republic declared and the city besieged for 10 months until June 1530; then followed some years of tyrannical rule by Alessandro de' Medici. It was not until 1537 that a more peaceful era was ushered in when Cosimo I was given the Dukedom of Tuscany. A young man of 17 from a cadet branch of the Medici family, he had much to do to restore the city to prosperity and to revive the popularity of his family.

In 1538 Duke Cosimo commissioned Niccolo Tribolo to lay out a new garden for the Villa Medici at Castello, a house of an earlier date. After Tribolo's death, responsibility passed to Giorgio Vasari, assisted by Bartolommeo Ammanati and Giambologna. The villa is at the foot of a gently sloping hillside; a pair of rectangular pools in front have long since gone, but the walled garden behind the house is still largely intact. To look up the sloping garden was to see a series of green patterns carved from box hedges interspersed with statuary and trees in pots. Whereas a Baroque designer would have terraced the garden by introducing walls and stairs and balustrades, Tribolo kept the garden green by limiting stonework to fountains, porticoes and the grotto.

Tribolo concentrated his physical plan on the axis from the centre of the villa, leading over fountains and a round basin up to a shallow terrace and the grotto; beyond the wall there is a wooded area and pool in which sits Ammanati's statue of January.

The gardens of the Villa Medici di Castello were laid out to a plan by Niccolo Tribolo. The sloping hillside garden is enlivened by fountains and a circle of statues, plus many rare varieties of citrus trees. According to the art historian Vasari, the garden was to have been filled with countless statues but only a small proportion was ever installed.

The main axis of the walled garden is enforced with parallel paths crossed by others at right angles, while box hedges surround square beds enhanced by fruit trees. In the plantations to the right a handsome domed pavilion once stood at the intersection of the main paths, the ideal solution to enliven this area on a slight incline.

By 1538, such a layout was no longer revolutionary. What was novel about Cosimo's garden was its glorification of Cosimo, its iconography celebrating his control over the state of Tuscany, for the fountains and the water system represent Florence, its countryside and Cosimo's good government. No doubt the political events of the previous decade and a touch of insecurity led him to encourage these flattering monuments. They are too sensitive to be sycophantic.

The iconographical programme is attributed to the scholar Benedetto Varchi, and centres on water flowing through the garden. It starts with the statue of January, an almighty being gazing with concern on the garden below, but beyond the garden wall. A fountain of unusual subtlety was incorporated into this sculpture, for from his hair and beard, water flowed like tears, drop by drop. Water from the pool around him is piped to the grotto below, begun in 1546, where the marvels of the natural world are assembled: animals,

shells and fossils, with a unicorn at the centre. They supposedly represent a legend of a fountain poisoned by a serpent and purified by the unicorn so that all the animals can drink safely, but in reality the grotto is an allegory of Cosimo's cleansing of Tuscany's past evils. Giambologna's stone and bronze animal figures are beautifully portrayed, some of them spouting water from their beaks, wings, ears and nostrils into the white marble basins carved by Ammanati. On the vaulted roof is an elaborate pattern of shells and stones, one of the earliest extant examples of a style of decoration that has remained popular ever since.

Water reappears in the central fountain with its wide basin, where a statue of Venus by Giambologna once stood, now in the nearby Medici villa of La Petraia. This basin was once fed by two other large fountains, representing the two mountains near Florence and their streams, the Rivers Arno and Mugnone, which water the city and the plain. A circle of cypress trees surrounded the basin, as shown in a lunetto by Giusto Van Utens *c.* 1599. Nearer the villa is another fountain, still in place, of Hercules strangling the giant Antaeus.

In contrast with the earnest iconography, there were also *giochi*

d'acqua, water jokes to surprise and amuse. In 1580, Michel de Montaigne and other French noblemen visited the garden in November and were duly sprinkled with water. Montaigne's manservant recorded the incident:

As they were walking about the gardens, looking at the curiosities, the gardener, having left their side for the purpose, while they were in a certain place contemplating certain marble statues, there sprang up from under their feet and between their legs, through an infinite number of tiny holes, jets of water, so thin as to be almost invisible, an excellent imitation of fine, trickling rain, by which they were thoroughly besprinkled by means of some subterranean spring, which the gardener manipulated more than two hundred paces from there, with such ingenuity that from where he stood he raised or lowered the outflow at his pleasure, turning and moving it just as he desired.[10]

The walled garden at Castello would still be recognisable to Cosimo. The arrangement of paths and beds has changed, but it is still based on a geometric plan; the small collection of orange trees started by Cosimo's wife, Eleonora of Toledo, has blossomed into a forest of trees and shrubs in pots; and benign January, the grotto with its spouting animals, and the fighting Hercules all remain in place.

At the far end of the main axis is the grotto; its façade was once encrusted with stalactites but these were removed when the exterior was remodelled in Neo-classical style.

In the bosco above the garden, the bronze figure of January by Ammanati, dating from 1565, sits on a mount surrounded by a fishpond. Also known as Appennino, the statue personifies the Appenine mountains, from whence flow the rivers watering Florence and Tuscany.

Peace, Profusion and Mannerism

Palladio's elevation and plan of the Tempo della Fortuna Virile *in Rome, from* I Quattro Libri dell' Architettura, *1570. This book and others by architectural theorists such as Serlio and Vignola were an invaluable source of reference for succeeding generations of garden architects.*

GGGG 2

With the exception of the garden of the Villa Medici at Castello, few villas or gardens of lasting merit were created in Italy during the second quarter of the 16th century. When the turmoil ended and prosperity returned, there was a spectacular burst of building activity from the 1550s onwards in Rome and in the countryside of Lazio. The Villa Guilia, the Quirinale, the Sacro Bosco of Bomarzo, the Villa d'Este, the Palazzo Farnese and the Villa Lante are the still-visible results.

The High Renaissance form had been carried on by architects like Antonio da Sangallo, while others had developed it beyond the purely Classical into a new style known as Mannerism. And Mannerism became the more popular style for garden embellishments.

Mannerism evolved from the 1520s onwards, after the peak of the High Renaissance, and was most widespread from 1550 until the end of the century. Like most styles, it was a reaction to its predecessor, in this case to the controlled logic of Renaissance architecture. The term itself derives from the word 'mannered', meaning artificial, affected or unnatural, and its essential principle was discord, in contrast to the harmony that Alberti and Bramante had embraced with such enthusiasm. Mannerism had no rules of its own, and its exponents used, adapted or discarded the Classical vocabulary according to whim; sometimes they pretended to defy even the basic rules of construction, for example by using a capital as decoration but omitting the column. It intended to confound, to surprise, to frighten, or even to amuse. In art Mannerism was expressed in varying ways by artists from Parmigianino to El Greco, so in architecture it was interpreted in many different ways, and the results could be refined, elegant, amusing, surprising, or even shocking. Yet despite Mannerism's tangential directions it was still closely related to the Classicism of Renaissance architecture.

As a movement, Mannerism flourished with decadent gusto but eventually began to lose favour towards the end of the century, partly because its diversity and frivolity lacked coherence, and also because it was associated with the decadence of its patrons, often the princes of the Roman Church. The Protestant ethics that developed during the Reformation had a more natural affinity with the severity of Classicism rather than the sensual pleasures of Mannerism, and towards the end of the century the debate in Italy led, temporarily, to a return to a purer interpretation of Classical rules.

The Villa Giulia, or the Villa di Papa Giulio, is one of the most perfect examples of a Mannerist villa and garden. Designed by Giacomo Vignola, in collaboration with Ammanati and Vasari, and built between 1551 and 1555, the clever ground-plan was based on the interplay between three descending courtyards, with vistas from one to the other and loggias to bond them together in an intimate variation of the Belvedere Court. A semicircular nymphaeum, complete with nymphs with water flowing at their feet, is the reward for progressing down a curved stairway from the second courtyard to the lowest level. In itself a satisfying form, the nymphaeum was also a reminder of the Roman Empire since it was inspired by a grotto from the 1st-century palace of the Emperor Domitian.

The nymphaeum at the Villa Giulia is considered to have inspired another version of the same idea at Palladio's Villa Barbaro at Maser in the Veneto. Palladio spent some time in Rome in 1554 and was sufficiently influenced by Roman Mannerist architecture to depart from the strictly Classical style he had followed until then. As far as gardens are concerned, this shift made little difference, for he seemed to ignore garden design. In spite of his many commissions for country houses, only one garden building survives that might be attributable to him – the nymphaeum at the Villa Barbaro, and even this is clearly not all his own work.

Palladio's clients were his good friends, the brothers Daniele and Marc'Antonio Barbaro. Both humanists, Daniele was an architectural historian, translator of the Roman Vitruvius and a keen gardener, Marc'Antonio an amateur sculptor. They sought the Arcadian ideal in a house that would relate to the countryside and its pastoral activities, and so the main façade of the villa Barbaro looks out across Barbaro estates, the wings contain a dairy and dovecots, and behind there is a little *giardino segreto*.

Palladio described it thus in his *Quattro Libri di Architettura: The first floor is at ground level behind, where a fountain with an infinity of stucchi and painted ornaments is cut into the neighbouring hill. The fountain makes a little lake and that serves as a fish pond, and from here the water runs into the kitchen, then irrigates the gardens . . .*[11]

The sculpture in the nymphaeum was largely by Allessandro Vittorio, except for the four larger figures, which are by a more primitive hand, probably that of Marc'Antonio Barbaro. The signature of Palladio is surely seen in the glorious sweep of the pediment as it curves round to a peak above an arched door.

The nymphaeum at the Villa Barbaro in the Veneto, designed by Palladio during the 1560s. Elaborately decorated in contrast to the plain façades of the villa, it is the centrepiece of the long and narrow giardino segreto *behind the villa.*

The Dragon in the Mannerist gardens of the Sacro Bosco at Bomarzo is not a diabolical foe but a humorous playful beast with the wings of a butterfly. In a garden where all the stone creatures had a symbolic rôle, the function of the Dragon was to ensure the purity of the fountains.

The greatest gardens often take decades to reach perfection. Many of the most significant gardens of the later 16th century, like the Boboli Gardens of the Pitti Palace in Florence, were conceived in the 1550s, and constructed over many years. Of all of them, Bomarzo is by far the most extraordinary. In its collection of grotesque figures, it is the most extreme manifestation of Mannerism in a garden. Its iconography is not merely an allegorical composition with symbolic statues but the model for a journey through the vicissitudes of life to reach an understanding of divine love; in its ground-plan, it overturns conventional geometric form in favour of twisting paths that herald the landscape movement; and in its humour, it mocks the pretentiousness of contemporary gardens and their owners.

The Sacro Bosco, or Sacred Grove, of Bomarzo, was started in 1552 by Pier Francesco 'Vicino' Orsini near Viterbo to the north of Rome. He developed it mainly from 1567 until his death in 1584. An aristocratic, intellectual soldier married to a member of the powerful Farnese family, he must have had a most original mind to conceive such a bizarre place. Although a terraced garden existed near the old fortified hilltop house, Orsini sited his new creation some distance away in the woods. More of an experience than a garden, it is full of creatures and urns of enormous size to belittle the confident, and wide-mouthed monsters ready to engulf the unwary. A tilting house adds to the confusion and alarm. At the end of the progress through horror and temptation, on a slope at the top of the garden, there stands the Temple of Divine Love, designed by Vignola.

Orsini expected his contemporaries to visit the Sacred Grove, for over the entrance, he wrote: *You who go wandering about the world in search of sublime and awesome wonders, come here where horrendous faces, elephants, lions, bears, ogres and dragons are to be seen.*[12] His words reflect the endless fascination with curiosities shared by all educated men of the time. They were thirsty for clues to a better understanding of nature and science, but also craved for reports of foreign lands and their inhabitants, customs, clothes and animals. They sought out and studied anything that was out of the ordinary, from coins to fossils to mummified animals. All over Europe, people kept collections of rarities, which they willingly showed to friends and acquaintances, and visiting travellers. Orsini's wild fantasy would have interested not only the regular garden visitors, but also those bewitched by the exotic.

Ironically, after Orsini's death, the Sacred Grove was ignored. It was not on the tourist route. Perhaps the reason for its omission lay in its separation from the villa, for the lack of any relationship between villa and garden did not conform to current taste. The dangers and discomforts of the road between Siena and Rome were perhaps another reason; travellers were always anxious to get south as fast as possible, so they stopped for the night in Viterbo, called in at the Villa Lante at nearby Bagnaia, and then hurried on. As a result the Sacro Bosco was smothered by trees and undergrowth for centuries until surrealist painter Salvador Dali rediscovered it in 1949. It has now been restored.

The most visited, admired, described, and painted Mannerist garden of this era was undoubtedly the Villa d'Este in Tivoli. Diplomats, visitors and travellers have left clear accounts of its glories. Guidebooks were available by 1580, and in 1611 Antonio del Re published a detailed description, *Dell'Antichita tibutrine capitolo v*; Salomon de Caus described the hydraulic systems in *Les Raisons des Forces Mouvantes*, first published in 1615, while J. Furttenbach depicted the Oval Fountain in his book on architecture, *Architectura Universalis*, published in Germany in 1635. Artists recorded it for posterity before it was even finished, and the first bird's-eye view engraving by Etienne du Pérac in 1573 was published repeatedly from 1575 until the end of the 17th century. Israel Silvestre, the French artist, produced a set of engravings in 1646, Venturini another in about 1675, while Isaac de Moucheron painted several views in 1694; in the 18th century, the most famous artists to immortalise the garden were Fragonard and Hubert Robert in 1760, and Piranesi in an etching in 1773; in the 19th century, Matthew Digby Wyatt made a bird's-eye view watercolour, and in the 20th century it has been photographed ad infinitum.

The Villa d'Este at Tivoli and its Mannerist gardens, as engraved by du Pérac in 1573. (Maps K.82.) The garden was dedicated both to Hercules from whom Cardinal d'Este was imaginatively descended and to Hippolytus, the symbol of chastity. Although some of the features have disappeared, such as the treillage tunnels, the pavilions in the fishponds and all the automata, several of the fountains are still intact. On the upper left side is the Oval Fountain, which is connected across the garden by the Walk of the Hundred Fountains to the model of ancient Rome on the extreme upper right. The neat little trees in the engraving have grown to huge proportions and now dominate the garden.

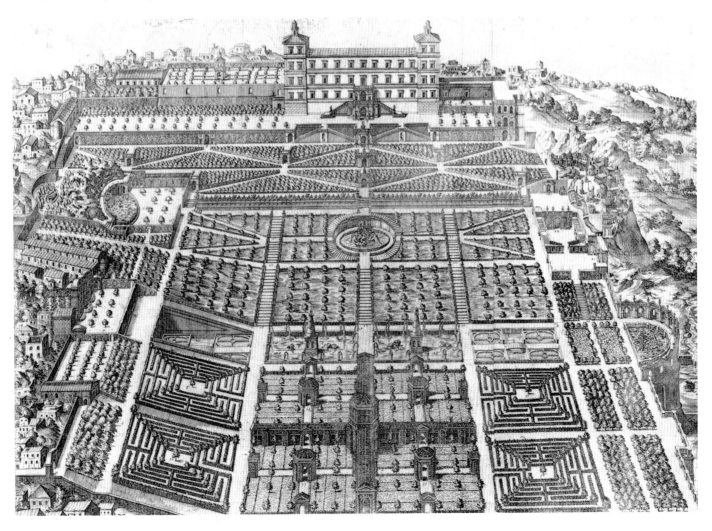

Why such interest in this garden? It was famed for its site, for its size, for its complexity, for its iconography, for its undoubted beauty, but most of all for its water. It was one of the most complex and original water gardens in Italy, the most frivolous version of Mannerist ideals. Water had played a central role in many gardens from the 14th century onwards. But at the Villa d'Este, the hydraulic engineers surpassed all previous achievements in creating an extravaganza of sparkling, moving and singing novelties.

The Villa was also famed for its owner, the rich, learned and ambitious Cardinal Ippolito d'Este of Ferrara. Ten years after the Cardinal had acquired an old monastery at Tivoli in 1550, near the remains of the Emperor Hadrian's villa, work started under the direction of Pirro Ligorio, and continued until 1575. Echoes of the Belvedere Court and the Villa Madama can be found in the tight architectural plan and the intensity of the structural element. The association with ancient Rome was there, too, since the garden was decorated with fine statuary, some taken from Hadrian's villa. The entire garden was made to glorify the Cardinal, and the iconography is a combined tribute to nature, art and the Este family. Both statuary

and iconography are extensive and complicated, and are described in David Coffin's thorough account, *The Villa d'Este at Tivoli*.

Ligorio's plan was a masterpiece of hydraulic engineering and produced an astonishing array of fountains, silvery and delicate and shimmering in the hot sunshine. In 1670, Daniello Bartoli described the watery effects as: *Extending so transparently and smoothly as to resemble the sheerest veils floating in the air, and spraying into minute drops that form a dewy cloud … They seem to gush from underground, to leap up and hover in the air, to moan like those in pain, to bellow like the enraged and sing like the merry.*[13]

The automata and their accompanying noises, which Bartoli records, had earlier made a deep impression on Michel de Montaigne when he went to Tivoli in April 1581. Of the Fountain of the Organ, which had been set up in 1568 by two French experts, Le Clerc and Vernard, he wrote: *The music of the organ, which is real music*

The Fountain of Rome, a model of the ancient city complete with a galley in the supposed River Tiber, intrigued and delighted visitors to the Villa d'Este.

The Fountain of the Goddess of Nature,
nourishing the garden through her abundant breasts,
symbolised the springs and rivers generated by
the earth.

and a natural organ, always however playing the same thing, is effected by means
of water, which falls with great force into a round arched cave, and agitates the air
which is there, and compels it to make its exit through the pipes of the organ and
supplies it with wind.[14]

An Englishman, John Raymond, who toured Italy in 1646 and
1647, was much impressed with the Fountain of Dragons, *which
vomit forth the Water with a most horrid Noyse.*[15] But he preferred the
Fountain of the Owl, which enchanted many visitors, for *amongst the
Branches of the Trees, Artificial birds move their Wings and sing sweetly; on a
sudden an Owle appears.*[16] John Evelyn, in May 1645, admired all the
fountains in their great and ingenious variety, including what must
be one of the earliest model gardens on record: *At the end of this, next
the wall the Cittie of Rome, as it was in its beauty, all built of small models,
representing that Citie with its Amphitheatres, Naumachia, Thermae,
Temples, Arches, Aquaeducts, streets & other magnificences, with a little
streame runing through it for the River Tybur, gushing out of the Urne next the
statue of that River.*[17]

Apart from the noise of organs, birds, dragons, cannon-shots and
muskets, there remain other delightful inventions, like the ship —
drenched with spray from the nearby rocks, it still responds with
twin jets that look like retaliatory fire hydrants.

This dazzling garden drew many comments from travellers from
abroad. *The whole is said to have cost the best part of a million,*[18] said John
Evelyn. Grandly did John Raymond state that *This shall be my
Patterne for a Country Seat,*[19] but Raymond disappeared into obscurity leaving only his good intentions on paper.

When garden fashions changed, and landscaped parks replaced
formal gardens, the waterworks were left to fill with silt and the
hydraulic machinery to creak to a halt. In the 19th century, some new
and powerful jets were were added at one end of the central pools;
thrusting frothy plumes high in the air, they seem crude beside the
delicate sprays of the 16th century. Some of the old fountains still
work, but the music has gone and the songbirds, owls and dragons fly
no more.

The waterworks at the Villa d'Este were exceptional in their time,
but there were others who were competing with the Cardinal in the
brilliance of their creations, for the Medici had made yet another
garden near Florence.

The Villa Pratolino, now known as the Villa Demidoff, was
built for Francesco de' Medici between 1569 and 1585. The gardens
were created by Bernardo Buontalenti on a dry, barren hillside,
which he turned into a celebration of water by piping it from a considerable distance; indeed some of the villa's fame rested on this
achievement alone. But it was the grottoes, with their automata and
water jokes, that enchanted everyone. For as at the Villa Medici at
Castello, visitors were showered by unexpected jets of water. There
was also a marvellous series of pools on either side of the garden, each
one of a different shape and size, with water dripping or cascading
into the one below in a completely asymmetrical fashion unique
in its day.

Pratolino had two other features for which the Villa d'Este had no rivals, a rocky Mount Parnassus and an amphitheatre in which sat a colossal statue of Appennino on an artificial mount surrounded by water. Appennino was vast because he symbolised the Appenines, the mountains of Tuscany. The statue was a fountain too, for the giant figure is pressing the head of a monster and forcing him to spew water from his mouth, while inside the giant there was enough room for a grotto. Far larger than the statue of January at Castello, it is Mannerist in scale and concept and was executed by Giambologna, the French-born sculptor who settled in Florence. Appennino is the most significant remaining feature of the 16th-century garden, for most of it was destroyed in 1819.

Montaigne had visited Villa Pratolino as well as the Villa d'Este:

Pratolino was exactly laid out in rivalry to this place [the Villa d'Este]. *In the riches and beauty of its grottoes, Florence is infinitely ahead; in its abundance of water, Ferrara* [the Villa d'Este]; *in the variety of jests and amusing movements by water, they are equal: except that the Florentine displays a little more elegance in the orderly arrangement of the place as a whole. Ferrara in antique statues and the palace; Florence in situation of place and beauty of prospect infinitely surpasses Ferrara.*[20]

The Oval Fountain, also known as the Fountain of Tivoli, was the principal fountain in the garden, much admired by Montaigne. Around the far side of the basin is an arcade, reminiscent of nearby ancient villas, behind which is a cool, refreshing gallery.

The gardens of the Villa Lante were perhaps the
most delightful of all those created in the later 16th
century, and much admired for their originality.
The water staircase takes the form of the elongated
body of a crayfish (gambaro in Italian), in
honour of the villa's owner, Cardinal Gambara.

Water was one of the essential elements in all Italian gardens. In the foothills of the Alps, at the Villa Cigogna Mozzoni at Bisuschio, is one of the loveliest water staircases of the 16th century. It is on a long steep slope, and cascades quickly down from a simple, elegant pavilion at the top of the hill to a stone-sculpted basin below, at the side of a wide allée. Aligned with the principal window of the first floor, the *piano nobile*, it has steps on either side all the way up to the pavilion.

Another famous water staircase, or *catena d'acqua*, is at the Villa Lante at Bagnaia in Lazio, near Rome. Beautifully edged with scrolls of stone representing the joints of the leg of a crayfish, the iconography refers to the owner, Cardinal Gambara – the Italian for crayfish being *gambaro*. Completed by 1573, the design of the water staircase and the rest of the garden is attributed to Giacomo da Vignola. Montaigne was very impressed by a fountain like a pyramid, around which were *four pretty lakes, full of pure and limpid water. In the centre of each is a stone boat, with musketeers who shoot and hurl water against the pyramid, and a trumpeter in each who also shoots water. You go round these lakes and the pyramid by the prettiest walks, with balustrades of handsome stone, very artistically carved.*[21]

Visitors still admire the pools and fountains, and are still sprayed regularly by hidden jets turned on by innocently smiling guides.

Many other gardens were renowned for their beauty or originality, among them the Palazzo Farnese at Caprarola, transformed from a fortress into a magnificent palace by Giacomo Vignola from 1559. Its gardens still boast many delights, including a water staircase of intertwined dolphins, and a vast fountain where jets in the form of the Farnese lily fill a gigantic urn, guarded by two massive tritons. In Florence, the ever-expanding Boboli Gardens, including the Mannerist grotto built between 1583 and 1588 by Bernardo Buontalenti, have always been enjoyed by citizens and visitors.

Most Mannerist gardens were lavishly decorated and much visited. Relying on artifice rather than nature, they were created for pleasure rather than for philosophy. They had an impudent sense of fun in their water jokes and musketeered sailors, but, like Pan in Arcadia, the giant, brooding figures were a reminder of the grotesque side of nature. While Villa Barbaro looked back to the humanism of the early Renaissance, the Villa d'Este looked forward to the even more sophisticated gardens of the 17th century.

Also at the Villa Lante is the Cardinal's Table, a vast stone table with a unique central canal, which served as a wine cooler. It incorporated water jokes, too, which the Cardinal could turn on when it pleased him to soak his guests. Beyond the table is the Fountain of the River Gods.

Henri d'Albret, King of Navarre, is pictured in the garden at Alençon in Normandy, c. 1527. (Ms 5096, fol.1.) The fountain inside the pavilion resembles medieval designs, yet the statue is in the Renaissance spirit. The pavilion is also Renaissance in outline, but the details of tapering columns and flat entablature reveal a hand inexperienced in Classical architecture.

When Charles VIII of France invaded Italy in 1494 to settle claims to the throne of Naples, the political results were slight compared with the intellectual and artistic consequences, for, although the Renaissance had spread through Italy, this was the first time that the creativity of Renaissance artists had been seen by large numbers of foreigners.

Charles VIII, his courtiers and generals, were entranced by what they saw in Italy, both by the art and architecture, as well as by the villas and gardens. Two villas in Naples, La Duquesa and Poggio Reale, made a deep impression on the King. Both had belonged to Alfonso II, whom Charles had usurped, and both had magnificent gardens.

Captivated by the theatrical extravaganza of Poggio Reale, Charles took a Neapolitan gardener, Pacello da Mercogliano, and a humanist and hydraulics engineer, Fra Giocondo, back across the Alps to start work on the royal gardens of France. Had he chosen an influential architect in the mould of Alberti, instead of a gardener and an engineer, French gardens might have developed with Renaissance unity from the beginning of the 16th century. To compensate, under the supervision of experts from other disciplines, they probably had a wider range of plants and more powerful fountains.

Some Italian ideas were adopted immediately, such as the geometric plan, the wide walks, the use of fountains and pavilions, an occasional flash of Mannerism, and an increase in the size of gardens. But the principle of designing house and garden together, or of designing the garden as the focus of an existing house, took decades to be generally accepted. French gardens of the early 1500s therefore lacked the architectural unity that give house and garden cohesion, an omission that was not rectified for half a century.

Despite this comparatively slow start in comprehensive design, buildings in the classical spirit appeared in French gardens soon after the turn of the century, although frequently classical detail was simply grafted onto gothic outlines. The pavilion seen in a portrait of Henri d'Albret, King of Navarre, *c.* 1527, was inspired by Roman architecture, as is the pedimented building in the background, and a classical stamp was added by the frame into which the artist set the picture. Yet the fountain and the Hortus Conclusus are distinctly medieval.

It is not known precisely what Pacello da Mercogliano achieved in the gardens of the fortress palace of Amboise on the Loire, although at Blois he is thought to have designed the principle parterre in the middle of which was a pavilion with arches facing four allées. He also designed an elaborate scheme at Gaillon in Eure for Cardinal Georges d'Amboise, a prince of the church who had also travelled to Italy with Charles VIII. No doubt the Cardinal added his own vision to that of Mercogliano for château and gardens became among the most esteemed in France.

Mercogliano divided the garden into three, a walled plantation of trees, an Upper Garden and a Lower Garden for fruit, flowers and vegetables. The prestigious Upper Garden, created between 1502 and 1509 while Bramante was building the Belvedere gardens for the Pope in Rome, was enclosed by high walls and entered through a screen of buildings nearly opposite the château entrance. At the far end of the parterre was a small, one-roomed, two-storeyed building with a steeply pitched roof, its style similar to the architecture of the château.

As at Blois, in the middle of the parterre was a wooden treillage pavilion painted blue and gold and decorated with coats of arms. Again, the medieval influence is apparent in the painting of the pavilion, for richly coloured decoration was an essential part of medieval life, be it in clothing, palace interiors or in the brilliant stained glass and painted walls of churches such as the Sainte Chapelle in Paris. Applying sapphire blue and gold to a garden pavilion was a logical extension of the desire for colour, and the practice continued in France in the early days of the Renaissance, as it did in England.

The Gaillon pavilion had a rippling gothic ogival roof and cupola. Aviaries were built into the four corners so that the Upper Garden could be filled with birdsong, while inside was a white marble fountain, a magnificent affair by Agostino Solario, ordered at enormous expense from Genoa. With water sparkling on white marble, and sun on the gilded edifice, the effect must have been remarkable.

The Upper Garden at Gaillon, illustrated by du Cerceau in Les Plus Excellents Bastiments de la France, *1576, was completed by 1509. As in many other contemporary gardens, the Italian concept of designing house and garden in one composition was ignored, and there is no axial relationship between the two.*

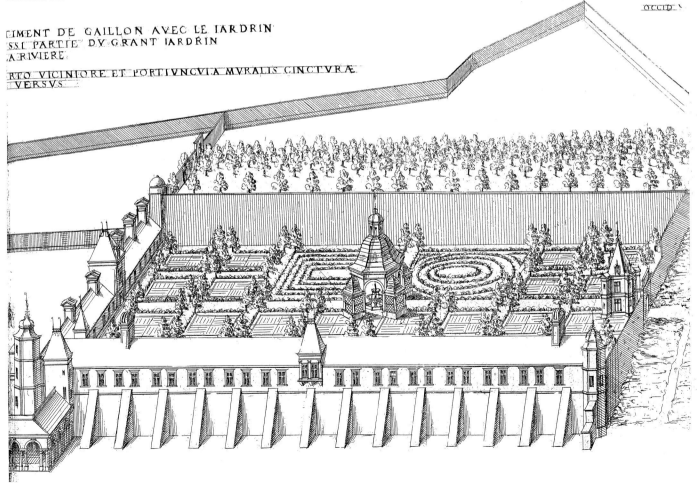

An aerial view of Fontainebleau (Maps 50·5·27) by Alessandro Francini, drawn in 1614 after Henri IV had extended the gardens to the right of and below the lake, and relaid the Grand Jardin above it. The Pavillon de Pomone is the tiny pavilion, below centre left, at the corner of a parterre.

An engraving of the Pavillon de Pomone at Fontainebleau (74B 65914), which was completed by 1541. Primaticcio painted a garden scene on one internal wall and Rosso the seduction of the goddess Pomona on another.

This *pièce de résistance* established the Cardinal's intention to rival Italian gardens and it is possible that Fra Giocondo's expertise added extra vigour and effect to the water displays, for all the fountains were beautifully conceived and executed, and amazed visitors with their magnificence.

The Cardinal's gardens at Gaillon were a great achievement, yet all three areas were completely separated from each other, and from the château, by a large courtyard. As at Blois, none of the gardens had any axial relationship to the château, and could only be viewed distantly from upper windows.

The gardens of Blois and Gaillon are known to us through the illustrations of Jacques Androuet du Cerceau, an architect who recorded the great houses of France in *Les Plus Excellents Bastiments de la France*, published in two volumes in 1576 and 1579. Du Cerceau's illustrations show how the flat terrain of France was used, for example at Beauregard and Fontainebleau, in comparison with the hillside sites of Rome and Tuscany. Each site had to have its own solution.

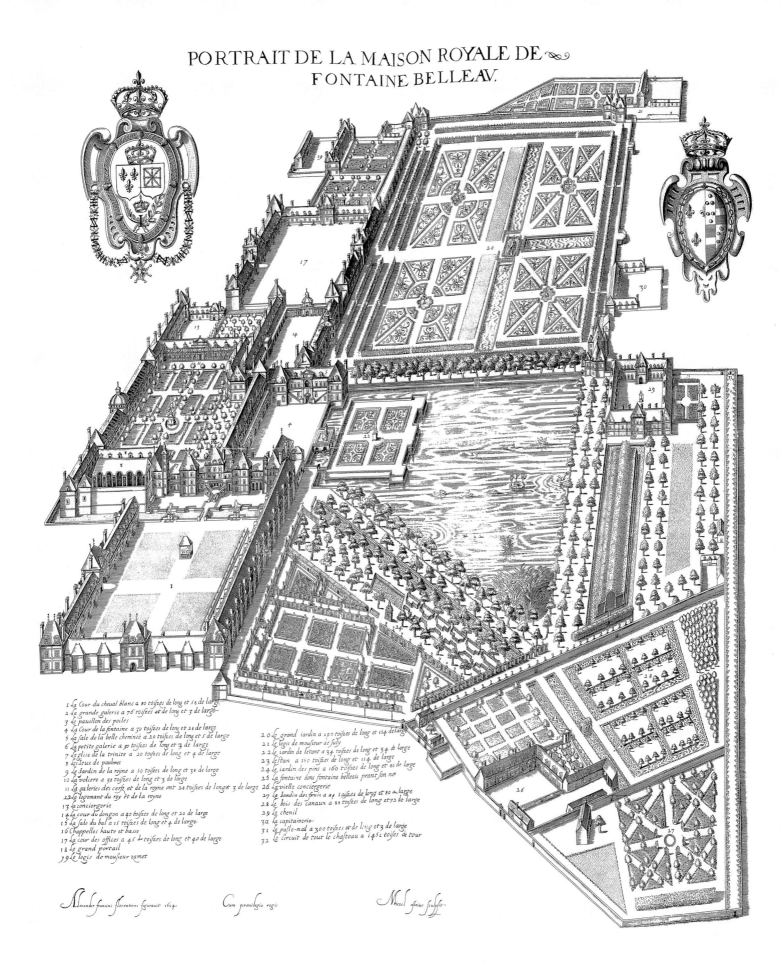

PORTRAIT DE LA MAISON ROYALE DE FONTAINE BELLEAV.

1 La Cour du cheual blanc a 80 toises de long et 58 de large
2 la grande galerie a 76 toises et de long et 3 de large
3 le pauillon des poiles
4 la Cour de la fontaine a 50 toises de long et 28 de large
5 la sale de la belle cheminée a 20 toises de long et 5 de large
6 la petite galerie a 30 toises de long et 3 de large
7 leglise de la trinite a 20 toises de long et 4 de large
8 les Ieux de paulmes
9 le iardin de la royne a 50 toises de long et 38 de large
10 la voliere a 38 toises de long et 3 de large
11 la galeries des cerfs et de la royne ont 28 toises de long et 3 de large
12 le logemant du roy et de la royne
13 la conciergerie
14 la cour du dongon a 40 toises de long et 20 de large
15 la sale du bal a 15 toises de long et 4 de large
16 Chappelles haute et basse
17 la cour des offices a 45 toises de long et 40 de large
18 le grand portail
19 le logis de mousieur zamet

20 Le grand iardin a 190 toises de long et 154 de large
21 le logis de mousieur de suly
22 le iardin de letant a 34 toises de long et 34 de large
23 lestan a 150 toises de long et 114 de large
24 le iardin des pins a 160 toises de long et 80 de large
25 la fontaine dons fontaine belleau prant son nom
26 la vielle conciergerie
27 la iardin des fruis a 24 toises de long et 80 de large
28 Le bois des canaux a 88 toises de long et 72 de large
29 le chenil
30 la capitainerie
31 le paslle-mail a 300 toises et de long et 3 de large
32 le circuit de tout le chasteau a 1456 toises de tour

Alexander francini florentinus figurauit 1614   Cum preuilegio regis   Micael lasnius sculpsit

Although the château of Fontainebleau remains, the royal gardens created for François 1 have gone. An earlier palace at Fontainebleau had been almost abandoned in the previous century, and work on the new palace started in 1528. Although the artists and architects assembled to create the King's palace have since been called the First School of Fontainebleau, many of them were Italian. François's links with Italy were strong, his mother being Louise de Savoie, and his military campaigns had revealed to him the splendour of Italian art and architecture. He bought many Italian paintings and possessions and also lured artists to France, among whom Leonardo da Vinci was the prize, and it was under François's patronage of the arts that the French Renaissance reached its height.

In 1530 the Florentine painter Gian Battista di Jacopo, known as Il Rosso, took up residence to decorate the interior of the palace; he was followed a year later by Francesco Primaticcio, a painter and sculptor who turned to garden architecture towards the end of his life. In 1540 Sebastiano Serlio was summoned to advise on architecture and stayed until he died in 1554. Giacomo Barozzi da Vignola was employed to cast statues in bronze.

Du Cerceau's view of Fontainebleau shows three main garden areas. To the north, the Jardin de la Reine had been developed by Primaticcio between 1560 and 1563; to the east of the lake, the Grand Jardin, a much larger area, was subdivided into neat rectangles with a canal across its width; to the west of the lake was the Jardin des Pins, a wooded area with wide allées. All three have been much altered over the centuries for Henri IV, Louis XIV, Napoleon and Louis-Philippe.

There is, however, one remaining structure of François 1's time – the Grotte des Pins. It is built into the corner pavilion of a long wing called the Galerie d'Ulysse, which was rebuilt under Louis XV, though the grotto was retained. Primaticcio was almost certainly the architect, and the four sturdy and twisted figures of Atlas that adorn its façade reveal his Mannerist leanings. Nearby was the Pavillon de Pomone, a small square structure with a roof tapering elegantly to a ball and finial. Some two centuries later, the pavilion was shown on a plan of Fontainebleau published in 1736 by Piganiol de la Force, but it no longer exists.

The royal gardens also boasted a statue of Hercules by Michelangelo, bought from Italy in 1529 at the order of François 1, and placed in the fountain courtyard overlooking the lake. Fontainebleau and Gaillon were not the only French gardens with Italian sculpture, for Donatello's *David* stood in the forecourt at the château of Bury.

However impressive it may have been in its time, Fontainebleau was not an architectural garden in the sense that much was constructed. François was more interested in the interior, on which he lavished fortunes. As the palace was irregular in plan, and the lake beside it trapezoidal, the garden had to be laid out at angles around the two. Various architects were involved in the building of the château – Giles Le Breton, Sebastiano Serlio, Philibert de l'Orme –

but it seems that at no stage was there a plan to unite the château and garden. The opposite was the case at the château of Anet, Eure-et-Loir, which was also recorded by du Cerceau.

Anet was built by Philibert de l'Orme for Diane de Poitiers, Henri II's mistress, between 1546 and 1552. De l'Orme had spent three years in Rome in the 1530s observing the products of Classicism and Mannerism, but retained his distinctly French style on his return to France. However, he designed the château and garden at Anet according to Alberti's principles of a single composition, and established in France by the middle of the century the benefits of a cohesive design. Architecturally it was more sophisticated than others designed about the same time, such as Serlio's plan for Ancy-le-Franc, Yonne, and there is an exuberant freedom in the Renaissance decoration applied to gatehouse, château entrance, walls, chimneys and terraces.

De l'Orme imposed a strictly axial garden plan to the north within a rectangular perimeter. The southern wall was dominated by a splendid gatehouse, on either side of which was a grove of conical trees, then a terrace approached between a pair of hemispheres, and finally a corner pavilion topped on one side by a sarcophagus that served as a chimney. A magnificent statue of Diana the Huntress was placed in a courtyard to the left of the *cour d'honneur*.

To the east, beyond the walls and the river surrounding the garden, was a Classical rotunda, which may have been inspired by Bramante's Tempietto in the cloister of San Pietro in Montorio, Rome, built in 1502. The tempietto is a small circular temple that was to have an enormous effect on the work of subsequent architects; it is two-tiered, with the upper *cella*, or tier, raised behind a balustrade, and finished with a hemispherical dome. Anet's rotunda is a single-tiered columned version, raised on a plinth to give it importance and a satisfying harmony of proportion. It may seem unnecessary to search Rome and Italian architectural treatises for clues to garden buildings in France, but French architects of the mid-16th century, especially Philibert de l'Orme, were departing from a gothic past, leaning heavily on Rome's ancient and modern architecture, and they liked the comfort of a precedent.

The rotunda no longer exists, and Anet's Renaissance galleried parterre, pavilions and bathing pool were destroyed by the great creator of the following century, André le Nôtre. One wing of the château remains, and the statue of Diana the Huntress is preserved in the Louvre. Gone, too, are the early gardens at Amboise, Blois and Bury, and at Gaillon, only the outline of the Upper Garden remains.

There was, however, a further addition at Gaillon in the 1550s. Called the Hermitage, in an early recorded use of this term, it was sited at the far end of a long canal, and was intended as a place of escape and repose – but with surprises. A wall built alongside the main canal was enlivened with arches of alternating size and interspersed with bands of rustication. Nearby, in the middle of a

The tempietto *in the cloister of San Pietro, Montorio in Rome, designed by Bramante in 1502 and illustrated by Palladio in* I Quattro Libri dell' Architettura, *1570.*

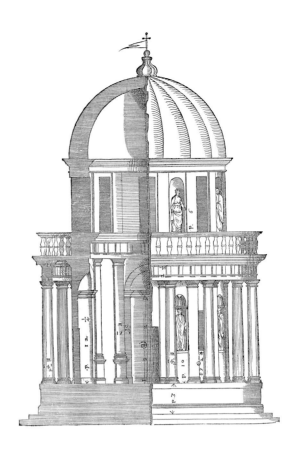

A view of part of the château of Anet (RF 78724), which was completed for Diane de Poitiers by de l'Orme by 1552. While the château was essentially French, to the right of it, in the centre of the drawing, can be seen a Classical temple, situated in an unusually naturalistic setting in a grove of trees. The cupola is surmounted with a crescent, the symbol of Diana the huntress with whom Diane de Poitiers was associated.

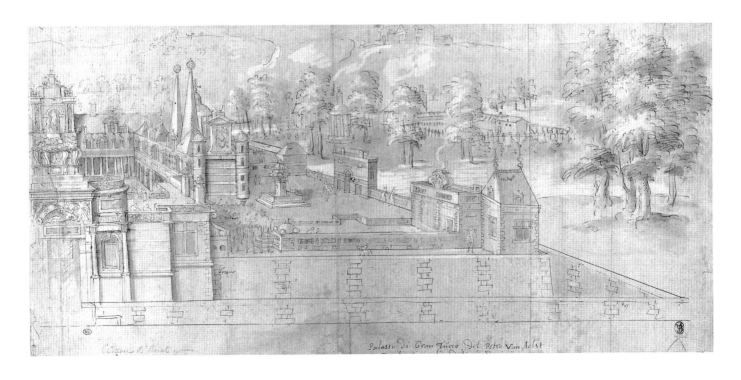

The Hermitage near the Maison Blanche
at Gaillon, and the Gallery at Montargis, both
illustrated by du Cerceau in Les Plus Excellents
Bastiments de la France, *1576.*

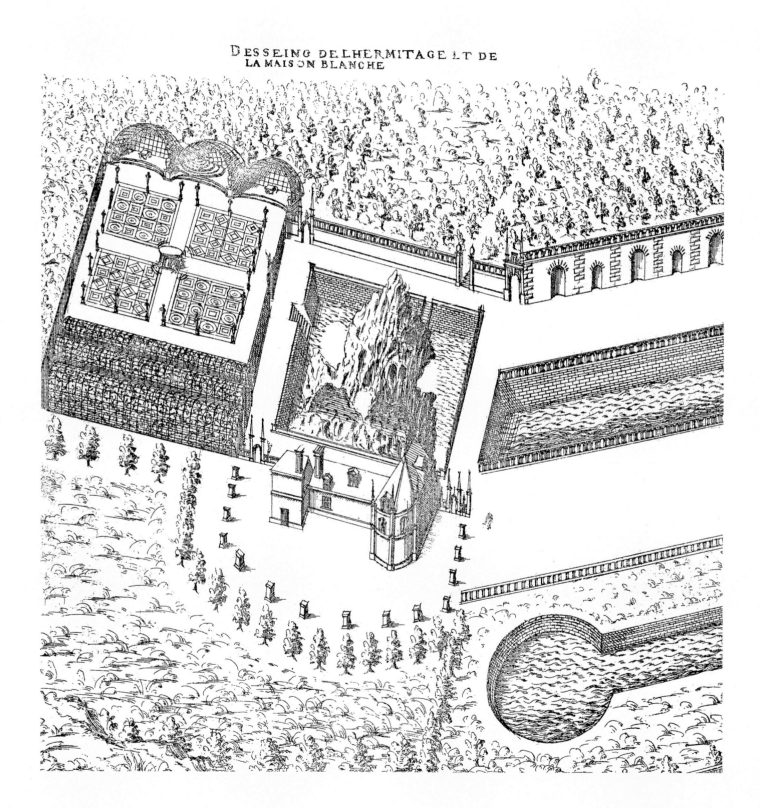

DESSEING DE LHERMITAGE ET DE
LA MAISON BLANCHE

sunken pond was a fantastic rock folly in the Mannerist spirit, known as the *Parnasse de Gaillon*.

Mannerism had been brought to France by the Italians employed at Fontainebleau. Apart from Primaticcio's Grotte des Pins, a prime example was the grotto at Meudon, a grandiose Mannerist conceit, also by Primaticcio, built in 1552 for the Cardinal de Lorraine. The Hermitage at Gaillon was another interpretation – a bizarre, man-made edifice designed to amaze spectators with its appearance and its mysterious caves and passages.

Although almost all the gardens illustrated by du Cerceau have been destroyed, some relics from the 16th century remain. There is a small half-hexagonal temple with fluted columns, decorated frieze and ogival roof at Les Beaux in Provence. At La Bastie d'Urfé in the Loire is a rotunda built for Claude d'Urfé, who had been French ambassador to the Holy See from 1549 to 1553, where he may have been inspired by the ancient Temple of Vesta in Rome or the Temple of Hercules and Zeus. His rotunda is a circular building with a ring of exceptionally tall fluted columns with Corinthian capitals; like the Temple of Vesta, its entablature is missing and it now has a low-pitched tiled roof rising to a point. As in other contemporary gardens, statues were brought from Italy to La Bastie d'Urfé and used to decorate the rectangular gardens surrounding the rotunda.

Apart from *Les Plus Excellents Bastiments de la France*, du Cerceau published several other architectural works, including one relevant to gardens – the second volume of *Les Trois Livres d'Architecture* – which appeared in 1561. It contains elevations and ground-plans for various garden buildings – prototypes the architect thought suitable for the new gardens of France. All the plans are classically inspired and on a grand scale, and some are Mannerist in spirit. Du Cerceau starts with a series of elaborate fountains that could form the centre-piece of the *cour d'honneur* or the parterre. One is covered with sculpted mermaids spouting water from their breasts, while others are decorated with strange beasts, satyrs and sphinxes.

Following the fountains and grand designs for wells, du Cerceau then moves on to six designs for pavilions, which he indicates should be made in wood or stone and placed in the middle of the garden or parterre. Some are more like small castles than pavilions and would dwarf any but the most massive parterre.

Du Cerceau's plans might have been widely used for new projects had it not been for the religious wars that tore France apart in the later part of the 16th century. Few were his commissions and none has survived. While Italian garden architects were reaching new heights of grandeur and frivolity, their French counterparts were short of work and little major building was started, let alone finished. The enthusiasm of the Queen, Catherine de Medici, for building châteaux and gardens, was largely frustrated, and her gardens at the Tuileries in Paris, completed in 1572, were a rare example of a finished project.

Surrounded by a high wall with access from the palace through a small door, the Tuileries Gardens comprised many rectangular plots within a very large approximate rectangle. On the principal axis, and at the opposite end to the palace, the wall curved into a wide semicircle. Within the walls was a grotto, famed in its time but of which no trace now remains, commissioned by Catherine de Medici from Bernard Palissy, a potter who evolved his own style of decoration with pottery figures of fish, reptiles and plants. In 1581, Catherine also commissioned a treillage tunnel or *berceau* along the length of one of the allées that must have resembled the *galerie* at Montargis, for it had pavilions at each intersection. Under the care of Pierre Le Nôtre, the Tuileries Gardens were open to the public, and have been much loved by Parisians from the 16th century to this day.

During the religious wars, du Cerceau, a Protestant Huguenot, escaped persecution under the protection of a royal princess, Renée of France. At her château at Montargis, he supervised the rebuilding of the castle and worked on his books. While political events prevented du Cerceau leaving completed projects, his major legacy is his record of French 16th-century architecture, and it is thanks to his considerable output that the glorious châteaux and gardens of 16th-century France have been recorded.

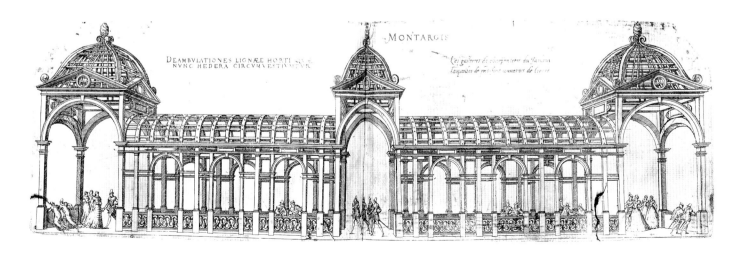

The Garden in Tudor England

Then in we went to the garden glorious
Like to a place of pleasure most solacious.

With Flora painted and wrought curiously,
In divers knots of marvellous greatness;
Ramping lions stood up wondrously,
Made all of herbs with dulcet sweetness,
With many dragons of marvellous likeness,
Of divers flowers made full craftily,
By Flora coloured with colours sundry.

Amidst the garden so much delectable
There was an arbour fair and quadrant,
To paradise right well comparable,
Set all about with flowers fragrant;
And in the middle there was resplendent
A dulcet spring and marvellous fountain,
Of gold and azure made all certain.

Stephen Hawes, *The History of Grand Amour and la Belle Pucelle*, 1509

A plan (CMP Supp.24) of the Elizabethan
gardens of the royal manor house at Hatfield,
c.1608. The orchard was in existence by 1583
and the pair of knot gardens are likely to have been
laid out well before the plan was made.

The architectural influence of the Renaissance did not reach England for many decades after it had percolated through France. Perpendicular gothic in its island mode continued to develop throughout the 16th century and it was not until the early 17th century that the first truly Classical Renaissance buildings were seen in England.

In the garden, medieval plans and features also evolved and developed at a leisurely pace in the early 16th century, with only occasional signs of Italian influence. Henry VII's Richmond Palace remains indistinct, with only the galleries or pergolas bordering the gardens visible in a rare illustration. Hampton Court in Surrey, the palace started by Henry VIII's Lord Chancellor, Cardinal Wolsey, also had a garden that is equally obscure. Henry confiscated Hampton Court from the unfortunate Wolsey in 1525 and started to redevelop the gardens in a grand manner from 1529 onwards. He had ambitions to prove England's importance on the European stage and to rival François I of France, and a palace that would compare well with Fontainebleau was essential.

Although he also improved the royal gardens at Whitehall, Hampton Court was Henry's first, and most influential, garden and he lavished considerable sums on expanding Wolsey's earlier plan, and in stamping his insignia all over it. Pennants, weathervanes and carved beasts had decorated the roofline of Richmond Palace and other important buildings, topping gables like superlative gothic pinnacles, but the Privy Garden of Hampton Court was dominated by heraldry and beasts carved in stone or wood, planted in the ground on twisted wooden poles. There were dragons, griffins, greyhounds, lions, horses, deer and antelopes, often bearing the King's arms or a Tudor rose, and holding a flag or a weathervane.

This was Tudor power gardening, this was a dynastic glorification of Henry and his claim to the throne of England. It was done for the same reasons that Duke Cosimo enhanced the Villa Medici at Castello with iconographical tributes to himself in the 1540s, and although Henry's way was hardly subtle, he was not alone in using his gardens for a display of power.

The beasts and heraldry in the Privy Garden were complemented by geometric or curving patterns fitted inside the railed beds. Designs for knots had already appeared in print in *Hypnerotomachia Poliphili*, a book that, as a Latin scholar, Henry might have read. As designs became more elaborate, the popularity of knots grew throughout the 16th century, yet they always adhered to to the principle of one band of colour, continuously turning, twisting, and interlacing with itself.

The source of inspiration for the endless movement in a knot garden came from the decorative arts, such as patterns of marquetry on tables, intricate designs on mirror frames, and patterns in brocade fabric and in embroidery. They were all part of the same taste in decoration, which developed in parallel until the final flourish of Rococo art and the demise of the parterre in the 18th century.

In the garden, the patterns were created out of vegetable or

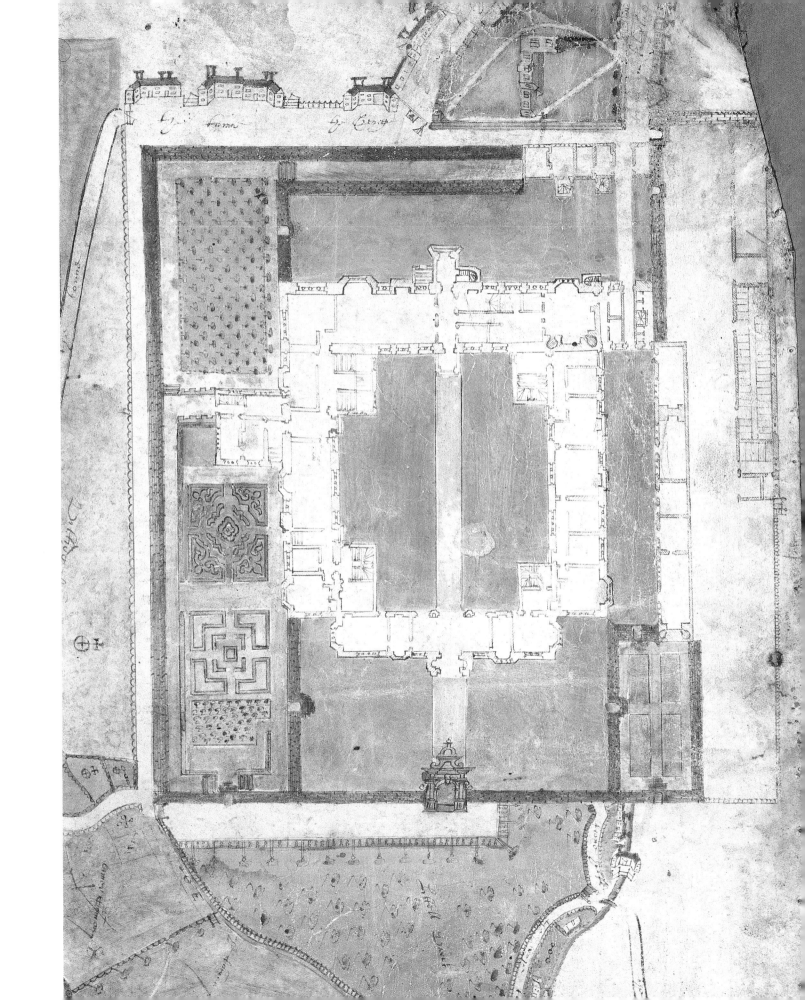

mineral materials, and scented plants, like rosemary, hyssop and thyme were added to give variety of texture and colour and to accentuate the pattern. At Hampton Court, a mixture of grass, white sand and red brick dust was laid out to resemble a chess-board.

Also remarkable at Hampton Court was the topiary, formed by growing shrubs through willow frames of men and animals, and clipping the foliage to make crisp, expressive shapes. It is not certain whether these were grown first in Henry's time or whether they date from after Elizabeth's accession in 1558, but a German traveller, Thomas Platter, who visited Hampton Court in 1599, was much impressed by them: *There were all manner of shapes, men and women, half men and half horse, sirens, serving-maids, with baskets, French lilies and delicate crenellations all round made from dry twigs bound together and the aforesaid evergreen quickset shrubs, or entirely of rosemary, all true to the life, and so cleverly and amusingly interwoven, mingled and grown together, trimmed and arranged picture-wise that their equal would be difficult to find.*[22]

Platter's account has a familiar ring to it; topiary creatures like these had been seen in the previous century at the Villa Quaracchi near Florence, as well as in the gardens of ancient Rome.

The garden at Hampton Court was designed in three principal sections: the Privy Garden with its Knot Garden, the Pond Garden, where fish were kept in pools, also marked out by the King's beasts, and the small triangular Mount Garden, the latter dominated by the mount itself, built during 1533–4. A spiralling path bordered with stone beasts led up to an exceptional building, known as the South or Great Round Arbour, said to be made largely of glass, an expensive commodity in Tudor times. Three storeys high, with a squashed onion dome made of lead, the Arbour was surmounted by a twisted pinnacle and a beast holding a standard.

The Great Round Arbour must have been a delightful pavilion, warmed in spring and autumn by sunshine through its leaded panes, and affording views of the knots in the Privy Garden and of the Thames.

The description of the Great Round Arbour recalls the *diaeta* that Raphael created at the Villa Madama, *c.* 1520. Was this by coincidence or by design? From 1527 Henry sent repeated envoys to Rome to plead with the Pope for a divorce, and he would certainly have questioned returning emissaries about art and architecture as well as papal negotiations, so it seems more likely that the Arbour was influenced by Raphael's building. Another tower, reminiscent of a *diaeta*, followed in 1538 at the royal palace of Oatlands in Surrey.

Despite Henry VIII's wish to rival Fontainebleau, the Hampton Court gardens never reached the same grand scale. However, its compact gardens had much to please: topiary, armies of painted beasts, coloured parterres, the mount with its outstanding Arbour, and the slowly gliding Thames.

What Hampton Court and Fontainebleau had in common was the fact that neither had been designed on the Alberti principle of house and garden conceived as one unit. The Palace at Hampton Court was not aligned with the river, which meant that the main area of the gardens was fitted into a large triangle, and, equally, Fontainebleau had developed in a similar haphazard way, its gardens at odd angles and with curiously shaped boundaries.

Anet and Ancy-le-Franc were the first châteaux and gardens in France to be designed to one overall plan. Both date from 1546, while Wollaton Hall in Nottinghamshire, started decades later in 1580, was among the first in England. Some of the reasons for the time lag in the English adoption of the new, unified approach lay in the

realms of religion and the Reformation. After Henry's break with the Catholic Church in 1536, contacts between England and Italy were interrupted, and the flow of ideas, artists and craftsmen slowed down. Furthermore, for over twenty years after the death of Henry VIII in 1547, political uncertainty inhibited building development. The great flowering of Elizabethan England did not start with Elizabeth's accession in 1558, but gathered momentum only after 1570. Unlike her father, Henry VIII, Elizabeth built no palaces or gardens for herself.

So Wollaton was a landmark. It was built for Sir Francis Willoughby, a rich eccentric with noble connections, a powerful intellect and a great library that contained copies of Danielo Barbaro's *Vitruvius*, Serlio's *Architettura*, Palladio's and Vignola's treatises, Philibert de l'Orme's *Nouvelle Inventions* and *L'Architecture*, as well as du Cerceau's *Les Plus Excellents Bastiments de la France* and at least two out of the three volumes of *Les Trois Livres d'Architecture*. Willoughby is also thought to have owned three of Hans Vredeman de Vries's pattern books. With this architectural interest behind him, Willoughby is considered to have had a significant influence on his new house, and to have designed it in conjunction with Robert Smythson.

A portrait by an unknown artist of Henry VIII and his family. (OM 43 HC510.) Through the arched doors, the twisted wooden rails and heraldic beasts on posts in the garden are clearly visible.

Hampton Court Palace, as drawn by Wyngaerde c. 1555 (EDB13), shows the Privy Garden and Mount Garden of Henry VIII and, to the right, behind the crenellated Water Gate, the squashed onion dome of the Great Round Arbour. The base of the mount is also visible, as is its spiralling path with yet more heraldic beasts.

Set on the flat top of a hill, Wollaton Hall is still intact, although the gardens have been much altered over the centuries. Smythson's plan shows a large square house with the garden divided into eight squares of equal size surrounding it, and, decorating the principal area, a fountain in a round basin.

The other great gardens of Elizabethan England belonged to leading figures at court: the Earl of Leicester's Kenilworth Castle in Warwickshire, Sir William Cecil's Burghley House and Theobalds. As Secretary of State and subsequently Lord High Treasurer to the Queen, Cecil purchased Burghley House in 1553, and Theobalds in 1564. Both gardens were developed over many years, largely to Cecil's own plans, for he was passionately interested in growing plants as well as in the aesthetics of design. Theobalds in Hertfordshire was probably the most elaborate. From 1585, when he had completed both the garden and the mansion, a massive pile of a place, the Queen stayed there regularly on her journeys to the north of England.

There are no contemporary plans of Theobalds but Sir John Summerson's research into surveys and plans of the following century, and accounts by visitors from the 1590s onwards, suggest that the garden was divided into two principal areas, the Privy Garden, which was for private use only, and the Great Garden.

The Great Garden was a vast square divided into nine huge beds edged with privet, some of which were planted with knots, some with flowers, some grassed, and in the centre bed a white marble fountain. What enchanted the German visitor, Paul Hentzner, in 1598, was another water feature, the canal surrounding the garden. Hentzner was able to see the garden from a boat, and he clearly enjoyed *rowing between the shrubs*.[23] This was a novelty in England, for at that time water had not played a major role in garden design.

Theobalds' other attractions, the Mount of Venus and two summerhouses, are all described by Hentzner. The first summerhouse was of an intriguing design: *we were led by the gardener into the summerhouse, in the lower part of which, built semi-circularly, are the twelve Roman emperors in white marble and a table of touchstone; the upper part of it is set round with cisterns of lead, into which water is conveyed through pipes, so that fish may be kept in them, and in summertime they are very convenient for bathing. In another room for entertainment, very near this, and joined to it by a little bridge, was an oval table of red marble.*[24]

Here was a garden with many entertainments. Apart from walking along the wide allées and crossing and recrossing the canal over a bridge or two, there was boating and bathing, and humanist links with the classical era in the collection of Roman statuary. Here was a garden to amuse, and to take the intellect along the paths of allegory. The Great Garden at Theobalds was a new departure in England, nudging towards the sustained programme of iconography that had evolved in the great gardens of Italy during the 16th century.

The great Nonsuch Palace in Surrey was also important for its innovations in the Italian style. Started in 1538 by Henry VIII, when his coffers were replete with the riches of the sacked monasteries, it was a large, ostentatious half-timbered house, encapsulating the romance of Tudor times. As its name suggests, it was without an equal.

After Henry's death, the Palace was acquired by John, Lord Lumley in 1579, and the gardens redeveloped during the following decade. A member of the Elizabethan Society of Antiquaries, a collector of books and portraits, Lumley was an intellectual and one of the few gentlemen of his generation who had travelled to Italy and seen the art, architecture and gardens of the Renaissance. He was also a Catholic, and his refusal to renounce Catholicism under Elizabeth subsequently restricted his political career.

At Nonsuch, Lumley removed Henry VIII's heraldic beasts on posts, replacing them with his own popinjays and falcons on marble columns, and a leaping horse; these decorations, not copied from Italy, were *de rigueur* in a Tudor garden. What was new were the materials of which they were made: painted wood in the gothic tradition had been replaced by coloured, polished marble and stone in a Classical design. While all these dynastic tributes at Nonsuch were lost with the demolition of the Palace, similar columns can still be seen on the garden front of Montacute House in Somerset.

To demonstrate his loyalty to the Crown despite religious adherence to Rome, Lumley also introduced a complex allegorical tribute to Elizabeth and among the many symbols of the Virgin Queen was a Mannerist fountain portraying a female figure under a royal crown.

At the centre of radiating paths in a woodland garden was another fountain where birds sprayed water from their beaks, and a *giocho d'acqua*, which involved a seemingly innocent pyramid that suddenly drenched anyone within sprayshot. On a mount stood a three-storeyed, half-timbered banqueting house with no less than eight rooms, as well as balconies from which to view the hunt. Paul Hentzner, who visited Nonsuch in 1598, also observed *groves ornamented with trellis-work and cabinets of verdure*.[25]

The source of these ideas must have been a garden in existence by the time of Lumley's trip to Italy in 1566. Evidence points heavily to the Villa Medici at Castello, since Lumley had been sent to Florence by the Queen to treat with Duke Cosimo I for the recovery of a debt due to Henry VIII. While in Florence, he no doubt visited churches and palaces, and is most likely to have included the ducal villa at Castello. The parallels with Nonsuch are there: allegorical symbolism glorifying the ruler, creatures spouting water, water jokes, and woodlands surrounding the formal garden enlivened by architectural points of interest.

Tudor gardens tantalise us with their secrets, for information about them is sketchy and incomplete. None of those described survives intact, and there was no English du Cerceau to record them. What emerges from these hazy pictures? First, colour, not on painted

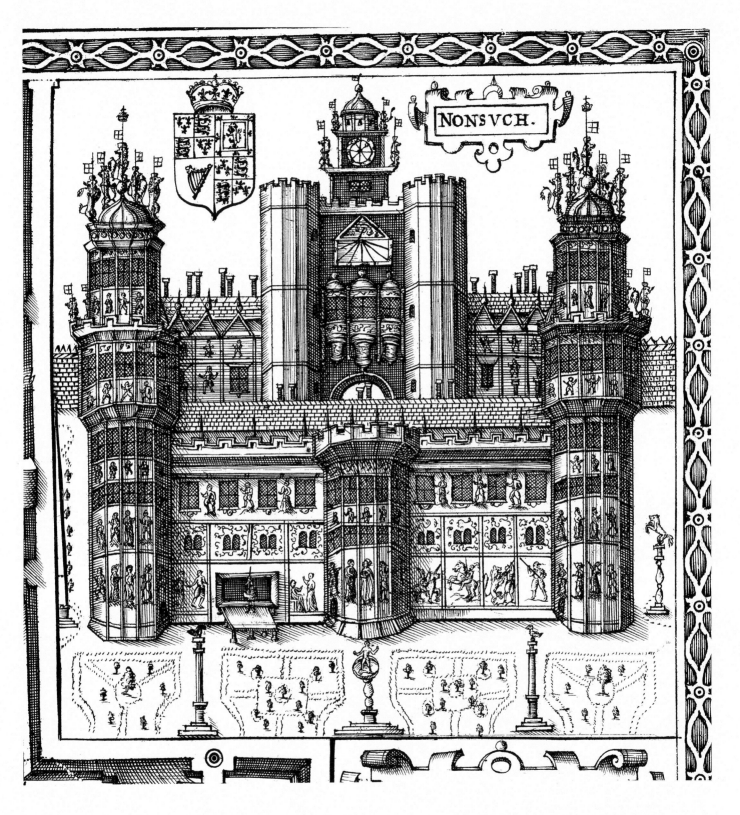

NONSVCH.

*The Privy Garden of Nonsuch Palace, illustrated
by Hondius in a Map of Surrey (Maps c.7.c.5).
The columns in front of Nonsuch have equivalents
still at Montacute.*

pavilions as in France, but on heraldry and animals. Next, the growing importance of allegory and a move from religious themes to glorification of gods and monarchs. Third, a comprehensive approach to geometric design and at the same time a gradual increase in size.

The features in these gardens changed too. The pleasures of sparkling, trickling and tinkling water were increasingly appreciated, as were the ever larger fountains, culminating in the magnificent Clock Court fountain at Hampton Court, erected by Elizabeth in 1590, which was surmounted by a statue of Justice and incorporated *giochi d'acqua*. By the end of the century, large impressive fountains and water jokes were an essential part of any garden of taste and enlightenment.

If moving water was ever more desirable, still water came to be appreciated only late in the century. Rather than turn it into one of the charms of the garden, in England the medieval moat had been abandoned. In Italy, it had hardly existed because of the undulating terrain, while in France it had played a vital defensive role, but had only just survived in rare instances to enhance a building by reflection, for example, at Ancy-le-Franc, where it encompassed the château, separating it from its gardens.

It also seems that statuary was not a feature of English gardens until late in the 16th century. Of Alberti's recognition of statuary as part of the decoration of a garden, and French enthusiasm for importing the best Italian sculptures, little response was seen across the Channel in England. The Dutch, too, were slow to follow the Italian lead, but by the end of the century, they were making their own contribution to garden design through the work of Hans Vredeman de Vries.

Hans Vredeman de Vries

Sixteenth-century Dutch gardens were geometric in design and Christian in symbolism. Humanist associations with classical mythology and pagan gods had been rejected in favour of allusions to Christ, St Peter and the Virgin Mary. Typically, a garden would be enclosed by a gallery or pergola painted with *trompe-l'oeil* plants and animals, and contain a central fountain surrounded by neat beds for plants. While the layout owed its formality to the Renaissance, the features were derived largely from the past.

Enter Hans Vredeman de Vries and his Mannerist ideas for grafting decoration on to the established features. De Vries was a painter, decorator and engineer who was fascinated by shape and design generally, and who published a series of ornamental pattern books that were highly influential abroad. *Hortorum Viridariorumque Elegantes et Multiplicis Formae*, to give it its cumbersome full title, is the part of this series devoted to gardens, published in Antwerp in 1583.

In a total of 29 engravings, de Vries showed gardens subdivided into compartments by fences, hedges and pergolas. There is no axial relationship between garden and house in most of the plans, so the garden is seen as sufficient unto itself, as it had been for centuries. Another reminder of the medieval garden is the fence that surrounds the entire garden, separating it from the area near the house, and screening it from the house as was the Gaillon Upper Garden from its château. A further relic from the past is the estrade, the tree clipped into horizontal discs.

The most significant features of de Vries' plans are the elaborate pergolas or berceaux, which are effectively architecture turned green by nature. Wooden tunnels with pavilions at their intersections, they are planted with climbers carefully pruned to conform precisely to the architectural outline. Not a leaf, not a shoot could be out of line to spoil the proportions. To demonstrate the importance he placed on the classical heritage, de Vries subdivided his plans into the orders of architecture: Doric, Ionic and Corinthian. Yet his creations have endless imagination that runs free of the rules of architecture, and delights in experimentation with shape and pattern. They are exuberant and extravagant and epitomise the Dutch interpretation of Mannerism.

The plots contained within the pergolas were patterned with maze-like designs in squares or curves, as complex as the strapwork patterns that decorated facades of buildings in the Netherlands and England at this period. Since they were not one continuous pattern, the designs were not, strictly speaking, knots, but rather cut-work, or *parterres de pièces coupées*, which overtook knots in popularity for 150 years or more until the parterre went out of fashion. An estrade was de Vries' preferred centrepiece for these parterres, although once he proposed a square pool and twice, a statue.

After the publication of *Hortorum Viridariorumque ...* , the author was invited to design the gardens at Wolfenbuttel for the Duke of Braunschweig in 1587, and for the Emperor Rudolph II in Prague in 1596. He also created garden pavilions and *trompe-l'oeil* panels of garden vistas in Antwerp and Hamburg. De Vries' greatest achievement in gardens, however, was the book itself, for it was most influential throughout Europe and must have been invaluable to the next generation of garden designers, men like Salomon de Caus and Jacques Boyceau.

The incredible inventive force of the Italians had given birth to the Renaissance, and then slowly stimulated their neighbours further north to copy, alter and develop the classical ideas in their own distinctive ways. By the end of the 16th century, although its influence in other areas of art was collapsing, the creative impetus of Italian garden design was still strong, and after 1600 more Italian gardens would be created to enchant, amuse and overawe, but the vocabulary of architecture was changing. The 17th century ushered in the age of Baroque.

Of the gardens illustrated in Hortorum
Viridariorumque…, 1583, some have tunnel
arbours that might have been the model for Lauro's
Roman garden (p.21), but most, like this one, have
a complex, controlled pattern of cut-work beds in
turf with a sparse collection of trees and flowers.

DORICA

4

The Birth of Baroque in Italy

Thou has thy walkes for health, as well as sport:
Thy Mount, to which the DRYADS *doe resort,*
Where PAN *and* BACCHUS *their high feasts have made,*
Beneath the broad beech, and the chest-nut shade;
That taller tree, which of a nut was set,
At his great birth, where all the MUSES *met.*

From 'To Penshurst' (the seat of Sir Philip Sidney) by Ben Jonson,
1572–1637

The Galley Fountain below the Belvedere
Gardens in the Vatican was designed by Carlo
Maderno very early in the 17th century.
A beautifully detailed model of a contemporary
ship that could spray delicate jets in every direction,
it was amongst the most famous of Rome's
celebrated collection of fountains.

Change in garden and architectural history never coincides precisely with the turn of a century. The themes of the grand gardens of the 16th century in Italy – assertion of power, portrayal of allegory and sophistication in water displays and hydraulics – evolved and expanded into the next century. As far as garden architecture was concerned, the spirit of design had moved from the High Renaissance of the Belvedere through to the Mannerist eccentricities of Bomarzo and the inventiveness of the Villa d'Este.

By the end of the 16th and into the 17th century, innovative architects like Carlo Maderno were moving on to develop subtle and not so subtle twists in the language of classical architecture. What was different after the turn of the century was that the first signs of Baroque were visible in some Italian gardens.

What is Baroque architecture? The term 'Baroque' is thought to derive from three possible sources: the Italian word *barocco* or *barroco*, meaning tortuous and useless knowledge; the style of the painter Federigo Barocci; or the Portuguese word *barrocco*, meaning a deformed pearl. As two of the derivations signify deviation from a norm, it is not surprising that 'Baroque' was first used as a term of abuse. In architecture, the word describes a style that flourished throughout Europe from the late 16th to the early 18th century, characterised by extensive ornamentation. To Classical purists, it is excessive, florid and pretentious.

Baroque architecture and decoration is powerful, grandiose and bizarre, tossing Classical restraint out of the window in favour of flamboyance of form, complexity of composition, and immensity of concept. There is occasionally a dark streak, too, a desire to shock by exaggeration and frighten by monstrosity, which is a legacy from Mannerism. The response to the drama of Baroque design was essentially emotional, just as it was to the art and sculpture of Bernini and other Baroque artists such as Rubens, Velásquez and Rembrandt.

Baroque, embodied in the work of Bernini and Borromini, was the principal architectural style in Italy in the 17th century; it also predominated in France, and lasted into the 18th century in Austria, Germany and Spain. British architects adopted it later in the 17th century, preferring a controlled version closer to Classicism rather than the curvaceous, swelling forms popular in the Hapsburg Empire, but they abandoned it early in the 18th century.

These themes of massive scale and abundant decoration were carried automatically into the gardens. Old-style gardens seemed constrained and cramped, so new ones engulfed the countryside, while at the same time the architect's contribution to garden design became steadily more important as the number of buildings in the garden increased. His responsibility now went far beyond the layout of paths in geometric patterns, interspersed with fountains, ancient statues and water jokes; it now also embraced the creation of garden

buildings, and major garden features in ornamental stone. Architecture is central in Baroque gardens; nature is the backdrop, never the foreground.

Early 17th-century plans had come a long way from the intimate formality of Alberti's gardens, the harmony with nature and the wistful desire for Arcadia. They were made to resound with music, not for the contemplation of philosophers. The grandeur of their scale shouts assertively: Long live man and his works! And because of the theatricality of their atmosphere, they demand an audience, a crowd of pleasure seekers to appreciate their delights.

Nowhere is this more evident than in the first Baroque garden in Italy, the Villa Aldobrandini, a composition of villa and garden for yet another prince of the church, Cardinal Pietro Aldobrandini. The estate at Frascati was a gift in 1598 from Pope Clement VIII to his nephew, the Cardinal, although Clement remained closely involved, the project being a symbol of family prestige. The Cardinal commissioned Giacomo della Porta to enlarge the existing villa, and after della Porta's death in 1602, Carlo Maderno and Giovanni Fontana were asked to complete the project. It was finished by 1603, while work in the gardens was continued until 1620. Both were badly damaged during the First World War, but much restoration has been undertaken recently by the owner, Prince Aldobrandini, and the architect, Clemente Busiri-Vici.

Built on a sloping hillside in the Renaissance tradition, the villa towers haughtily above Frascati, looking across the now great conurbation of Rome and beyond to the Appennines, its height a dramatic embodiment of power, reminiscent of the fortress Farnese Palace at Caprarola.

What gives Villa Aldobrandini and its garden a Baroque label is della Porta's experimentation with new decorative architectural devices that, after modification, came to be called Baroque, and the fundamental importance of the structural element in the garden. Architecture is at the core of the garden composition, and nature is, quite literally, pushed to the sides.

Carlo Maderno, the architect for the gardens, was assisted in the creation of the hydraulics by his uncle Giovanni Fontana, and by Orazio Olivieri, who had been in charge of the fountains at the Villa d'Este and who designed the new waterworks. A reliable source of water had been secured in 1603 when the Pope was given a present, doubtless for a papal favour, of an aqueduct. It was 12 kilometres long and brought copious quantities of water to supply countless fountains. Fontana and Olivieri, together with the Pope and the obliging donor, were the heroes of this garden, for Frascati is notably dry.

The original entrance to the villa was along a tree-lined avenue on the central axis, an approach that intensified its height, for it was intended to overawe. The visitor then reached a series of three terraces, linked by a pair of wide oval ramps and decorated with rows of clipped orange trees in pots so neatly and regularly arranged

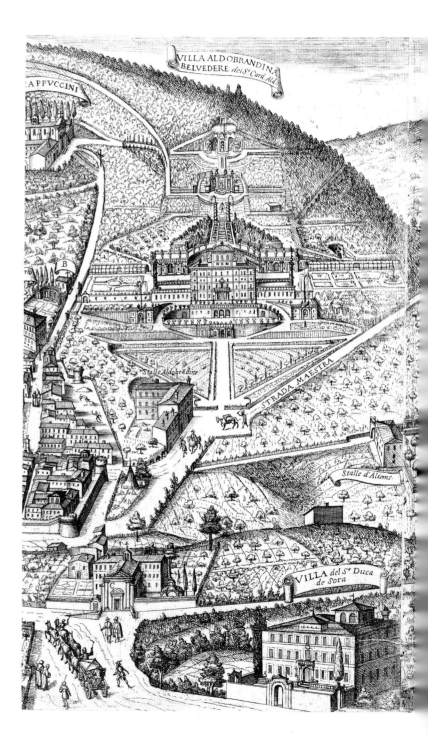

An aerial view by Matthias Greuter of half of the town of Frascati, 1620 (Maps K.82), in the vicinity of which, according to John Raymond, 10 cardinals had their country seats. On the left, the garden of the Villa Aldobrandini, showing not only its architectural axis rising up the hillside but also, to the right of the villa, a giant stone face with an open mouth similar to one at the Sacro Bosco at Bomarzo. It was an Orc, a devouring monster which symbolised one of the gods of the Underworld.

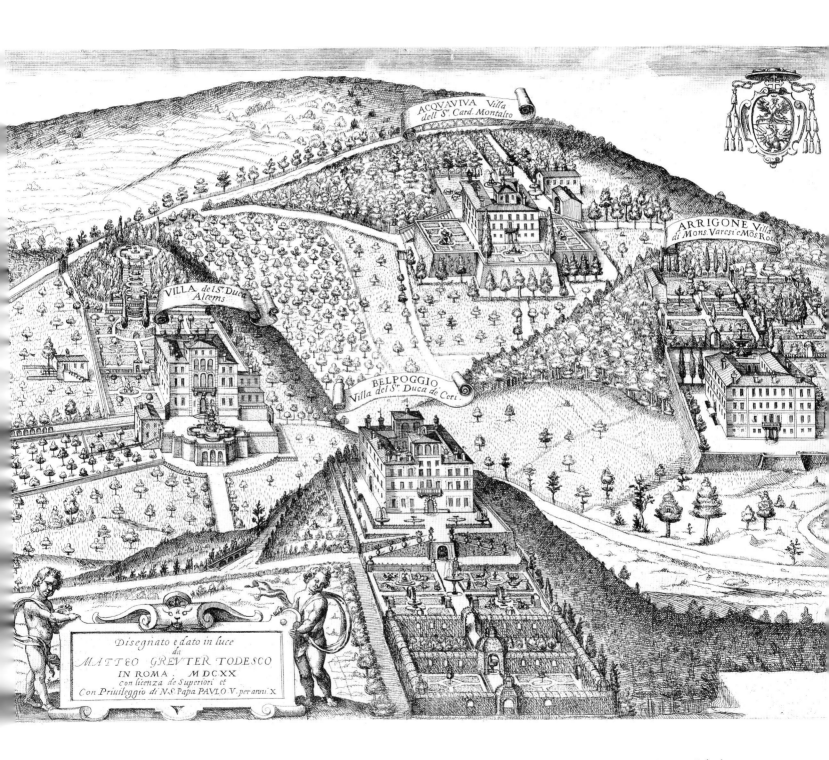

ACQVAVIVA Villa
dell S.r Card. Montalto

ARRIGONE Villa
di Mons. Varesi e Mōs Roc.

VILLA del S.r Duca
Altems

BELPOGGIO
Villa del S.r Duca de Ceri.

Disegnato e dato in luce
da
MATTEO GREVTER TODESCO
IN ROMA. MDCXX
con licenza de Superiori et
Con Priuileggio di N.S. Papa PAVLO V. per anni X.

The rear elevation of the Villa Aldobrandini, as engraved by Falda in Il Nuovo Teatro, *1665, is seen from the Water Theatre. Visitors are scurrying away from the steps to escape the sprays of the water jokes.*

as to seem part of the architectural plan. A grotto at the centre of the lowest terrace and another on the oval middle level were other major features. This was all splendid, but not novel.

The real drama lay on the other side of the villa, hidden behind its tall façade and tucked into the hillside out of sight. High up the slope, the composition starts with first one water staircase, which descends to a second, and then to a truly brilliant third that drops curtains of water in wide shining steps. The cascades have been designed to give maximum drama through the effect of light reflecting on falling sheets of water. Here is an altogether more powerful use of light on water than the delicate patterns created in the cascades of the Villa Cicogna Mozzoni, the Villa Lante or the Palazzo Farnese at Caprarola.

Flanking the head of the third staircase is a pair of mosaic-encrusted columns of breathtaking originality, for from the top water runs round and round and down the outside of the columns in helter-skelter channels. Allegorically, they represent the pillars of Hercules; visually, they draw the eye of the beholder upwards, and frame the two upper *catene d'acqua*.

Below these shimmering falls stands the nymphaeum, or water theatre. This is a reminder not only of Vignola's internal courtyard at the Villa Giulia, but also of ancient Rome's pleasure houses

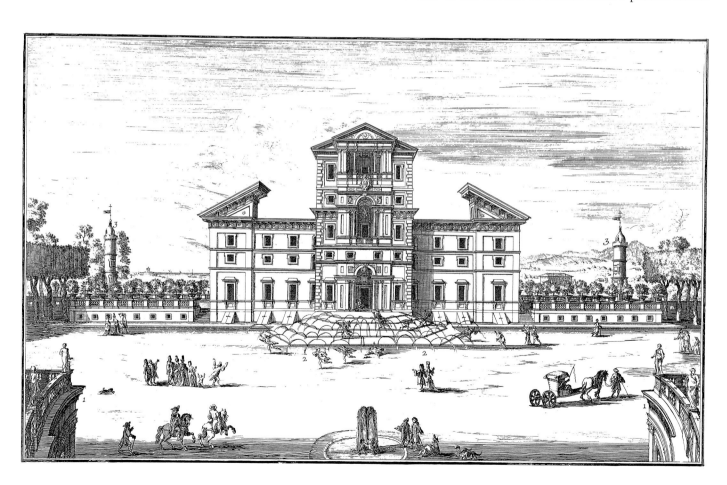

adorned with fountains and statues. The nymphaeum is built in a semicircle, close to the villa, on a level with the first floor, and is a most dramatic frontispiece to the gardens.

This water theatre was an invention of pure delight built to impress and amuse. John Evelyn, the eminent scholar and diarist, described it in his visit to the villa in May 1645, when all the hydraulic fantasies were operating to perfection: *We tooke coach, and went 15 miles out of the Cittie to Frascati, formerly Tusculanum, a villa of Cardinal Aldobrandini built for a country-house, but surpassing, in my opinion, the most delicious places I ever beheld for its situation, elegance, plentifull water, groves, ascents and prospects.*

In Rome, Evelyn had already visited the Villas Medici, Borghese, the Belvedere, and the Pope's Palace at Monte Cavallo, but saw the Villa d'Este the next day, and Pratolino later. He continued:

Just behind the palace (which is of excellent architecture), in the centre of the inclosure, rises an high hill or mountaine all over clad with tall wood, and so form'd by nature as if it had been cut out by art, from the sum'it whereof falls a cascade, seeming rather a greate river than a streame precipitating into a large theater of water, representing an exact and perfect rainbow when the sun shines out. Under this is made an artificiall grott, wherein are curious rocks, hydraulic organs, and all sorts of singing birds moving and chirping by force of the water,

Directly opposite the villa is the Water Theatre, from Falda's Le Fontane di Roma, *1675; its sophisticated architectural façade is further enlivened by water and statues and bursts with Baroque vigour.*

with severall other pageants and surprising inventions. In the center of one of these roomes rises a coper ball that continually daunces about 3 foote above the pavement by virtue of a wind conveyed secretely to a hole beneath it; with many other devices to wet the unwary spectators, so that one can hardly step without wetting to the skin. In one of these theaters of water is an Atlas spouting up the streame to a very great height; and another monster makes a terrible roaring with an horn; but above all, the representation of a storm is most naturall, with such fury of raine, wind and thunder, as one would imagine ones self in some extreme tempest.[1]

Evelyn's only reference to nature other than the wooded hillside is very brief: *The garden has excellent walkes and shady groves, abundance of rare fruit, oranges, lemons &c., and the goodly prospect of Rome, above all description.*[2]

Water jokes abounded. John Raymond, on the Grand Tour in Italy in 1646 and 1647, said that any spectators, *whosoever they be, must looke to goe away wet to the Skinne, as we did.*[3] It was an observation, with not a hint of complaint.

In 1685, Bishop Gilbert Burnet was fulsome in his praise: *The Water-works in the Aldobrandin Palace have a magnificence in them beyond all that I ever saw in France, the mixture of Wind with the Water, and the Thunders and Storms that this maketh, is noble.*[4]

By 1740, the hydraulic machinery had suffered with time. In his *Lettres Historiques et Critiques sur l'Italie*, written during a visit in 1739, the Président de Brosses lamented the condition of the automata in the grotto of the Mount Parnassus and found the music melancholy. The Nine Muses, made of stone and daubed with colour, were a chilling sight, since the machinery that had once made them seem to play their violins in time with the music was no longer working.

After nearly four centuries, most of the statues have gone and the machinery has long since disappeared, but Atlas' powerful arms still hold the globe aloft while water cascades around his head.

By 1904, Edith Wharton, writing in *Italian Villas and their Gardens*, found the water theatre *pompous* and *a heavy and uninspired production.*[5] Had she been able to see the figures moving and the water spraying, and hear the music and the thunder, she might have been more impressed. A water theatre with no dramatic action and only a little water lacks a significant part of its *raison d'être*. Would that such hydraulic figures could be fully restored, to give a true impression of the designers' intentions, and of the type of attraction that was to be found in the principal gardens of Europe. Made of stone, wood or bronze and often painted, they must have made an amazing impact in that pre-industrial age.

Wharton also criticised the Villa Aldobrandini's juxtaposition of villa and water theatre. *It suffers from too great proximity to the villa, and from being out of scale with the latter's modest elevation: there is a distinct lack of harmony between the two facades.*[6] Others have felt the same, but perhaps the closeness of the two is part of the concept of Baroque, for the tension between them adds greatly to the drama of the composition.

The cascades and water theatre were constructed to be admired from the villa as much as from the garden, observed Geoffrey Jellicoe. He noted that: *If you enter the villa itself, and climb to the topmost loggia which looks back upon the hillside, you will see how cleverly the cascade has been planned to give the illusion of an almost vertical fall of water. This is one of those exercises in the arts of perspective in which the Italians have always delighted.*[7] The designers, Carlo Maderno, Giovanni Fontana, and Orazio Olivieri had thought it all through very carefully.

Villa Aldobrandini was one of the main attractions on the tourist map of Rome, a map dotted with villas and churches as well as the sites of ancient Rome. Inevitably, it was soon known beyond the confines of Rome and Italy, and its influence spread to designers abroad. Its enviable reputation might have caused the lips of Cardinal and Pope to curl with pleasure.

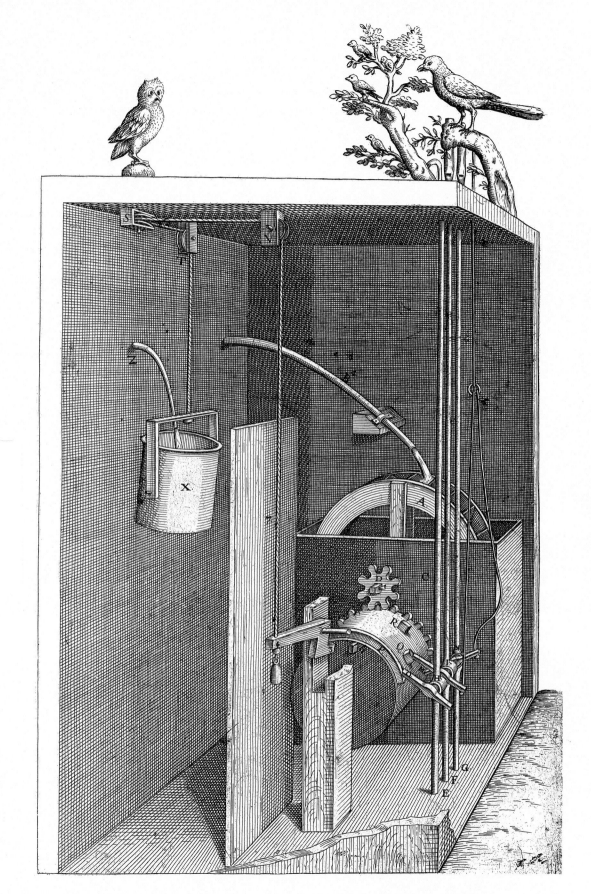

Two of the many automata at the Villa Aldobrandini: the Fountain of the Owl, right, was modelled on an earlier version at the Villa d'Este at Tivoli. Left: the copper ball that balanced on top of a jet of water was another feature that intrigued visitors, and both were illustrated by de Caus in Les Raisons des Forces Mouvantes, *1624.*

PORTRAIT. DES. CHASTEAVX. ROYA — VX. DE. SAINCT. GERMAIN. EN. LAYE.

Early Baroque in France

The château and gardens of St. Germain-en-Laye (Maps K.66.4.d), illustrated by Francini in 1614, were Italianate in design. The water parterre on the lowest level was never completed, and now only part of the terracing remains.

An engraving of a Swiss garden in Riehen near Basle by Matthäus Merian, 1620. (Wüthrich Nr.404.) Entitled Breakfast by the Swan Lake, *it shows how precise architectural features such as a square pond and a clipped arbour were sometimes set in a natural landscape.*

Italian pre-eminence in garden design led Henri IV of France to employ a Frenchman familiar with Italian gardens, Etienne du Pérac, and the brothers Francini from Florence. Du Pérac, also known as Duperac, and with his first name sometimes Italianised as Stefano, had published the first engraving of the Villa d'Este in 1573, and his experience of Italian gardens led to his appointment as *architecte du roi* in 1595. As for the Francini brothers, Henri IV and his Italian wife, Marie de Médicis found in Tommaso and Alessandro Francini engineers with artistic eyes, for they had been responsible for the impressive waterworks in the Medici garden at Pratolino.

Thus it was that du Pérac and the brothers Francini were charged by the King with designing the royal garden overlooking the Seine west of Paris, at St. Germain-en-Laye. An older building, the Chateau-Neuf, had been started by Philibert de l'Orme for Henri II, and Henri IV now wished to complete it.

The site at St. Germain-en-Laye was unusual in France, in that the château was sited on the top of an escarpment; it therefore had a fine view, like the summer villas around Florence and Rome. The gardens obviously had to be terraced, and were set out by du Pérac in six or seven layers down to the level of the river. Work was under way by 1599, and continued for a decade. Since château and terraces have largely disappeared, illustrations do not always tally, and records are contradictory, some details are in doubt.

What is clear, however, is that although it was more extensive than its Italian equivalents like the Villa d'Este, St. Germain-en-Laye is an Italian garden in France. The concept is grander, the size is greater, and the terraces are therefore wider. Its magnitude gives it a Baroque flavour, as does the way that the flights of stairs and terrace

The gardens at Tanlay, Yonne, boasted a very theatrical grotto, also known as the Château d'Eau; it was designed by Pierre Le Muet and completed by 1648. The canal narrowed as it approached the grotto to increase the illusion of distance.

Profp. du Parc. et du Canal de Tanlai

La Grotte.

walls are heavily decorated with architectural features. From the level of the river, the effect of the elaborate terrace structure was to increase the appearance and importance of the château. Only the walls on the lowest levels were kept comparatively plain.

Into the terraced walls was built an *orangerie*, a greenhouse for storing orange trees in winter, and, of course, the inevitable grottoes.

Mythology supplied the subject matter for some of the automata, which were made of bronze or brass; in one, Neptune, his chariot drawn by sea-horses, sounded his trumpet, in another Orpheus played a violin and in another Perseus freed Andromeda from the clutches of the dragon. As was the custom, these ancient gods and heroes usually symbolised the King.

The most original automata related directly to the royal family, and comprised a succession of scenes showing the sun, followed by a storm, after which the royal family processed in front of a representation of the palace, while the Dauphin descended from the heavens in a chariot.

Although the terraced gardens and resplendent grottoes echoed Italy, in respect of water features St. Germain-en-Laye was inferior to Italian gardens. Lack of a reliable water supply meant there were no water staircases, no large basins and few fountains. It took the determination of Louis XIV to ensure his gardens had water in abundance, a determination that meant that French gardens could rival Italian gardens in sparkle.

The best water displays in France at that time were at Liancourt in Oise. With a plentiful supply of water to hand, the gardens that had been laid out around the château of 1580 were enlarged and enhanced by new fountains and cascades by Roger du Plessys and his wife Jeanne after they inherited the estate in 1620. These included a single jet that reached 15 metres in height on the Grand Parterre, as well as fountains, canals and basins, a rectangular pool called the Nappe d'Eau (tablecloth of water), and another huge square pool with an island in the middle. There was also the famous cascade, or rather line of 22 cascades built side by side into a terrace retaining wall, each one with water tumbling from tier upon tier of shells of rose-grey marble. Denis Godefroy II, the eminent French historian, described it in 1637 as most unusual and reminiscent of the finest pleasure gardens in Italy. After the Revolution these intricate and complex gardens were destroyed to make way for a landscaped garden in the English style.

The Francini established their reputation at St. Germain-en-Laye and subsequently became French citizens, known as Thomas and Alexandre Francine, their descendants serving the kings of France until the Revolution. Although not trained as an architect, Alexandre was an engraver with a creative eye, and in 1631 he published his *Livre d'Architecture*, a catalogue of designs for massive triumphal arches and gateways in the Mannerist style. A second edition appreared in 1640, and it was eventually published in London in 1669.

Because of its similarity with drawings in this book, Alexandre Francine is thought to have been the architect of the Grotte du Luxembourg, or Fontaine Médicis. For the same reason, the Grotte de Wideville, built between 1630 and 1636, is also attributed to Alexandre Francine, or his influence. Both were built as the focal point at the end of an axis, and both are rich with decoration, but while Wideville is Mannerist, Luxembourg is Baroque.

Rueil, Hauts-de-Seine, was another great garden that has disappeared. In 1633 Cardinal Richelieu purchased an existing château, and proceeded to spend a fortune on the gardens ... *though the house is not of the greatest, the gardens about it are so magnificent, that I doubt whether Italy has any exceeding it for all rarities of pleasure,*[8] wrote John Evelyn *en route* to Italy in 1644. It would have been interesting to have Evelyn's comment on his return, but he did not refer to Rueil again.

Evelyn was impressed by this *paradise* with its variety of vineyards, cornfields, meadows and groves as well as by the triumphal arch, brass fountains, a vast orangery, or *citronière*, and a cascade *of astonishing noyse and fury*[9] – there was no shortage of water here, thanks to two kilometres of ducts. The cascade, designed by Thomas Francine, was the prototype for other great cascades in France, notably the Grandes Cascades at St. Cloud and Chantilly, though because it rose from a flat terrace the cascade at Rueil appeared awkward and angular in profile. Rueil also had its grottoes and original water jokes, including a pair of musketeers who shot jets of water from their barrels. Visitors must have speculated, nervously, about the source of the next shower.

The Grande Cascade at St. Cloud has survived. Built for the Duc d'Orléans after 1661, it was probably designed by Antoine Le Pautre and enlarged in 1697 by Hardouin-Mansart. It is a massive set-piece, perhaps a little ponderous but definitely impressive as water froths and bubbles down three wide staircases of vases and basins. Built into the hillside, its situation is more comfortable than the cascade at Rueil.

At St. Cloud a free-standing grotto, like a small classical temple with a domed roof and a cupola on top, bristled with statues in the style of Bernini. Built near the Grande Cascade it was approached up a long wide flight of steps, down the middle of which rushed a flow of water. The grotto was almost certainly built for Jean-François de Gondi, Archbishop of Paris, who acquired St. Cloud in 1620. He was an extravagant, worldly character of an Italian family, not averse to splashing out on his properties to keep up with his Italian counterparts. Besides, rivalry about possessions was part of the archepiscopal tradition, and critics distressed by the squandering of church funds could be soothed by arguments of the employment given to craftsmen and labourers. This grotto was surely the Archbishop's reply to Cardinal Aldobrandini's water theatre at Frascati.

Jacques Boyceau, Seigneur de la Barauderie, was another leader in French garden design in the early part of the 17th century.

Two amongst many designs for parterres de broderie that appeared in Traité du Jardinage *by Boyceau, 1638. Originating in Italy, variations on this ornate type of pattern could be found in textile design, on wall coverings (see the patterned columns in Henry VIII's family portrait on p.50), and on decorated objects of all sorts. Much admired, it was also applied to the garden, and is still frequently seen on the tourist souvenirs of Florence.*

Frises du Jardin des Tuilleries   *Desoubs la terrace des meuriers*

Intendant des Jardins for Louis XIII, he is thought to have designed the Luxembourg gardens for Marie de Médicis, Louis' mother, although probably his most important and lasting contribution was a book on the art of beautifying a garden. Published in 1638, five years after Boyceau's death, *Traité du Jardinage selon les Raisons de la Nature et de l'Art* was most influential, reprinting four times, in 1640, 1678, 1689 and 1707.

Writing of ground-plans, Boyceau states that while long straight allées have the advantage of perspective they could become boring; circles and curves should not be forgotten since they allow the variety that nature demands. Curves have their place, provided they are disposed according to the nature of the place, *la nature du lieu*,[10] which is often constrained by hills and rivers. For centuries, conventional practice had separated landscape from garden by high walls, allowing views to the countryside but no aesthetic relationship with it. The countryside was untamed, while the garden was firmly under control. Now Boyceau was suggesting an understanding between garden and landscape, an empathy that was to be developed by Le Nôtre in the second half of the century.

Boyceau also praised the use of carpentry berceaux or pergolas covered with clipped foliage, which would give shade and act as partitions, and advocated important garden buildings of stone or carpentry, free-standing or built into a terrace. The latter could be decorated inside and out with paintings and sculptures, and could be the winter home for tender plants such as orange trees.

As far as water was concerned, Boyceau found moving water more attractive than still water, and preferred twisting streams to straight canals. He seems to be gently leading opinion to consider an alternative to strict geometrical plans, suggesting a type of design where nature was not entirely subjugated to man's will.

Might he have influenced gardens abroad? Quite possibly. Isaac de Caus's design for Wilton, begun *c.* 1632 and described on p.89, follows Boyceau's principles exactly, even though it was probably finished by the time *Traité du Jardinage ...* was published. News travelled surprisingly fast between those who shared an interest.

Could Boyceau have directly inspired Kent, Burlington, Pope and Bridgeman nearly a century later? Probably not, for his book was not translated into English and would have been thought very out of date by the early 1700s. He simply edged towards the same ideas for the same reasons as did the Englishmen, the difference being that the latter went on to develop a completely new concept of garden design, the English landscape garden.

Other influential leaders in the world of gardens in France included members of a great garden dynasty, the family Mollet. Jacques Mollet had been head gardener at Anet; his son Claude became gardener to Henri IV, covering the Tuileries as well as Fontainebleau, Montceaux and St. Germain-en-Laye, and *Théâtre des plans et jardinages*, his invaluable account of French gardens of the late 16th and early 17th centuries, shows great variety in the designs for *parterres de broderie*. Published in 1652 after his death, it was reprinted in 1663, 1670 and 1678.

Of Claude's sons, André, Pierre, Claude II and Jacques II all looked after royal gardens, but André was the most successful of them all. His experience was international, for not only was he employed by the French King, but he also managed to work in England at St. James's Palace in 1630, at Wimbledon Manor for Henrietta Maria in 1642, in Holland at Buren and Honselaarsdjik for two years from 1633, and in Stockholm for Queen Christina for five years from 1648. His published work, *Le Jardin de Plaisir*, appeared in 1651 and described the principles of classic French garden design.

This book covers the essential features of a pleasure garden: statues, grottoes, terraces, aviaries, fountains and canals, and there are plans for *parterres de broderie*, in swirling, elegant patterns very similar to those in Boyceau's book. There are, however, no new ideas for buildings to enhance the gardens, since Mollet was essentially a horticultural designer, not a would-be architect. Nevertheless, from the death of Salomon de Caus until the rise of André le Nôtre, he and other members of his family were the most renowned gardeners and leading designers in northern Europe.

This garden design incorporating the shape of a hippodrome was by André Mollet and published in Le Jardin de Plaisirs, *1651; it resembles the gardens at Honselaarsdijk in the Netherlands, which Mollet designed, c. 1633. The idea of surrounding the perimeter with four rows of trees had originated in the gardens of ancient Rome, and it was a feature that would be publicised later by Félibien des Avaux.*

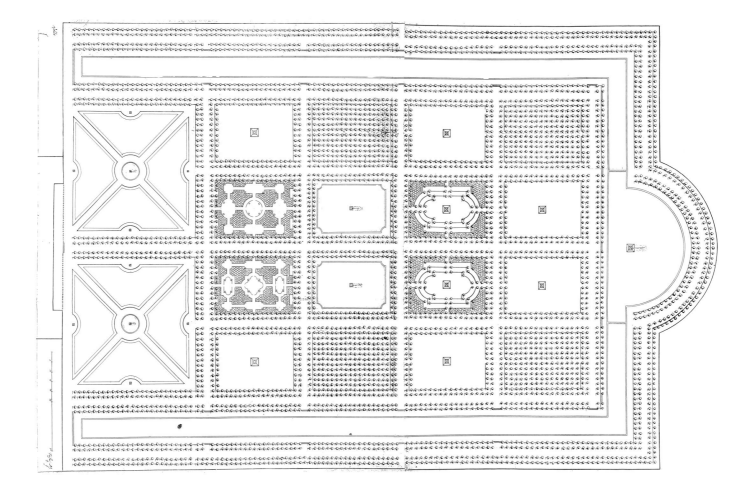

Iacob Fecquier
pinxit
Matthæ Merian fecit

Salomon de Caus

Expertise in elaborate hydraulics and automata was not confined to the Italians. A French Huguenot mathematician and engineer by the name of Salomon de Caus, internationally renowned for the gardens he created and the books he wrote, was without doubt one of the leading experts in the business of hydraulics. He had spent three years in Italy between 1595 and 1598, and must have examined the gardens of Florence and Rome in detail; he then worked for the Archduke Albert in Brussels from about 1601 to 1608, when he moved to London at the invitation of James I.

While there are few visual records of his work to prove it, de Caus is also credited with introducing to England the Renaissance concept of house and garden designed as a single composition. Although he came to gardens via engineering, not architecture, he clearly had a brilliant eye for architectural proportion and detail. Since gardens required designers skilled in both engineering and aesthetics, de Caus was soon employed to design gardens for existing palaces: the Prince of Wales appointed him as gardens and engineering adviser at Richmond Palace, and the Queen, Anne of Denmark, employed him at Greenwich and Somerset House.

At Somerset House, the gardens extended to the Thames, and were given the fashionable Italian touch by de Caus, the principal feature being a Mount Parnassus. The many forms of this fantastical and popular garden feature are explained in detail later in this chapter, but, briefly, a Parnassus was a huge pile of boulders decorated with statues of Apollo and the Muses.

The Parnassus at Somerset House was 10 metres high. At the summit, Pegasus pranced with wings outstretched, while below Apollo played a violin, surrounded by the Muses, moving gently under a thin mist of spray from jets around the edge of the pool. Powered by hydraulics, it must have made a profound impression on visitors.

The gardens at Heidelberg as engraved by Merian and published in Hortus Palatinus *by Salomon de Caus, 1620. Although never completed, they were planned to have a great variety of patterns in the various parterres. From right to left, starting next to the maze, some are cut-work as illustrated by de Vries, (p.55), others are like embroidery or broderie, as in Mollet's plan (p.68), while yet others have a strapwork pattern. The screen to a grotto, in the foreground on the left, is pure Baroque extravaganza.*

This grotto at Heidelberg in Les Raisons
des Forces Mouvantes *by de Caus, 1615,*
is traditional, with water cascading over stone in
the centre and falling like a curtain on the left;
a humorous touch is added by the servants on either
side complete with pitcher and tray.

Giant statues, a relic of Mannerism, were also part of de Caus's specialities, and in 1610 he designed two for Prince Henry at Richmond. They were positioned on islands in the Thames just off the palace gardens, and although the statues have gone, the pair of Flower Pot islands are still there, covered with trees.

De Caus was also employed by James I's Secretary of State, Robert Cecil, Earl of Salisbury, at Hatfield House in Hertfordshire. Hatfield was one of the great architectural achievements of the Jacobean age, a house designed by the surveyor Robert Liminge, with additional advice from Simon Basil and Inigo Jones. In 1611, de Caus's task was to improve an existing garden by the addition of cascading fountains. Unhappily, Salisbury did not live to enjoy it, for he died in 1612, deeply in debt.

Although de Caus was highly revered in England, he has left no body of work in his own country, where perhaps his Huguenot convictions militated against acceptance. Possibly, too, it was easier to accept the artistic talents of a foreigner rather than those of native experts. While familiar with the works of the Francine brothers in France, de Caus had consolidated his ideas and experience in Belgium and then in England, and it was this combination of experience and observation that led to his greatest commission, the design of the gardens for the royal palace at Heidelberg in the Palatine, known subsequently as the Hortus Palatinus.

In 1613, Princess Elizabeth of England, daughter of James I, married the Elector Palatine, Frederick V. With the death of her brother Prince Henry in 1612, de Caus had lost his main patron, so he was free to accept the Princess's summons to Heidelberg, and the instructions to design and construct a new garden round the schloss. His scheme is known through *Hortus Palatinus*, a detailed description of the gardens published in 1620 in both France and Germany, and through the work of artists and engravers. *Hortus Palatinus* was reprinted in full in *The Castle of Heidelberg and its Gardens* by John Metzger, published in 1830, together with an account of the garden's history in English.

De Caus's plan involved massive movement of earth in order to create flat terraces, five in all, out of the hillside site, each terrace with superb views to the schloss and down to the River Neckar below.

Conventional taste was satisfied by the usual features of statuary, fountains, pools of water, and pergolas or trellis tunnels like those of Vredeman de Vries. The design, artistic yet practical, romantic yet humorous, and endlessly inventive, then went far beyond tradition; a handsome gallery was built into one of the terrace's retaining walls to create a cool, shady walk, with a façade of 10 bays divided by rusticated columns. Fish tanks were planned where *the fish wanted for the use of the Court are kept*,[11] to be built into rooms within the terraces, and also a *Bathing Hall, together with adjoining chambers*, designed *to afford the conveniency of bathing in all seasons, by means of two stoves by which the water was to have been heated*.[12] There was also to be a greenhouse, built into a terrace, for winter protection of orange trees, for which de Caus drew columns like rustic tree trunks, entwined with ivy.

The greenhouse designed for Heidelberg from Les Raisons des Forces Mouvantes*; in romantic mood, de Caus has used tree-trunks entwined with ivy in place of Doric or Ionic columns.*

Eschelle de 10 pieds.

But de Caus surpassed himself in the quantity and originality of his automata and hydraulics and their musical effects. Dedicated to detail, he even composed music for the water-organs. All were to be displayed in the many grottoes within the terraced walls, many of which also had carved animals, tufa, coral and decorative stones. Each feature was loaded with significance, too, for the iconography glorified the Elector and the Palatine state in great detail.

Only the terraces remain in outline today, together with the arcaded terrace wall. Some bare grottoes, and the bathing hall still exist, but many of those planned may never have been built, since the Thirty Years' War started in 1618, and de Caus wrote in 1620 that work had been stopped. In a further comment on the gardens in 1830, Metzger wrote that the tufa, corals and stones had all been removed to the gardens of another Palatine palace, Schwetzingen, in 1770. Although the gardens at Heidelberg were hailed as the Eighth Wonder of the World, their reputation relied essentially on the plans illustrated in *Hortus Palatinus*.

It is on the combination of *Hortus Palatinus* and his other great work, *Les Raisons des Forces Mouvantes*, that de Caus's fame has rested, and rightly so. The latter, published in Frankfurt in 1615 with a second edition in 1624, is primarily a book about hydraulics, and includes engravings and technical descriptions of all manner of fountains, automated figures and the machinery to operate them; it even anticipates the steam engine. De Caus seems to have improved and refined existing technology, and used his machines and figures in

countless new scenes of enchantment born of his fertile mind. His automata were carved from stone, and painted as life-like models of people or animals, but none have survived the passage of time.

One of his ideas was a copper ball perpetually balancing on a jet of water, somewhat like the one held aloft in the Villa Aldobrandini. The trick must have seemed magical, and is still compelling. A version is still in operation in the grotto of the Old Castle at the Hermitage near Bayreuth, but, instead of a plain copper ball, a crown balances on top of the water jet.

Les Raisons des Forces Mouvantes also illustrates one of de Caus's finest grottoes. Neptune, standing in a shell boat, is pulled around a rocky isle by two horses, with sea heralds ahead blowing conch shells and a pair of dolphins astern, while a reclining goddess watches from the isle. Imagine the delight of this scene, with Neptune's endless progress around the island, the bow wave from his shell boat, the spouting dolphins and spurting rocks, the stream gushing from the goddess's urn.

The Heidelberg garden and his books were de Caus's last great works, for he died in 1626. As far as German gardens were concerned, the Thirty Years' War had a devastating effect on the Palatinate and other states, with the result that no major gardens were created during most of the 17th century. It was not until the end of the century, with the assurance of peace and the inspiration of Versailles, that fortunes were again spent in creating new gardens in Germany.

One of de Caus's many designs for fountains, from Hortus Palatinus, *1620.*

This design for the grotto of Neptune at
Heidelberg by de Caus in Les Raisons des
Forces Mouvantes, 1615, was slightly adapted
a century later by Dezallier d'Argenville in
La Théorie et la Pratique du Jardinage.

Mounts and Mounts Parnassus

The mount and the Renaissance Mount Parnassus are both so little known today that they require some explanation. Their place in the list of garden features was well established in the early 17th century and, considering that they were large, solid and difficult to dismantle, it is surprising that so few have survived.

The conical mount or mound had been known since medieval times, and maintained its popularity in England through the 16th century. Apart from the royal mount topped by the Great Round Arbour at Hampton Court Palace, *c.* 1533, and another with its banqueting house at Nonsuch Palace in Surrey, the gardens of New College in Oxford were enhanced by a mound in 1529. A rarity from Tudor days, in 1594–95 the New College mound was reshaped into a three-tiered pyramid, and has fortunately survived to recall one of the most significant features of bygone centuries.

In his famous essay, 'Of Gardens', Sir Francis Bacon recommends simple conical mounts. The ideal garden should have *in the very middle, a fair mount, with three ascents, and alleys, enough for four to walk abreast; which would have to be perfect circles, without any bulwarks or*

The mount in the gardens at Enghien (157.*a.17) was illustrated by Romain de Hooghe, c. 1687. The mount remains but it has lost its hedged superstructure reminiscent of a Tower of Babel by Hieronymus Bosch. Although called a Mount Parnassus at the time, it lacked the essential figures of Apollo, Pegasus and the Muses; terminology was not always precisely applied.

embossments; and the whole mount to be thirty foot high.[13] Not satisfied with one, he then advised building two more mounts, each at the end of long allées running down the sides of the garden.

Eventually to become Lord Chancellor and Viscount St Albans, Bacon was a barrister and had chambers at Gray's Inn, where he laid out the gardens into tree-lined walks between 1597 and 1599, and then, following his own advice, in 1608 he built a mount. Like Henry VIII's mount at Hampton Court, with which Bacon would have been familiar, it was topped with a building, in this case a wooden open-sided banqueting house. The slate roof, with its ogee-shaped cupola, was again reminiscent of the Great Round Arbour at Hampton Court.

Due to his rank and expertise in all matters horticultural, Bacon became the main amateur arbiter of taste in gardens in England. His *Essays* were reprinted several times and translated into French in 1619; what he proposed in 'Of Gardens' and built in his own gardens would be followed by those with pretensions to good taste and the means to indulge it. Mounts were thus an integral element in garden design, and it may be due to Bacon that they were especially popular in England.

A contemporary mount was built at Montacute House in Somerset for Sir Edward Phelips, Speaker of the House of Commons from 1604, and a legal colleague of Bacon. The house was completed in 1601, and the garden probably laid out in the latest taste during the following years. A mount constructed in the *best garden* to the north-east of the house survived at least until 1782. A 1697 engraving by Kip shows another example, tiered with circular paths, at Dunham Massey, Cheshire, which may date from *c.* 1616, when the Jacobean house and gardens are said to have been built.

Mounts were, however, also found on the Continent. In France in 1600, Olivier de Serres produced a design for a mount in *Le Théâtre d'Agriculture*. Largely a practical, horticultural guide, the only man-made element de Serres illustrated is a *montaignette*.[14] This is a gently sloping conical mount, with a path spiralling slowly upwards supported by a wall with grass between the paths. The summit is flat, edged with a balustrade, and in the middle stands a small fountain.

In Italy, a grand tiered mount was constructed in the gardens of the Villa Medici in Rome, and planted in true Italian fashion with cypress trees. It was described as a mausoleum and illustrated by G.B. Falda in 1683. With a flash of originality, the Dutch poet and statesman Jacob Cats combined a mount with a maze in his gardens at Zorgvliet, in the Netherlands, in the 1650s. And a mount with a spiral path was built in the 1730s by the Margrave of Bayreuth at the Eremitage in Bavaria.

Conical mounts gradually went out of fashion during the 17th century. They had been built only in grand gardens, and after the middle of the century they were no longer considered desirable features. Many had become smothered with vegetation, like John Evelyn's brother's *mountaine overgrowne with huge trees and thicket*[15] at

The mound at Wadham College, Oxford, from an engraving by David Loggan published by Macartney in English Houses and Gardens, *1908. It is crowned by a giant Atlas struggling to support the world.*

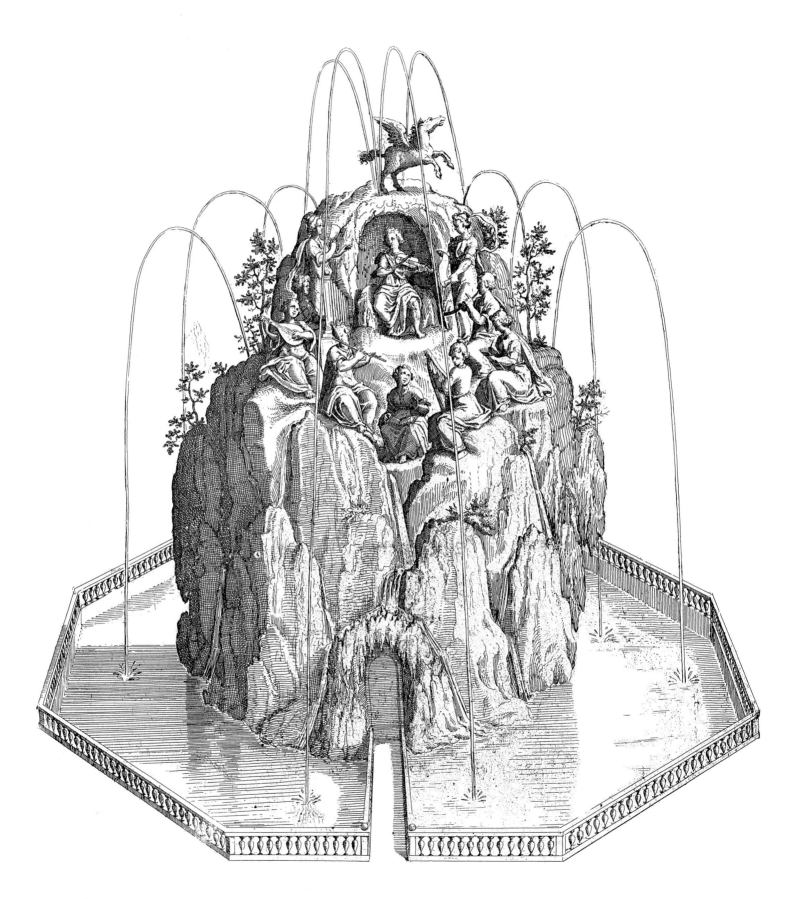

Wotton in Surrey, which was levelled in 1652, while the mount at Hampton Court and the Great Round Arbour at its top were demolished in 1697, when the new Privy Garden was completed. When formal gardens were replaced by landscaped parks in the 18th century, few mounts remained; of the 156 gardens illustrated in the two volumes of *Britannia Illustrata*, published in 1720 and 1740, mounts are shown in only five gardens: Haughton, Dunham Massey, Sundridge, Wentworth Castle and Boughton.

Nevertheless, as late as 1715, in *The Nobleman, Gentleman, and Gardener's Recreation*, Stephen Switzer recommended the building of mounts in new gardens. A mount, he wrote, would give views of the garden and estate and should be planted with evergreens. Perhaps it was the influence of Switzer, whose garden designs enjoyed the highest reputation, which encouraged the 3rd Duke of Marlborough to commission a mount in the gardens of Little Lodge in Windsor Park, *c.* 1735. It was vastly expensive to construct, and was doubtless one of the last to be built before formal Renaissance gardens were swept away.

Today, the mount at Dunham Massey is still intact, though now only about three metres high, and others remain in Cheshire at Little Moreton Hall, in Warwickshire at Packwood House, *c.* 1650, and in Oxford at New College. On the Continent survivors include the mount in the Veneto at the Villa Pisani, the Spiral or *Schneckenberg* at the Eremitage near Bayreuth, and the mount at Enghien in Belgium.

Conical mounts were simple affairs compared with the fantasy of a Mount Parnassus, which was derived from ancient Greek mythology. The real Mount Parnassus, overlooking the Gulf of Corinth, was considered sacred to Apollo and the Nine Muses, hence the statues gracing the Mount at Somerset House. To build a Mount Parnassus was to imply, at the least, a knowledge of the classics, and, at best, that Apollo and the Muses lived in the garden and that by their presence the earthly inhabitants would be lifted into the intellectual sphere of the gods.

Early examples of this fantastical concept were created at the Hermitage at Gaillon, built after 1550 and at the Villa Pratolino, built after 1569, but there had been others, at Chenonceaux in 1563 and the Tuileries in 1573, both built by Catherine de Medici for great fêtes and not meant to last. It was Salomon de Caus who seems to have developed the concept, inspired perhaps by Gaillon but more likely by his observations in Italy. Wedded to his Protestant faith, while religious wars were waging in France, de Caus is unlikely to have knocked on the door of the Catholic Archbishop of Rouen to ask permission to see the gardens.

De Caus's version of a Parnassus was a tumble of boulders piled 10 metres high and decorated with statues of Apollo and the Muses, while he also shows a rocky version called a Mount Tmollus complete with a giant statue. Another illustration shows mount and a reclining male with his hand on an urn from which gushes forth a great burst of water representing a river. De Caus proposed a grotto

De Caus's design for a Mount Parnassus, suitable, he wrote, for a royal garden, with space enough for several grottoes. It was identical to the Somerset House Mount Parnassus, except that the latter had four additional figures representing the rivers of Great Britain. It would have been at least 10 metres high, with larger than life-size figures of Apollo, the Muses and Pegasus.

De Caus also designed a Mount Tmollus, inspired, he said, by the great Cyclops (Appennino) at Pratolino. Its height may have been exaggerated, a custom adopted by many artists to enhance their designs, for it dwarfs the figures on the right; if built to scale it would have reached over 20 metres. The actual Mount Tmollus in Greece was famed for its sweet air and mentioned in a fable by Ovid, but was not associated with the gods of mythology. A garden version of Mount Tmollus may have been started by de Caus for Prince Henry at Richmond Palace, but otherwise this feature, not surprisingly in view of its size, was probably never copied. Both designs were illustrated in Les Raisons des Forces Mouvantes, *1615.*

This mount by de Caus in Les Raisons des
Forces Mouvantes, *1615, was planned as the
centrepiece to a garden; it too had grottoes within
and would have measured some 17 metres in height.*

for Orpheus inside the giant figure, and drew him playing a cello, complete with moving arm and automated organ music, surrounded by an arrangement of animals reminiscent of the grotto of the Villa Medici at Castello.

With his reputation for creating Mounts Parnassus, it might be expected that de Caus would have included one in the gardens at Heidelberg, but he did not. Publication of his engravings in *Les Raisons des Forces Mouvantes*, however, may have encouraged others to be built. Diarist John Evelyn saw an overgrown version in Cardinal Richelieu's gardens at Rueil in 1644; sited on an island in a pond, it was *built of vast pieces of rock, neere 50 feet high, growne over with mosse, ivy, &c., shaded at a competent distance with tall trees, in this the fowles lay eggs and breede*.[16] This neglected mount probably dates from earlier in the century, after Jean Moisset, known as Montauban, bought the château in 1606, for the moss and ivy would hardly have had time to smother it had it been built after Richelieu bought the property in 1633. Evelyn also recorded a Mount Parnassus at St Cloud, a grotto inside a Classical temple on top of a mount.

A Parnassus was the centrepiece of a vast pool in the gardens at Aranjuez, the royal palace near Madrid. And at the Eremitage, near Bayreuth, a Parnassus of tufa was created at the late date of 1718, complete with Pegasus, Apollo and the Nine Muses. The outlines of those at Aranjuez and the Eremitage still exist, but the statues have gone.

Another was made in the 1650s at Zorgvliet for Jacob Cats, who, as we have seen, had also built a conical mount with maze. His Mount Parnassus was not, however, a pile of rocks but a four-sided grass pyramid with a tree on top and a tall, tapering cypress-like tree at each corner. Something of a hybrid, it was called a green Mount Parnassus.

What amazing follies these mounts were! But no fashion lasts for ever, particularly not one that is so costly. While making a gesture to nature in the rough arrangement of stones and pretending to an Arcadian ideal, de Caus's mounts were utterly contrived. They lost favour as the century progressed, partly because of the initial expense and partly because of the cost of maintenance, for the exterior had to be kept free of weeds and the grotto inside in working order. But Mounts Parnassus were such curious and fabulous creations that their disappearance raises many tantalising questions. Perhaps in the current climate, which rightly values the garden heritage, an accurate version will reappear in some noble old garden.

Conical mounts had had a logic in a flat garden, but were overtaken by less precise undulations when gardens were landscaped in the 18th century. Perhaps the simpler conical mount will swing back into fashion. In 1990, the late architectural historian Gervase Jackson-Stops raised a mount in his garden at The Menagerie in Northamptonshire. It is nearly three metres high and planted with *Aceana microphyllus* through which a spiral path of closely mown grass winds its way to the summit. It is crowned by a stone obelisk. Is this the start of a revival of a major feature of medieval and Renaissance gardens?

The fashion for mounts was spread around Europe by books and travellers. This Swedish version, at Jacobsdahl, was called the Mount of Perseus and Andromeda, and there was another mount in a lake at Gröneborg, both illustrated by Perelle in Suecia Antiquae, 1723.

Repræsentatio Montis Persei et Andromedæ in Horto Jacobs Dahlenfi

Stuart Gardens of England

One of a pair of gazebos at Montacute. Probably dating from the first decade of the 17th century, they are exceptionally fine examples of Jacobean garden architecture. They are at the far corners of the East Court or Privy Garden, built into garden walls which also include a pair of delicate ornamental turrets. The Renaissance tradition of uniting house and Privy Garden in a single concept has resulted in a very harmonious composition.

After the initial uncertainties following the accession in 1603 of James I, the first Stuart king of England, there was a rush of new building of both houses and gardens. New gardens were laid out at Worcester Lodge, Ham House, Chastleton, and Hatfield House, all completed by 1614.

Salomon de Caus, creator of the garden at Hatfield, although renowned for his work, was not the only respected figure in the field of garden design; there were others who were influential and none more so than Francis Bacon, who was a man of towering intellect, great prestige through his office as Lord Chancellor, and a dedicated amateur gardener.

His much-quoted Essay, 'Of Gardens', starts with a splendid affirmation: *God Almighty first planted a garden. And indeed it is the purest of human pleasures. It is the greatest refreshment to the spirits of man; without which, buildings and palaces are but gross handyworks.*[17]

Then follows advice on flowers, shrubs, fruit trees and design, including the use of wide allées and sheltering walls. Bacon thought topiary childish and statues unnecessary, but recommended mounts, banqueting houses, fountains, bathing pools and covered allées or pergolas. There is no doubt that the essay profoundly affected the form of gardens under the early Stuart kings.

Because house and garden were designed to an integrated plan and structure in the garden was seen as part of the embellishment, features such as banqueting houses and fountains were items of focus, located at strategic points as in the Renaissance gardens of Italy. In 1608 Bacon built a banqueting house in the centre of the water garden at his country estate at Gorhambury in Hertfordshire. Described by John Aubrey in 1656 as being *of Roman architecture*,[18] it was a square building, set on a square island within a square lake, and surrounded beyond by a further canal on four sides. It was infinitely grander than Bacon's Gray's Inn version, for it was on three floors, with a terrace on top above an open supper room, while below were dining-room, bed chamber, cabinet and music room.

A noble banqueting house was designed by Robert Liminge, *c.* 1620 for Sir Henry Hobart at Blickling Hall in Norfolk. This was to be set into a wall on a terrace that formed part of a new formal garden. When Sir Baptist Hicks started building his new house and garden at Chipping Camden in 1613, a pair of banqueting houses were an integral part of the plan, for they are at either end of the main cross axis in front of the house. The latter was destroyed during the Civil War, but the banqueting houses escaped and stand there still, their façades decorated with a Jacobean strapwork frieze, arched windows and soaring chimney-pots.

Whereas banqueting houses were to be found in the grandest Stuart gardens, much more common were the gazebos built into the corners of a walled garden. Remaining versions can be seen in many gardens, for instance at Coombe Manor in Berkshire and Packwood House in Warwickshire. At Montacute House in Somerset there is a particularly handsome pair of ogee-roofed gazebos built for Sir Edward Phelips *c.* 1601.

Markham's plan for a garden from
A Way to get Wealth, *1623.*

*A summer house at Chelsea (Smythson
Collection I/9) by Robert Smythson, 1609,
or John Smythson, 1619.*

During the first decades of the 17th century, word of the glories of Italian and French gardens spread steadily to England, consolidating the teachings of de Caus. John Aubrey, writing *Brief Lives* at the end of the 17th century, insisted that *'Twas Sir John Danvers of Chelsey who first taught us the way of Italian gardens: He had well travelled France & Italy, and made good Observations.*[19] Sir John had created an Italian-style garden at his Chelsea house as early as the 1620s. However, in respect of design and features, new English gardens caught up quickly with Italian and French gardens, even if they lacked the scale and splendour of the major gardens on the Continent.

Professionals leave the greatest mark and de Caus's contribution to English garden design was more than matched by Inigo Jones's momentous contribution to English architecture. Jones visited Italy, France and Germany before 1603 and then spent a further 21 months abroad, mainly in Italy, from 1613, stopping *en route* at Heidelberg to see the Schloss and de Caus's emerging plan. He returned imbued with the Palladian spirit and a profound knowledge of the buildings of ancient Rome, and then proceeded to introduce Classical architecture to England. In adopting Palladio as his mentor, Jones rejected the excesses of Mannerism and Baroque in favour of a restrained yet inventive Classicism; not for him the Mannerist style of Alexandre Francine, his contemporary in France. It is important to remember that Jones was not only an architect, he was also an antiquarian, a military engineer, and a painter; he had started his career as designer of theatrical masques, and this too remained an important and influential part of his work. Only in the freedom of this latter more light-hearted activity did he show signs of Mannerist and Baroque influence.

Jones's rare intellect made him a pre-eminent figure in the talented Stuart courts of James I and Charles I. As Surveyor-General of the King's Works from 1615, his major projects were for the Crown, for example, the Queen's House at Greenwich and the Banqueting House in Whitehall, but because of lack of resources, neither James I nor his successor Charles I were able to commission projects on the scale of the Villa Aldobrandini or St Germain-en-Laye, so what Jones might have produced for an integrated palace and garden can only be imagined. He did build a small banqueting house at Theobalds for the King, but no trace of it remains, and he is said to have influenced the design for Wilton House in Wiltshire, but his work in gardens is tantalisingly limited.

Designs for gates and doorways are amongst surviving items of Jones's work relating, albeit loosely, to gardens. An early example was the *greate gate* to the vineyard for Oatlands Palace, built in 1617 for the Queen. Supporting a pediment over the entrance are rough-cut blocks of stone, the first example in England of rustication. In this Classical technique, massive blocks of masonry are separated by deep joints, the surface of the stone being either dressed till smooth, left rough-hewn, or vermiculated, that is, carved with shallow curly channels like worm casts or the coat of a Persian lamb.

A Summer House at Chealsea

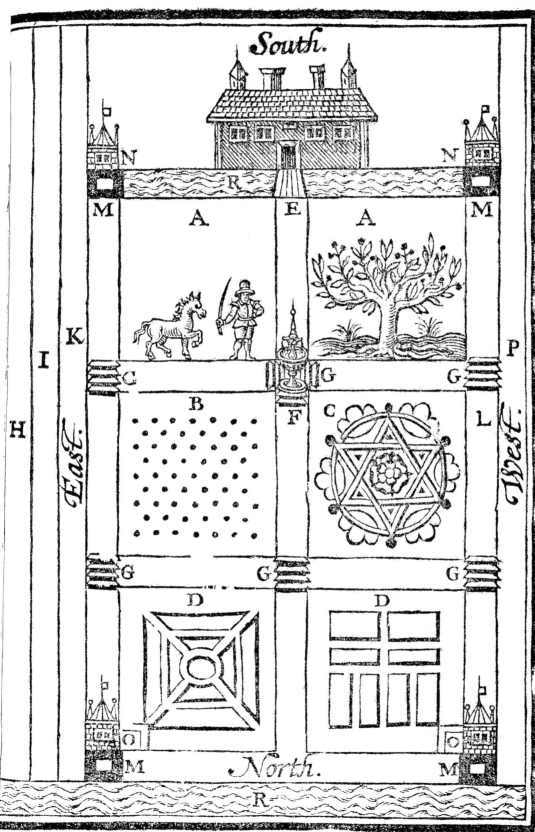

A. All thefe fquares muft bee fet with trees, the Gardens & other ornaments muft ftand in fpaces betwixt the trees, & in the borders and fences.

B. Trees 20. yards afunder.

C. Garden knot.

D. Kitchen garden.

E. Bridge.

F. Conduit.

G. Staires.

H. Walkes fet with great wood thicke.

I. Walkes fet with great wood round about your Orchard.

K. The out fence.

L. The out fence fet with ftone fruit.

M. Mount. To force earth for a mount, or fuch like, fet it round with quick; and lay boughs of trees ftrangely intermingled, tops inward with the earth in the middle

N. Still-houfe.

O. Good ftanding for Bees, if you haue an houfe.

P. If the Riuer run by your doore, and vnder your mount it will be pleafant.

The garden at Wilton, designed by Isaac de Caus and illustrated in
Wilton Garden, *1645, was the most prestigious Italianate garden in
England at the time. With the passage of time and changing tastes, the patterns
for the parterres near the house had evolved since those at Heidelberg, and the
trees planted at each corner were tall and tapering rather than the rounded
bushes of the earlier garden. All of the garden in this view was destroyed in the
18th century when the fashion for formal gardens was replaced by the desire for
a natural landscape. The River Nadder that crosses the garden was dammed
downstream to make it more significant, and in 1737 a Palladian bridge was
added on the left.*

*An elevation of a Doric gateway at Beaufort House, Chelsea, by Inigo Jones,
1621. With rusticated stonework behind the columns, it is Classical in the
simple grandeur of its proportions, compared with the more elaborate
decoration of Baroque buildings, such as the Water Theatre on p.61 or the
grotto façade on p.70.*

The grotto at Wilton, which terminated the main axis, also from Wilton Garden, *1645. The influence of Inigo Jones and therefore of Palladio is evident in the façade, a fine example of restrained Classicism compared, for example, with that of Salomon de Caus's Baroque grotto at Heidelberg, shown on p.70. The interior followed tradition in its associations with the sea and the stalactite effect.*

The Royal Institute of British Architects (RIBA) holds a surviving elevation for a garden entrance designed in 1621, together with Jones's drawing of the gateway which still stands at Chiswick House. A valuable example of the work of this English genius, it is a simpler, more delicate version of some of his other designs, the order being Doric, the rustication smooth in plan but vermiculated in execution.

Despite Jones's close involvement in masques and stage sets, there is no evidence that he designed grottoes and automata. But grottoes and moving figures were not unknown in English gardens, and, as far as hydraulics were concerned, those at Enstone in Oxfordshire were famous. They were made about 1630 by Thomas Bushell, a mining engineer who had been page and secretary to Francis Bacon and, therefore, a man about the Court. An eccentric with an impish sense of humour, water jokes were the centrepiece of his country garden, and Charles I visited them twice, in 1634 and 1636.

On his second visit Charles was accompanied by the Queen, and Bushell turned on all the taps and cocks to give them *an entertainment of artificial thunders and lightenings, rain, hail-showers, drums beating, organs playing, birds singing, waters murmuring all sorts of tunes &c. ...* [20] According to John Aubrey, Enstone also had *a Neptune neatly cutt in wood, holding his Trident in his hand, and ayming with it at a duck which perpetually turned round with him, and a Spanniel swimming after her — which was very pretty.* [21]

Bushell's gardens were on John Evelyn's route in October 1664. But Evelyn, now in his forties, had lost his youthful enthusiasm for water jokes and made no mention of them: surprise jets of water are not as funny when you are middle-aged and cold in England in October instead of youthful and warm in Italy in May.

Around the time that Charles I and Henrietta Maria were visiting Enstone, another de Caus, Isaac, a brother or nephew of Salomon, was recognised as the leading garden designer in England. His best documented work was for the 4th Earl of Pembroke at Wilton House near Salisbury, where he designed both house and garden *c.* 1632. Wilton already had a literary pedigree, for it was here that Sir Philip Sydney wrote *Arcadia*, a romantic tale in prose and poetry including pastoral eclogues set in the ancient landscape of its title.

Isaac de Caus had already established a career in England, and may have been responsible for the celebrated garden at Moor Park. He also designed the grotto at Woburn Abbey in Bedfordshire, completed before 1627 and still a fine example of the art of grotto decoration. Built within the house, fountains once played in niches set in shell-encrusted walls, and mermaids still sport playfully above the billowing waves.

According to John Aubrey, at Wilton de Caus took advice from Inigo Jones. The house was built with encouragement from Charles I, who had a fondness for the location, and *His Majesty intended to have it all designed by his own architect, Mr. Inigo Jones, who being at that time ... engaged in his Majesties buildings at Greenwich, could not attend to it: but he recommended it to an ingeniouse architect, Monsieur de Caus, who performed it very well; but not without the advice and approbation of Mr. Jones.* [22]

Isaac's other influence was Salomon, and following his relative's example he published in 1645 a book of his Wilton plans, called simply *Wilton Garden*. This contains 24 elevations, ground-plans and a bird's-eye view entitled *Hortus Pembrochianus*, providing information on the architectural details and showing how deeply Salomon de Caus's design for Heidelberg had influenced Wilton. The plans show, too, that Isaac was mainly a follower, not an original creator. Two of the designs for treillage are closely related to illustrations in *Hortus Palatinus*, and there are other echoes of Heidelberg in the detailed drawings of Wilton, although the latter plan is far less

complex. As seen in the bird's-eye view from Isaac's book, the river is the garden's most original feature as it meanders across the flat floor of the valley in front of the house. De Caus chose to subdue it into a canal, and then ignore it by carrying on regardless with the geometric ground-plan, a successful solution.

The Wilton grotto with its rusticated pilasters was the focal point of the Great Walk at the far end of the centre of the garden. It had *a Portico of stone* on either side of which was *an assent leading up to the terrase upon the Steps whereof instead of Ballasters are Sea Monsters casting water from one to the other from the top to the bottome and above the sayd Portico is a great reserve of Water for the Grotto.* [23] Inside the grotto, merman, mermaids and nymphs perched on shells, and a rockwork frieze dripped with stalactites.

The pergolas were planted with hedging clipped into an architectural form, as illustrated in 1583 by Hans Vredeman de Vries, with pilasters and arched mouldings around the entrances, and arched windows cut out of foliage walls. They were a more sophisticated version of Francis Bacon's *covert alley upon carpenters work*, [24] which was about 3.5 metres high. Turning nature into stone in this manner was a fashionable garden conceit well into the 18th century; at the recently recreated gardens at Het Loo in The Netherlands berceaux planted with clipped hornbeam are similar to the foliage walls designed for Wilton. Like Mounts Parnassus, such contrivances were another way of showing off the achievements of man rather than the glories of nature.

Wilton was much appreciated by Charles I, according to John Aubrey. *King Charles the first did love Wilton above all places, and came thither every summer. It was HE that did put Philip (1st) Earle of Pembroke upon makeing this magnificent Garden and Grotto, and to new build that side of the House that fronts the Garden, with two stately Pavilions at Each end, all al Italiano.* [25]

Although Wilton was on a smaller scale than Heidelberg and lacked the architectural opportunities of terraces, it was the largest and most handsome Renaissance garden created in England before the Civil War cast its long shadow. Nowhere else had nature been controlled to this extent, nowhere else was artificiality and illusion celebrated so effectively. Missing is the Baroque theatricality of an almost exact contemporary, the extraordinary Villa Aldobrandini, or of St Germain-en-Laye or Isola Bella on Lake Maggiore, but this is because Wilton is a Palladian garden under the influence of Inigo Jones. Despite the fact that Wilton and Isola Bella were started at roughly the same time, there are few parallels between the two, for Wilton exemplifies restrained Classicism while Isola Bella revels in all the exuberance and excesses of Baroque.

Isola Bella

The island garden of Isola Bella on Lake Como was illustrated by many including Le Rouge in Détails des nouveaux jardins, Cahier VII, *c. 1779. It is a masterpiece of man's manipulation of nature. There has been little change to the architecture in the garden, but some of the parterres have been turned into lawns while others have been planted with trees and shrubs. The reservoir is under the extensive balustraded platform at the highest point. Of the pair of hexagonal pavilions, one was a pump house and the other a summerhouse.*

Any description of Isola Bella on Lake Maggiore has to be a catalogue of superlatives. The secret of its startling effect is the marriage between this island palazzo and garden and its setting on Lake Maggiore, the powerful bond between its Baroque drama of mimicking a ship at sea, and the majestic spiky white peaks of the Italian Alps that surround it. It is an island built over by man, its natural outlines lost forever underneath the village, the palazzo and its terraced gardens. As at the Villa Aldobrandini, architecture is at the core of Isola Bella.

On the highest ground of the island is a magnificent, extravagant amphitheatre, loaded with fountains, statues and finials that seem to soar ever upwards. It is built facing north against a vast viewing platform, which is also the roof of a reservoir of water. The reservoir is a practical necessity, but also a secure base behind the elaborate façade, avoiding the awkwardness of a free-standing structure like the cascade at Rueil, built about the same time. Where the ancient Greeks would have set a temple at the highest point, medieval designers would have crowned it with a basilica, and 18th-century landscape architects would have planted a clump of mighty trees or built an obelisk, 17th-century man gloried in his own works and needed to admire them. Hence this balustraded terrace, on which grand festivities were staged.

Below to the south are a parterre, two hexagonal towers and serried terraces with oleander-clad walls, while to east and west are walks, flowerbeds, shrubberies and groves of trees. North of the amphitheatre is a series of cool grottoes through which the gardens are entered.

The instigator of this extraordinary project was Count Carlo Borromeo, who started developments in 1632. Over the ensuing 40 years, he and his son, Count Vitaliano Borromeo IV, transformed the island garden aided by the architects Angelo Crivelli, Carlo Fontana and Francesco Castelli.

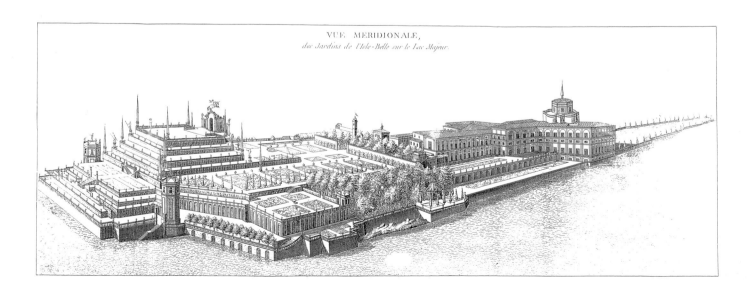

VUE MERIDIONALE,
des Jardins de l'Isle-Belle sur le Lac Majeur

Anything as spectacular as this proud ship of an island was quickly on the traveller's map. In 1685 Bishop Gilbert Burnet observed that *the freshness of the Air, it being both in a Lake and near the Mountains, the fragrant smell, the beautiful prospect, and the delighting Variety that is here makes such a habitation for Summer that perhaps the whole world hath nothing like it.*[26]

Bishop Burnet's account of his travels, *An Account of what seemed most remarkable in Switzerland, Italy, &c*, was published in English in Rotterdam in 1686, and by 1752 had run to a further 16 editions. It was also translated into French and German, so Isola Bella's existence would have been known across Europe to thousands of readers.

A later visitor to Isola Bella, the Président de Brosses, had read Bishop Burnet's book, as he noted in his account of his 1739 visit to Italy, *Lettres Historiques et Critiques sur l'Italie*. The Président embarked on his tour convinced that French gardens were vastly superior to Italian ones. However, he conceded that he had seen none more original nor in a more unusual situation than Isola Bella, and he fell under its magic spell. *Cet endroit est digne des fées*,[27] he wrote, and suggested that the fairies must have transported to this island a corner of the Garden of Hesperides.

With gardens amongst the best kept in Europe, Isola Bella still retains intact its air of extravagant Baroque fantasy, while white peacocks mince and shimmer on the lawns.

The amphitheatre, with its immense vertical thrust provided by the statues and finials, seems almost ready to explode with its own exuberance. Part of the magic of Isola Bella lies in the unusual combination of a garden surrounded by water, where sculpture is frequently offset by the blues of a lake rather than the greens of grass and foliage or the greys of stone.

From the top of the reservoir, the view to the south includes yet more statues and a parterre with swirling patterns in box.

The Gardens of Spain

Probably because they have been on the receiving end of foreign influences and have never given birth to a movement that has spread to other countries, Spanish and Portuguese gardens have often been ignored by European garden historians. Nonetheless, with the added spice of an Arab heritage, their gardens have a richness of decoration and an originality that gives them a unique character.

In 1600, the gardens of southern Spain owed more to the Moorish or Mudéjar tradition than to the Italian Renaissance. Although the Arabs had been expelled from southern Spain in 1492, their influence on architecture persisted, and Moorish features linger in Spanish gardens to this day.

The Arabs were skilled and devoted gardeners. For them, gardens were a vital part of life, a means of expressing joy and beauty, and a foretaste of the delights of Paradise. Water was an essential component, in limpid cool canals, in playing fountains and for irrigation. Gardens had to be kept watered during hot summers, and for this reason the Arabs developed great skills both in irrigation and pressure control of water; they are said to have invented the fountain jet in medieval times, and made a fountain in Córdoba with a jet far higher than any other in Europe.

Many of the features of Spanish gardens can be seen in the early Arab gardens of the Middle East, and were brought to Spain by the Moors. Long narrow canals with flowers on either side are the principal features of the best-known Moorish gardens, the Generalife in the Alhambra at Granada and the Alcazar at Córdoba, though the arched jets of water that line the edges are a 19th-century addition. The lotus fountain, modelled on the oriental lotus flower, is another favourite element of Moorish gardens, and one that is still reproduced. The Arabs favoured a shallow version carved in marble or alabaster, with open petals that seem to float on the surface of the water. Examples can be seen in the garden of the Generalife at the Alhambra in Granada, as well as in many other gardens. Often fountains were simple water spouts on ground level or in a low basin.

The Torre de las Damas in the garden of the Alhambra at Granada, where water laps close to the base of the columns to ensure an uninterrupted reflection.

The Charles v pavilion in the Moorish gardens of the Alcazar in Seville was built in the 1520s in a Moorish style. The walls behind the arcades are superbly decorated with azulejos featuring heraldic motifs, centaurs and fauns.

The intimate gardens of the Generalife, the old summer palace of the sultans of Granada, rejoice in water and architecture. In summer, the beds on either side would be bright with flowers making patterns to resemble a Persian carpet. The fountain with its low open basin and single, burbling little jet is typical of Mudéjar design.

A Mudéjar garden of *c.* 1350, built in the Alcazar at Seville for King Pedro the Cruel, contains a rare Moorish pavilion built for the Hapsburg Emperor Charles v in the 1520s. Its Mudéjar style emphasises Spanish acceptance of the architecture of their previous Arab overlords. Overall, the gardens of the Alcazar soon became a rich mixture of Spanish, Moorish and Italian traditions, a hotch-potch of cultures as Italian influences percolated into Spain. Dates of individual items are obscure.

In the first part of the garden the Mercury Pond, a raised square pool with iron balustrades, takes its name from the bronze statue of Mercury in the centre. The statue was cast in 1576 by Bartolomé Morel after a design by Diego Pesquera, although the pool is probably of a later date.

Behind the pool is the Grotesque Gallery, or Grotto Wall, which encloses the garden of Charles v on one side, separating it from later developments. This is a unique Spanish creation, rooted in classical architecture but with an added individuality by virtue of the painted panels within arches and the bands of pseudo rockwork applied later to the façade. It is these bands, carved in high relief, almost like excessive rustication, which give the wall its 'grotesque' appearance. This is the dark side of Baroque, the menacing streak that makes the wall all-dominant in the tranquil Arab garden.

Inevitably, water jokes and fountains were added, and unlike those at the Villa Aldobrandini, for example, these were kept in good working order into the 19th century. Henry Swinburne visited the Alcazar at Seville on 9 April 1776, and praised the excellent effects of the waterworks:

You have often heard me launch out in praise of some hanging gardens in Italy, so refreshing and voluptuous in the summer evenings; this of the Alcazar is exactly such another; several parterres surrounded by galleries and terraces, intersected by myrtle hedges and jasmine bowers, and perfumed by clumps of orange trees, have also the advantage of abundance of water. A large party of sprightly damsels and young men that were walking here, were much indebted to us for making the water-works play, by means of a small bribe to the keeper. Nothing can be more delicious than these sprinklings in a hot day; all the flowers seemed to acquire new vigour, the odours, exhaled from the orange, citron and lemon trees, grew more poignant, more balsamic, and the company ten times more alive than they were; it was a true April shower. We sauntered near two hours in the groves, till we were quite in ecstasy with sweets. 'Tis a most heavenly residence in spring.[28]

The Alcazar obviously had powerful attractions. An 1803 visitor made an interesting comparison between formal Renaissance gardens and the later landscape style, in which the old Alcazar was much preferred:

The garden is full of jets d'eau, *cascades, fountains, and water tricks and devices … The English taste for simplicity and nature, which places a house in the midst of a grazing field where the sheep din* ba ba *all day long, has, by offending me so much, perhaps driven me into the opposite extreme, and made me prefer to the* nature *of a grass field and round clump the* built *gardens of two centuries ago.[29]*

Two images of the Fountain of the Harpies at Aranjuez: an engraving from Les Délices de l'Espagne et du Portugal *by Alvarez de Colmenar, 1707, and a recent photograph. They demonstrate how artists often exagerated the scale of the features they were drawing. The engraving suggests that the columns topped by harpies were nearly 9 metres high; in reality they measure about 3 metres. The bench in the background of the photograph gives a clue to their height.*

Vuë de la Fontaine des Harpyes, autrement nommé de l'epine dans le Jardin D'ARANJUEZ.

This was the opinion of Lady Holland, wife of an English diplomat who moved in Court circles and travelled widely in Spain. It was an unfashionable view in the early 19th century, when conventional wisdom abhorred formality and saw beauty only in supposedly natural landscapes.

The Alcazar was an old garden partly modernised, but there were new palaces and new gardens to be made by Charles v's son, Philip II. The royal hunting box at Aranjuez, near Madrid, had plenty of scope for development, and it was here that the first great Renaissance garden in Spain was created by Juan de Herrera. Philip had grown up in The Netherlands and, like his father, appreciating Dutch gardening skills, employed a Dutch gardener, Jan Holbeq, and several Dutch assistants. As a result, at Aranjuez, he had a garden laid out in old-fashioned rectangles and squares edged with box in the Dutch style. Known as the King's Garden, it has recently been restored to its original plan.

The first gardens in Spain to rival the great gardens of Italy were designed at Aranjuez by Juan Bautista de Toledo for Philip's wife, the French-born Elizabeth of Valois. Work started in 1562 and continued for 100 years. The garden, called the Jardin de la Isla, was not aligned with the palace, but, within its irregular river boundaries, was laid out geometrically with long walks and avenues of trees, and was handsomely decorated with exquisite fountains. With a constant supply of water from the River Tagus, Aranjuez had water jokes and the finest fountains in Spain. To add to its ornamentation, Italian sculptors were brought across the Mediterranean to meet demands of quality and quantity.

After Philip's death, some fountains were installed at Aranjuez by his son, Philip III, and further changes to the ground-plan were made in 1660 by the architect Sebastian Herrera Barnuevo, but since then the basic plan has changed little. In 1665, the French engraver L. Meusniers published a book of views of houses and gardens *Veuë du Palais Jardins et Fontaines D'Arangonesse, Maison de plaisance du Roi d'Espagne*. Most of the illustrations are, in fact, of French houses and gardens, but seven of Aranjuez and the Jardin de la Isla are included, a mark of the garden's renown, and among them is a view of the palace, of the parterre with fountains and trellis tunnels, and individual illustrations of the Fountain of Neptune, the Fountain of the Tritons, the Fountain of Don Juan of Austria, and the Fountain of the Harpies.

Writing in 1707, Don Juan Alvarez de Colmenar declared Aranjuez to be the finest garden in Spain. *Les fontaines, les allées, les parterres, les berceaux, les cabinets, les cascades et les grottes, sont d'une beauté merveilleuse, & font de ce lieu un Palais enchanté.*[30] Everywhere one went, he said, it was possible to see five or six fountains at a time, ornamented with bronze statues and marble basins. He admired the Fountain of Diana, the Mount Parnassus, and the Dragon Grotto, which was decorated with automata and dated 1607. He also disclosed an intriguing fact, that the Don Juan of Austria Fountain was so named because the main statue was carved from a stone found in a Turkish ship after the Battle of Lepanto in 1571. The dedication of a fountain in a garden to a national hero, in this case the victor of Lepanto, was unusual for the time.

Even though the island garden was not aligned geometrically to the palace, Aranjuez demonstrated that mainstream thought in garden design had reached Spain by 1600. In the case of Aranjuez, topography was the reason palace and garden were separated, but at another great Hapsburg palace and garden, Buen Retiro, the essential Renaissance concept of unity within a geometric plan was effectively ignored.

The palace and gardens of Buen Retiro were started in 1631 for Philip IV on the eastern edge of Madrid by the Conde Duque de Olivares. Only one wing of the palace remains, the Cáson, or ballroom, designed in 1637 by Alonso Carbonel, and now housing the Army Museum. The gardens were designed in part by an Italian, Cosimo Lotti, who had been involved in the design of the Boboli Gardens in Florence. Unfortunately, there was never an overall plan for palace and garden, and the gardens were enlarged later through further purchases of land, parcels that could not be easily integrated into the existing plan. As a result, there was no unity of composition, no central axis, and no view of the vast square lake from the palace. In 1712, an attempt was made to improve the design by inviting French expert René Carlier to Madrid, but the task was fundamentally impossible.

Nonetheless, Buen Retiro made a splendid Baroque pleasure garden for Court entertainments. The King and Queen presided over lavish festivities, during which aquatic festivals, naval battles and comedies were staged on the lake or in the Cáson, and in 1639, 12 gondolas were brought from Naples for court promenades. The cost of these entertainments provoked caustic songs from the poor of the city, but the diplomatic community was impressed. The British Ambassador, Sir William Ashton, wrote: *In the festival at the Buen Retiro in 1636, rare gardens and new water devices were inaugurated. The entertainment was the most original and brilliant I have ever attended, with three scenarios, each illuminated in the newest and most ingenious way, all due to the imagination of the Conde-Duque.*[31]

On the edge of the great square lake stood seven pavilions, known as hermitages: these were inhabited by so-called 'hermits', each one receiving an allowance to act the part. Interestingly, this is one of the earliest instances of paid hermits occupying hermitages in a garden, a fashion that spread to the rest of Europe; hermitages in a variety of styles sprang up in distant corners of countless gardens, and hermits were paid to think in peace, or at least to pretend to do so.

The hermitages at Buen Retiro were charming and it is not surprising that in 1707, according to Alvarez de Colmenar, members of the Court at Buen Retiro usurped the hermits and used the buildings themselves. He reported, too, that the gardens were delightful, noting that the King visited them nearly every day, especially when it was hot.

Several other much larger buildings also known as hermitages were to be found within the grounds of Buen Retiro, each within its own garden. The Hermitage of Saint Anthony was a plain building encircled by a canal, which the King would visit by gondola, while the Hermitage of St Paul was much grander, with an ornate Baroque façade, three fountains in front and pergolas on either side.

Despite its haphazard development, Buen Retiro was laid out on a grand scale. Illustrations suggest a certain Spanish severity about the design and buildings, and, in comparison with contemporary gardens, it lacked the profusion of buildings of Rueil, the theatricality of Isola Bella, the unity of Wilton, and the abundance of fountains of Aranjuez, but it had many delights of its own and, with its fountains, lakes, wide allées and paths, it answered a vital need for pleasure gardens in the capital.

In the 19th century, the gardens of Buen Retiro suffered from lack of water and neglect, and in 1868 the royal estate became a public park. By 1902 the French poet Théophile Gautier was scornfully dismissive, writing in *Voyage en Espagne* that he considered Buen Retiro to be like the dream garden of a rich grocer, filled with common flowers, fake wooden swans on the lake, ridiculous automata and other examples of bad taste.

Apart from the Cáson, all the former garden buildings as well as the palace have gone, but Buen Retiro is nowadays a delight to the inhabitants of Madrid. Under the aegis of Carmen Anon, a programme of rehabilitation was started in 1993, with the intention, where practicable, of restoring the gardens to their original condition, bearing in mind both cost and the needs of the public. The total concept is one of the most ambitious in Europe and will take decades to complete, but work is under way.

Le Grand Étang du BVEN-RETIRO.

Louis XIV

If there be any tolerable share of Happiness *and* Content *to be anywhere enjoyed by an Innocent Man, out of the hurry and noise of the World, a compleat and spacious* Garden, *furnished with a variety of* Walks *and* Groves, *and adorned with* Fountains, Cascades *and* Grottoes *&c. must do very much towards the obtaining of even a* Paradise *upon Earth.*

Walter Harris, *A Description of the King's Royal Palace and Garden at Loo,* 1699

Louis XIV was born in 1638, succeeded his father at the age of five, took over the government in 1661 and reigned until 1715. An autocratic, all-powerful giant of a monarch, he reigned longer than any other French king, and clearly left a massive imprint on French and European history. His imprint on garden history is massive, too, for although he created a stifling city of courtiers at Versailles, he surrounded it with an amazing garden.

A countryman at heart, Louis was a dedicated huntsman and first-rate shot, and enjoyed observing the natural world. But he also had a passion for building, and spent much of his life poring over plans for palaces and gardens, watching them take shape, changing them again and again if necessary, and finally standing back and admiring them when he thought they could be improved no further. He combined this discerning eye with the ability to choose the best professionals.

Vaux-le-Vicomte and Versailles were the two most important gardens created during Louis XIV's reign, Versailles having, for long after its completion, the additional reputation of being the single most-admired garden ever created; it is probably still better known than any other garden on the Continent, possibly in the world.

Both Vaux and Versailles were the brainchildren of André Le Nôtre, the third generation of a family of gardeners to French kings. Born in 1613, the young André chose painting as his first career. It was when he had entered the studio of Simon Vouet that he met another artist with whom he was to work closely in the future, Charles Le Brun. André must have had an obvious talent for garden design as well as for art, since, in 1637 at the age of 24, he was appointed gardener in charge of the parterres at the Tuileries in Paris in succession to his father, Jean Le Nôtre. Thereafter he was also employed at the Luxembourg Palace, and at Fontainebleau in 1645, and was appointed Contrôleur Général des Bâtiments du Roi in 1657. In 1656, Nicolas Fouquet engaged him to design the gardens at Vaux-le-Vicomte.

Château and gardens were designed from scratch by a team of three, Louis Le Vau, architect, Charles Le Brun, painter and interior decorator, and André Le Nôtre, garden designer. It was Fouquet's ambition that his new château and garden should be the most brilliant in France, and with this talented trio and his own fortune, made largely through lending money to the government, he achieved his ambition. He would have been familiar not only with all the royal gardens, as well as with Rueil, Wideville, Fresne and others, but also with the reputation of Italian gardens; furthermore he probably knew the books on Heidelberg and Wilton by Salomon and Isaac de Caus, as well as Boyceau's work. He was indeed a knowledgeable patron.

Vaux-le-Vicomte is a superb creation. Encircled by a moat in the French tradition, the architecture of the château is emphasised by the

La Montagne d'Eau, *1693, one of many wondrous fountains at Versailles captured by J. Cotelle in a series of 21 paintings, now on display in the Grand Trianon. Situated in one of the smaller salles de verdure, at 'K' on the plan on p.107, it is more intimate than the majority of fountains.*

A bird's-eye view of Vaux-le-Vicomte
(K.66.23.K) shows the gardens much as they
are today, although only some of the parterres
de broderie have been restored. The design was
Le Nôtre's first masterpiece and defined the majestic
scale of French gardens for many decades.

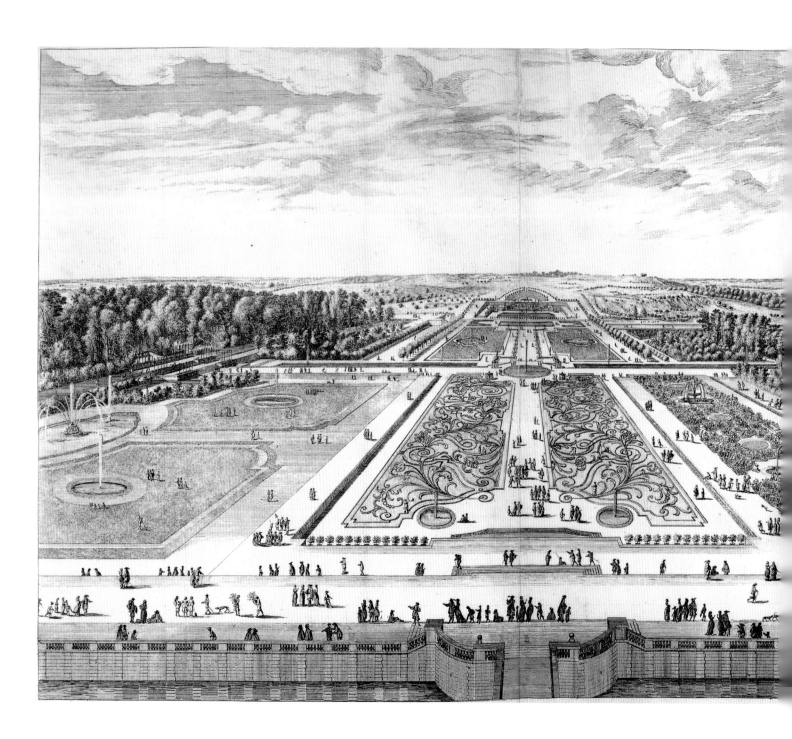

level parterres that surround it, as well as by the proportions between the building, the parterres and the plantations of trees beyond on either side. Intersected by cross allées, the spacious central allée leads past parterres, fountains and basins down to the *Miroir d'Eau*, and then on to another, wider *miroir*; this second stretch of water is part of a long canal running at right angles to the main axis. Behind it is the grotto, whose façade is beautifully embellished with sculpted torsos on rusticated pilasters, between which are seven niches filled with rockwork fountains. It bears a distinct resemblance to the grotto at Wilton, although it exceeds the latter in size and grandeur.

Above the grotto is a balustraded terrace, approached up wide staircases on either side; in the triangles below the steps, the sculptor Lespagnandel set great river gods, reclining and gazing back towards the château. The central axis continues beyond the grotto and up a slope to a statue on the skyline, now a copy of the Farnese Hercules in gilt lead, executed by Tournois and cast by Thiebaud in 1891.

Vaux-le-Vicomte is not a garden that relies mainly on architecture, but rather on a triumph of proportion in the management of space and levels. Le Nôtre made use of a natural river and valley, and controlled them into flat surfaces, ramps and a canal. The vista from the château is uniquely satisfying, because the ground falls and rises, and the entire composition is at ease with the wider landscape. Many of the main features are visible from the château, yet there are hints of others just out of sight in the wings. It departs from the older, Italian manner of treating a flattish site by dividing it into separate sections, and dotting buildings about the place as features, as in the Villa Borghese in Rome and at Rueil. Here, there is no structure to distract the eye between the château and the grotto and the distant statue. The garden is one single composition, complete and controlled, created by a supreme landscape artist. It was the finest château and garden in France.

The story of how the château and gardens were finished within five years, and of Fouquet's sumptuous fête in August 1661, is well known. It was one of the most glittering parties ever thrown, with outrageously expensive gifts for all the guests, a magnificent dinner, a play commissioned specially from Molière, and a sparkling display of fireworks.

Within three weeks of the fête, Fouquet was arrested, tried and finally, after three years, condemned to life imprisonment. The charge was financial irregularity, but Louis' envy was probably the root cause. Fouquet's lifestyle was ostentatious, his new château superb, and his attentions to Louis' mistress overt. The King was angry and jealous, as were others at court, who produced evidence of Fouquet's excessive profits from Crown business; it was they whom Louis chose to believe. Fouquet died in gaol in 1680. After his imprisonment, lavish parties went out of fashion – except for those thrown by the King. Louis XIV's reaction to the glorious achievement of Vaux was to expropriate the château and remove everything that was movable, from furniture to orange trees, and to employ Le Vau and Le Brun as well as Le Nôtre on his own behalf. Although the trio worked together again, it was never on such a perfect, single, surviving project.

Versailles was the site where Louis chose to develop the most remarkable palace in Europe. The concept and building progress were quite the antithesis of Vaux, since there was no overall composition from the start. Its haphazard development was wildly extravagant and appallingly wasteful, but the end result was far more magnificent than Vaux.

The story of the building of Versailles, a tale of great complexity, has been unravelled by Guy Walton in *Louis XIV's Versailles*. Le Vau's first transformation of the old royal hunting box into a château was torn down and replaced by a larger version by Jules Hardouin-Mansart in 1678. The same fate befell Le Vau's Orangery of 1664, when in 1685 Hardouin-Mansart replaced it with the colossal U-shaped building that still houses tender plants in winter. The Grotto of Thétis, a delectable free-standing pavilion designed by Charles Perrault, was built near the north façade of the château, but demolished in 1684 to make way for Mansart's north wing of the château. Le Nôtre's first parterres and terraces were laid down and then ripped up on several occasions, as the King's ideas grew and grew. *There is not a place in Versailles that hasn't been changed ten times, often for the worse*, wrote an envoy from the Palatine.[1]

By 1664, when Louis staged his first *grande fête*, Plaisirs de l'Ile Enchantée, Versailles was already a delight. *Tout y rit dehors et dedans … Sa symétrie, la richesse de ses meubles, la beauté de ses promenades et le nombre infini de ses fleurs, comme de ses orangers, rendent les environs de ce lieu dignes de sa rareté singulière*, wrote Madame de Marigny.[2] Further splendid fêtes followed in 1668, and again in 1674, when there were concerts, buffet suppers, fireworks and dancing in various locations in the gardens.

In 1688, after a quarter of a century of building, both palace and gardens at Versailles were more or less finished. They were awesome. The interior was gloriously decorated by teams of artists. The Galerie des Glaces glittered spectacularly, with its chandeliers, candelabra, consoles all silver, its woodwork all gilded and its ceiling all painted, the whole lit by a thousand candles reflected in the mirrored wall.

The gardens were equally amazing. The length of the central east–west axis sets the massive scale as it continues beyond the Apollo Fountain along the Grand Canal, the end of which seems to disappear into distant mists on all but the clearest of days. Parterres sweep wide on either side of the château, on a scale much larger than at Vaux-le-Vicomte, and with a rich variety of patterns and fountains. A huge lake, the Lac des Suisses, extends to the south beyond the Orangery.

Crossing the main axis at right angles are the allées, while others radiate out from the round pool at the end of the canal. The main

This plan of Versailles, the ultimate in Baroque gardens, was published in Les Délices de Paris *by Piganiol de la Force, 1717. The gardens are vast, stretching 3 ½ kilometres on the main axis from the château to the boundary. The Menagerie was to the left of the cross-canal and the Grand Trianon to the right, while most of the fountains were in the* salles de verdure *closer to the château. The 18th-century gardens of the Petit Trianon are outside the boundary of this plan, on the right. The vast reservoir was to the right of the château and gave its name to the road below it.*

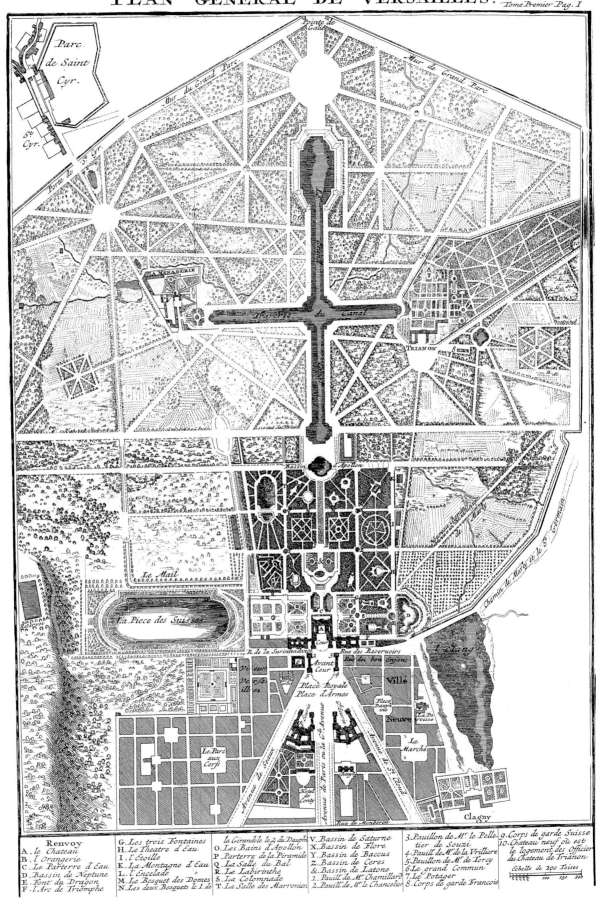

PLAN GENERAL DE VERSAILLES.

Tome Premier Pag. I

Parc de Saint Cyr.

St. Cyr.

Pointe de Galie

Mur du Grand Parc

Mur du Grand Parc

Mur du Grand Parc

Porte de St. Cyr

LA MENAGERIE

TRIANON

Travers du Canal

Chemin de Marly et de St. Germain

Chemin de Marly

Bassin d'Apollon

Le Mail

La Piece des Suisses

Chemin de Marly

R. de la Surintendance   Rue des Reservoirs

Cour   Avant Cour   Rue du bon Enfant

Place Royale   Place d'Armes   Ville

Place Dauph ine   Neuve

Le Parc aux Cerfs   Le Marché

L'Etang

Avenue de Seaux   Avenue de Paris ou la Gd Avenue   Avenue de St. Cloud

Hotel de Conty   Rue de Monboron   Clagny

Renvoy				
A. le Chateau	G. Les trois Fontaines	la Girandole le 2. du Dauph.	V. Bassin de Saturne	3. Pauillon de Mr. le Pelle-
B. l'Orangerie	H. Le Theatre d'Eau	O. Les Bains d'Apollon	X. Bassin de Flore	tier de Souzi
C. Le Parterre d'Eau	I. l'Étoille	P. Parterre de la Piramide	Y. Bassin de Baccus	4. Pauill. de Mr. de la Vrilliere
D. Bassin de Neptune	K. La Montagne d'Eau	Q. La Salle du Bal	Z. Bassin de Ceres	5. Pauillon de Mr. de Torcy
E. Font du Dragon	L. l'Encelade	R. Le Labirinthe	&. Bassin de Latone	6. Le grand Commun
F. l'Arc de Triomphe	M. Le Bosquet des Domes	S. La Colomnade	1. Pauill. de Mr. Chamillard	7. Le Potager
	N. Les deux Bosquets le I. de	T. La Salle des Marroniers	2. Pauill. de Mr. le Chancelier	8. Corps de garde Francois

9. Corps de garde Suisse
10. Chateau neuf où est le logement des Officiers du Chateau de Trianon

Echelle de 200 Toises
100   150   200

Louis's first great fête, Les Plaisirs de l'Isle Enchantée, *lasted for three days in May 1664. There were sumptuous banquets, this one captured in an engraving by Silvestre, and a magnificent display of fireworks, illustrated by Le Pautre, in which the château is shown as it was before Louis started to expand it. Both these illustrations are taken from* Les Plaisirs de l'Isle Enchantée *published under the direction of Louis XIV and the Cabinet du Roi.*

axis has parallel allées on either side, and countless crossing walks to subdivide the parterres and the bosquets, the wooded areas. It is in these bosquets, behind walls of clipped hedges, that further delights were to be found, green rooms, *salles de verdure,* or a smaller version, a *cabinet de verdure.* In each was an intricate path plan, a fountain, a pavilion or a trellis structure. They were imaginative and enchanting, each room with its own character, and each a surprise, for they were hidden from view until the *salle* was entered.

In one bosquet, the amphitheatre of La Salle de Bal, was one of Le Nôtre's later and finest inventions for Versailles. It was begun in 1680 and completed five years later, Le Nôtre collaborating with the Francine family of hydraulic fame, assisted by Denis, and a rock expert called Berthier. At one end is a curved wall of cascades, wildly elaborate and theatrical, with water shooting up and spilling down over tiers of carved stone and shells, brought by the French Navy from the Red Sea and the Indian Ocean. At the opposite end and round the sides are banks of stone seats, and in the middle a ballroom floor in the shape of a trefoil surrounded by water. The orchestra played above the cascades. La Salle du Bal was a great Baroque composition, like the cascade at St Cloud, and would have

Premiere   Journée

Festin du Roy, et des Reynes, auec plusieurs Princesses et Dames, serui de tous les mets et presens faits par les Dieux et les quatre saisons.

been a brilliant sight when torches lit up dancing figures and glittering waterfalls. Now, without water, music and dancers, it looks as
dejected as a faded wallflower, and only partially revives when the
taps are turned on again. Like so much of Versailles, it needs the
throngs of elegant ladies and gentlemen for whom it was created.

In yet another bosquet is the Colonnade, an exquisite invention,
this time by Mansart, completed in 1685 and still standing. It is an
elegant peristyle, a circle of marble columns of differing colours. In
the spandrels above the columns are low relief carvings in white
marble of children playing musical instruments, while white marble
urns decorate the upper rim. It is a presage of the 18th century, when
Baroque was generally suceeded by a return to a pure form of
Classicism.

Versailles also had a menagerie, a labyrinth, and a major collection of statues for which Le Brun was responsible. The sculptors
included Girardon, Coysevox, Tubi, Monnier, Buirette, Clérion,
Laviron, Desjardins, Hutinot, Regnaudin and Guérin. The Italian
Domenico Guidi was responsible for the statue in the Fountain of
Fame, and Bernini was commissioned to make an equestrian statue
of Louis XIV for the Orangery.

The great circular Colonnade was designed by Mansart and measures 32 metres in diameter. In each arch there is a fountain in a shallow basin on a pedestal, and in the middle, Girardon's statue of the Rape of Proserpine, *which was placed there under Louis's direction in 1699.*

Following the Italian tradition that water was an essential ingredient in a grand garden, so the garden of the great Louis XIV had to have more water than any other. Although a network of reservoirs was constructed by 1678, the supply had proved inadequate, and the River Seine, on the other side of a hill and some kilometres away, was the only possible never-failing source of water. Thus it was that two engineers, Arnold de Ville and Renequin Sualem, were responsible for building one of the engineering miracles of the day, the Machine de Marly at Bougival, whereby the waters of the Seine were hoisted 162 metres up the hill by 14 giant waterwheels, and then flowed along an aqueduct to Versailles to fill the reservoirs. So important were the reservoirs that when the ambassador of Siam visited Versailles in 1686, he was taken to them as well as around the gardens. When the ambassador from Moscow toured the gardens in 1681, he suggested that there was so much water that it seemed as if the sea had been brought to Versailles. Whether a genuinely amazed spectator or an unctuous diplomat, he could hardly have been more flattering.

Fountains played throughout the gardens – the great Fountains of Apollo and Latona, Neptune and the Dragon, the *Bassin de l'Encelade* with its amusing frogs, and *Isle Royale*, and many more, some in prominent positions, others tucked away in bosquets. There are now only 300 fountains at Versailles, where once there were 1,400. They refreshed and cooled the gardens in summer, and added gaiety throughout the year. François and Pierre de Francine, who had succeeded their forbears as engineers in charge of hydraulics, ensured that the fountains near the château played continuously, while those further away were only turned on when the King or important guests were approaching.

Their only drawback was the occasional smell from the water. Because it was kept in holding tanks where it could become stagnant, it was, according to Walter Harris, *liable to cause an ill-stench in the Gardens*,[3] so it was essential to run the fountains for a day or two before an important visit or event.

This breathtaking garden, with its fountains, buildings, statues and walks, epitomised the all-powerful monarch of France, just as the gardens of 16th-century Italy had displayed the power and riches of the princes and cardinals. In the same tradition, there was a bold iconographical plan at Versailles, which would have been easily understood by the educated classes familiar with classical mythology. It centred on Apollo, god of the sun, symbolising Louis XIV as the Sun King, and included statues to Apollo, the great Fountain of Apollo, and the god's head set in a sunburst emblazoned all over the palace, all in honour of King Louis. Apollo's mythological sister, Diana the Huntress, was glorified, too, as was the hunter Nimrod, to whom the Bourbons were also compared. The iconography was as profound as the gardens were vast.

Louis' personal enthusiasm for the gardens at Versailles is shown by his careful itinerary for showing them to visitors. Between 1689 and 1705, he wrote no less than six versions, one in his own hand, parts of which were published in 1982 in Louis XIV: *Manière de montrer les Jardins de Versailles*. Over the years, there are variations in the routes, but all start outside the west front, and most take in the Orangery, all the delights of the bosquets and the great fountains. The second and third versions include visits to the menagerie and, by boat, to the Grand Trianon on the Grand Canal.

One of the remarkable aspects of all versions is the quiet language Louis used. He did not command the beholder to admire, he modestly suggested that the visitor should stop to consider: *en arrivant aux Sfinx on fera une pause pour voir le parterre du midiy, et après on ira droit sur le haut de l'Orangerie d'où l'on verra le parterre des orangers et le lac des Suisses.*[4]

The Machine de Marly, *illustrated by Piganiol de la Force in* Les Délices de Versailles, *1717, was such a curiosity that it became a tourist attraction in itself. Thanks to the machine, water was raised from the Seine and transported via an aqueduct to supply the fountains of Versailles.*

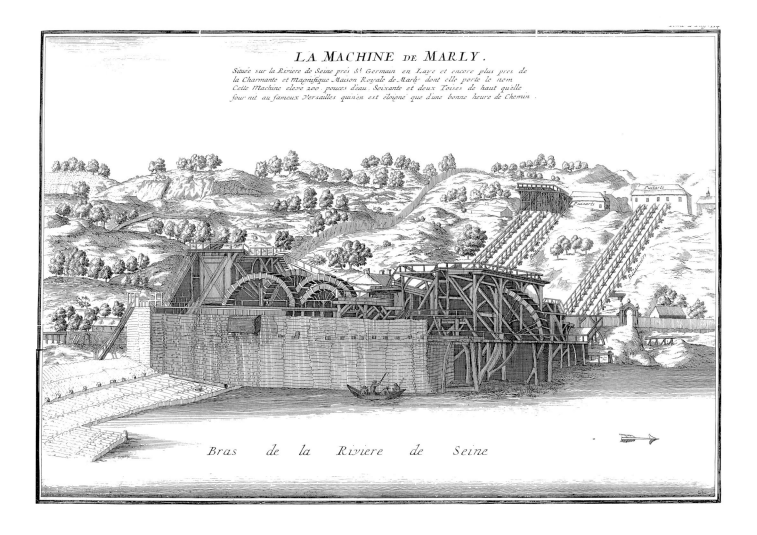

The Marais d'Eau *in the Bosquet du Marais was started in 1670 to a plan drawn by Madame de Montespan. The tree in the fountain sprayed water from every leaf, but it was too fragile to survive and was dismantled in 1704. It was illustrated in Perelle's* Vues des Belles Maisons de France, *1685.*

This was the largest Orangery in the world by far, and an enormous man-made lake, but there is not a word of their grandeur.

Within the boundaries of Versailles, to the north of the Grand Canal, is the Grand Trianon, or the *Trianon de Marbre*, a miniature palace complete with its own garden. The first building on this site was the *Trianon de Porcelaine*, built in 1670 and covered with blue and white Delft tiles. It was said to be in the Chinese taste because of the colours of the tiles, but at the time understanding of Chinese architecture was limited and the structure was French in form. It was surrounded by parterres of the brightly coloured flowers that Louis loved. Le Nôtre on the other hand considered bright colours vulgar, fit only to be seen by nurserymaids; they should not, therefore, be grown in the parterres near the château. Banished out of sight from Versailles, the garden of the Trianon specialised in flowers, including tender plants like orange trees, which were grown in the ground and covered up in the winter. In 1687 the *Trianon de Porcelaine* was pulled down and replaced by the Grand Trianon, whose architects were probably a combination of the King and Mansart, together with staff in the King's Building Office.

The sumptuous decoration of the Grand Trianon places it beyond garden architecture and classifies it as a palace. Although far too impractical for royal living, it became an idyllic place for escape from burdensome court rituals, as well as for entertaining favoured members of the aristocracy. Two new parterres were developed by Le Nôtre when the Trianon was rebuilt, both using nature with original flair: the Jardin des Sources had an irregular plan of mean-dering streams and the Trianon-sous-Bois focused on the beauty of foliage and twisting branches.

Profusely enhanced by man-made additions to the beauties of nature, Versailles lacked certain other man-made features that had been an essential part of earlier French and Italian gardens. After the destruction of the Grotto of Thétis in 1684, there were no grottoes and no hydraulic machines to turn figures, play music and make birds sing. Why this omission? The royal automata at St Germain-en-Laye, which Louis would have known as a child and during his early days as King, were installed *c.* 1600, but 60 years later they would have seemed dated and may have been troublesome to operate successfully. Nor are there any water jokes. The hidden jets that sprayed visitors in Italy and at Rueil were omitted at Versailles. A possible explanation for these singular omissions might be that Louis did not wish to fill his new gardens with old ideas, for he was instinctively a leader of taste, with the talents of innovative artists at his disposal.

Apart from developing new approaches to design, Versailles was a conscious demonstration of the most refined taste and of French superiority in the arts. It set the standard of European design for a whole era. Distinguished visitors, both French and foreign, were welcomed, and accounts of its glories were featured in journals, such as *Mercure Galant*, which circulated in France and abroad. Descrip-tions were published frequently by Le Sieur Combes, André Félibien, Piganiol de la Force and R. le Testu; illustrations were published, too, including an important series of 25 engravings by the leading topographical engraver, Israel Silvestre; there were bird's-eye views by Liévin Cruyl, J.B. Martin, Pierre Denis Martin, Dumas and Pierre Patel, and engravings by Perelle, Thomassin, Pierre Le Pautre, Aveline, Allegrain, Meusniers, de Poilly, Swidde and many others. All aspects of Versailles were fascinating to the public.

On the other hand, the cost of Versailles was phenomenal, especially in the 1680s. In the gardens, the construction of the enormous Orangery was a major expense, as was the digging of the Lac des Suisses, partly done by soldiers with no enemy to fight at the time. Throughout Louis' reign, wars cost France dear, and expendi-ture at Versailles rose and fell according to the demands of the military budget. Even in time of war, however, there were still some funds for building. Marinier's *Table of Annual Expenses for the Château of Versailles* shows how expenditure rose steadily, with a brief hiccup at the start of the war against the Dutch between 1672 and 1678, rocketed to a peak in 1685, and then sank again after the start of the

Nine Years' War in 1688. These figures cover expenditure on both château and gardens.

MARINIER'S TABLE OF ANNUAL EXPENSES
FOR THE CHÂTEAU OF VERSAILLES[5]

	£	s	d	Brought	£	s	d
1664	834,037	2	6	Forward	19,553,003	14	8
1665	783,673	4		1678	2,622,655	3	10
1666	526,954	7		1679	5,667,331	17	
1667	214,300	18		1680	5,839,761	19	8
1668	618,006	5	7	1681	3,854,382	2	
1669	1,238,375	7		1682	4,235,123	8	7
1670	1,996,452	12	4	1683	3,714,572	5VI	1
1671	3,396,595	12	6	1684	5,762,092	2	8
1672	2,802,718	1	5	1685	11,314,281	10	10
1673	847,004	3	10	1686	6,558,210	7	9
1674	1,384,269	10	3	1687	5,400,245	18	
1675	1,933,755	8	1	1688	4,551,596	16	2
1676	1,348,222	10	10	1689	1,710,055	10	
1677	1,628,638	11	4	1690	368,101	10	1
Carried Forward							
	19,553,003	14	8	Total	81,151,414	6	4

Funds, or a lack of them, postponed rather than curtailed the King's plans; it was up to the Surintendent des Bâtiments du Roi, first Colbert, then Louvois, to find the money through taxes, and to allocate it between the King's two great passions, building and military campaigns. France was by far the richest and most populous nation in Europe at the time, and Louis was very conscious of national prestige, and of Versailles as its manifestation. Had he not spent so prodigiously on Versailles, his subjects would have been less harshly taxed and he would have avoided sowing what some historians suggest were the seeds of the French Revolution. On the other hand, the stimulus to the *beaux-arts* and the manufacture of tapestry, porcelain and fabrics was immense, not only giving employment at home but also bringing foreign currency income through exports. Through succeeding centuries, the benefits to France of one of the greatest tourist attractions in Europe have been unquantifiable.

Towards the end of his reign, when his creative obsession turned to Marly, Louis opened the gates of Versailles to the public. Parisians thronged through them, but over the years left a sad trail of damage and destruction: statues were mutilated, urns removed, and taps, nozzles and piping for the fountains spirited away. Some of the treillage disintegrated with age. By the time of Louis' death in 1715, the Sun King's garden had lost a little of its lustre, yet none of its majesty.

An aerial view of Marly, painted by P.D. Martin, showing how it nestled into a narrow secluded valley from the head of which flowed the famous Rivière. In Mansart's plan, the château and its 12 guest pavilions are perfectly integrated into the gardens and focus on the Grande Pièce d'Eau, *which still exists. Below it were* Les Nappes, *a series of lacy little waterfalls over which water slipped to the basin below. The gardens were enriched throughout with fountains and statues of the highest quality, some of which were moved later to the Tuileries. Deprived of all its original features except some water and allées, the site is now a public park.*

Marly was never a rival to Versailles. The château and gardens, only a few kilometres away, on the Seine nearer Paris, were much too small for that. Instead it was an exquisite retreat where Louis could escape from the rigid etiquette imposed at Versailles, to which the Court had moved from Paris in 1682. Louis claimed that he built Marly for the courtiers, but it was probably much more his need for privacy and his irresistible urge to build that set Mansart, Le Brun and Le Nôtre to work again. Le Nôtre's contribution to Marly, however, was probably limited, not only because he was in Italy during the early planning stage, but also because of his age, and Mansart was ambitious and talented enough to fulfil the role of garden designer as well as that of château architect.

Marly was started when expenditure on the gardens at Versailles – in particular on the Orangery – was ever increasing. It was complete in outline by 1685, but as usual the gardens were altered regularly over the following years, with a major burst of activity around 1700. The final cost of château and garden is said to have been even greater than that of Versailles.

Compared with Versailles, Marly was intimate and secluded. It was set in a narrow wooded valley, the main axis running down the valley towards the Seine, with a delightful view across the river to St Germain-en-Laye. The château was a small, elegantly proportioned house that could accommodate only the King and the immediate members of his family, so the courtiers were lodged in 12 little pavilions, ranged on either side of the valley and nestling into the wooded hillsides. Elaborate berceaux covered the terraced allées on either side, and on the valley floor water basins were shaped with geometric precision. Fountains by Coysevox and others and round-headed orange trees in tubs completed the meticulous architectural arrangement. The effect of this open, sunlit area was heightened by the contrast with the dark foliage of the surrounding woods. Above the house, a fast-flowing and intricate cascade, known as *La Rivière*, was built into the hillside, and to satisfy the many thirsty fountains, water from the Seine raised by the *Machine de Marly* was diverted from Versailles.

The plan could hardly be said to encourage simplicity or informality, but Marly did have an extra charm through Louis' relaxation of Court etiquette. The pleasure of Marly also lay in its comparative intimacy compared with Versailles, and in the beauty of the gardens themselves and the surrounding woodlands, while the dolls' house pavilions, each representing a sign of the zodiac, charmed the bewigged and silken guests. An invitation to Marly was the most coveted prize that Louis could award.

A fairy palace, unique in Europe as to form, still more unique for the beauty of its fountains, unique in the character and reputation . . . making it an object of curiosity to foreigners of all stations who visited France.[6] Such was the assessment of the Duc de Saint-Simon in his memoirs.

No one could deny that Marly is really beautiful, much lovelier than Versailles,[7] wrote Madame, the Palatine Princess Liselotte who was married to Monsieur, Louis' brother. Two years later, in July 1701, she wrote from Marly to a correspondent:

I have been here since Sunday night. The King received me with great kindness. He came to meet me, and then took me for a walk. He has made many improvements since I was last here; there is a new mail [an area where the forerunner to golf was played] *so shady that one can play at high noon without feeling the sun. We made a tour of the entire garden, and climbed a small hill to see the new waterfall. It is very fine, and constructed in quite a new way: it has three steps right at the top, a large fountain spurts a great gush of water, and the heads of sea-monsters spit out more. This water forms the cascade. In the centre of each step there is a low jet, and on each side, at the top, bronze children play with the sea-creatures.*[8]

This cascade was *La Rivière*, which Saint-Simon considered Marly's greatest charm. The upper part is said to have been designed by Hardouin-Mansart, but it is more likely that it was devised by Le Nôtre's nephew, Claude Desgots, in consultation with his uncle.[9] Like much of the construction at Marly, it was not well made and

leaked badly, and did not survive the reign of Louis' successor, who covered it with grass. The rest of the gardens and château fell into ruin during the Revolution and were pulled down early in the 19th century.

Louis was as deeply attached to Marly as he was to Versailles. He would accompany a lady on the tour of the garden, she in a chair mounted on wheels and pulled by four men while he walked beside her. Later in life, he took to the wheeled chair himself, both at Marly and at Versailles, so that he could still enjoy his gardens.

Inspecting his creations remained one consolation in sad old age, when his heirs and other close relatives had all died. To his five-year-old great-grandson, the future Louis XV, he said on his death-bed: *Do not copy me in my love of building or in my love of warfare.*[10] As far as building was concerned, did he regret the money, the mistakes, the time or the energy? It would be a great sorrow had he regretted the results, for he created two of the most astonishing gardens of their time in the world. The pity is that neither is complete today.

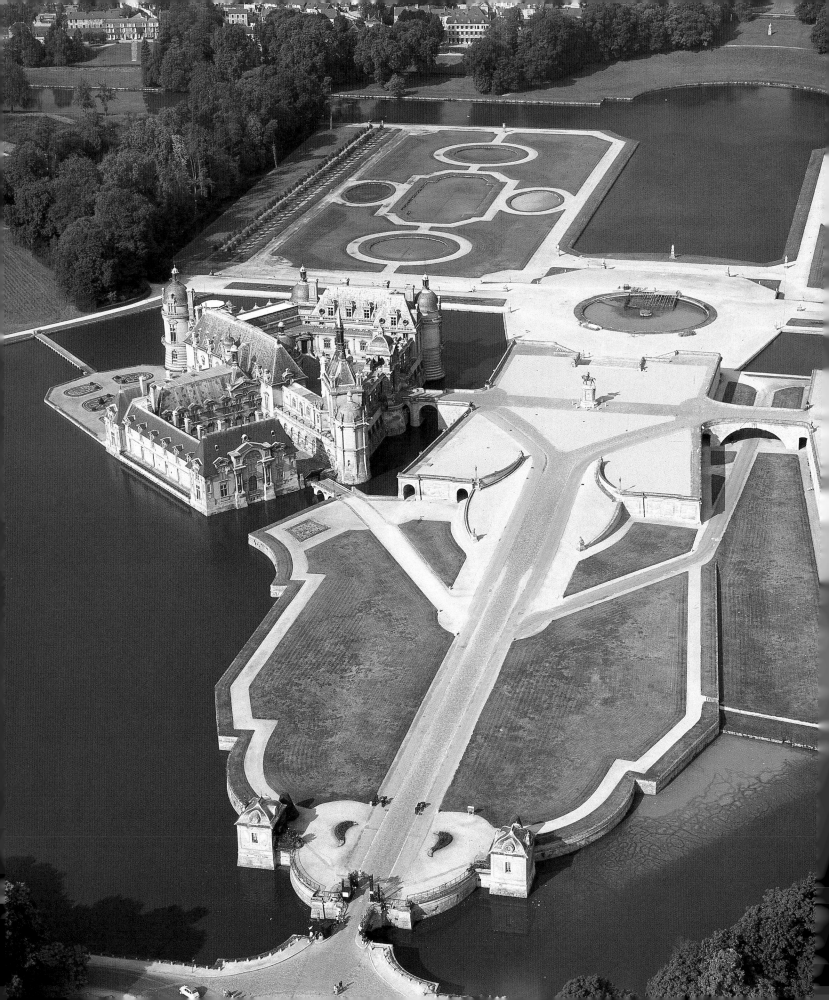

Le Nôtre and his Influence

Le Nôtre's reputation rested not only on his work for Louis XIV at Versailles and Marly, but also at Fontainebleau, where he redesigned the Grand Parterre in 1661 and at St Germain-en-Laye where he made the great terrace in 1669. Despite his continuing responsibilities at the Tuileries and his appointment in 1657 as *Contrôleur Général des Bâtiments du Roi*, he was free to accept commissions from others. The Prince de Condé, head of one of France's most illustrious families, commander of the French army, and a guest of Fouquet at the ill-considered fête at Vaux-le-Vicomte, was one of his most important clients, and Chantilly one of the achievements of which Le Nôtre was most proud. His involvement started in 1663 when the Grand Condé invited him to redesign the grounds at his estate in the Oise.

A strong central axis was always the first element that Le Nôtre established. At Vaux-le-Vicomte with a green field site in which to place the château and gardens, this was easily accomplished, while at Versailles he had a symmetrical house and as much space as he could wish for. But at Chantilly, the château buildings were impossibly irregular.

His plan was, therefore, to leave the château well to one side, concentrating on the immense width of the central axis, as well as its length, stretching as it did up over a raised terrace, down to the Grand Canal and on to the *vertugadin*, a semicircular space defined by trees, and up an avenue cut out of the wooded hillside. To relieve the monotony of even ground, Le Nôtre raised a terrace and made a new entrance to the château at a higher level.

By the time the Grand Condé died in 1686, Chantilly had been given all the features essential for magnificence. Water abounded on this marshy site; it was channelled into a sculpted lake on either side of the main approach and contained in a strait, known as La Manche, on the main axis, then stretched into the Grand Canal that formed a great cross axis some 2,800 metres long overall. There were countless fountains in the Grand Parterre, the Parterre de l'Orangerie and other smaller parterres, all supervised by a member of the Francine family. A machine to pump water was built by the hydraulic engineer Jacques de Manse, while treillage made by Dutch craftsmen was used to create berceaux within the gardens and gateways from one area to another. An orangery was designed by Jules Hardouin-Mansart, a labyrinth by Claude Desgots and two cascades by Daniel Gittard.

At Chantilly, laid out by Le Nôtre in the 1660s, the château is effectively incidental to the plan. The designer made best use of plentiful supplies of water in his clear-cut patterns of green, blue and sand, patterns easily appreciated from the raised central terrace or from the vertugadin beyond the canal, as well as from the air.

The cascade at Sceaux, illustrated by Perelle in
Vues des Belles Maisons de France, *1685,*
is another example of Baroque theatricality. It was
designed by Le Nôtre for Colbert, Louis XIV's
minister, and flowed into a great Octagon Lake.

No wonder Le Nôtre was contented with this magnificent Baroque triumph, this remodelled landscape. It was for this ability to manipulate a challenging site into a successful garden that he was most admired, at Chantilly and elsewhere: Anet, Castries, Clagny, Conflans, Dampierre, Gaillon, Meudon, Pontchartrain were all by Le Nôtre, and his genius influenced many more gardens that followed.

Water was a vital component of all these designs, and the variety of ways in which Le Nôtre handled it was endless. The shape of the basins, the width of the canals, the originality of the sculpture, the strength and angles of the jets, the tinkling or rushing sounds, all were aspects that the designer and his engineer could use in endless permutations. At Castries in Hérault in southern France, water was not readily available, so a seven-kilometre aqueduct was built to supply Le Nôtre's fountains. At Sceaux, he tamed water into a Grand Canal and a cascade to rival those at Rueil and St Cloud.

Cascades were often the most elaborate feature in the 17th-century French garden. That cascade at Sceaux is a tumbling froth of water, once ornamented with statues by Girardon and Coysevox. Another

surviving cascade in working order is at the château of Villette, in Val d'Oise. It formed part of the plan devised by Jean Dyel from 1665 onwards, and is the focal point of the garden as seen from the château.

The great cascades of 17th-century French gardens, culminating in La Rivière at Marly, epitomise the theatrical climax of French Baroque gardens, the ultimate control of water. Being wider, often longer, and more elaborately decorated, they were more majestic than their Italian antecedents, even more so than the *catene d'acqua* at the Villa Aldobrandini. Because of the difference in natural topography, French cascades lack the drama of a steep drop so useful in Italian gardens, but they make up for this in grandeur. If they tend to pretentiousness, it is because they reflect the spirit of Baroque architecture. If they look dull and heavy now, it is because too often their waters are turned off, or flow merely at a trickle.

These vastly grand, ornamental cascades did not, however, travel widely beyond the boundaries of France, although there are a handful of spectacular examples elsewhere. In Vienna, in the 1690s, Fischer von Erlach's first plan of Schönbrunn for the Emperor

The Tuileries in Paris, redesigned by Le Nôtre in 1664 and shown by Perelle in Vues des Belles Maisons de France, *1685. The name derives from their location on the former site of tile factories, and they adjoin the palace of the Louvre. From the palace Le Nôtre designed an uninterrupted view along the main axis of the Tuileries and up the Champs Elysées, to the end of which the Arc de Triomphe was later added. In recent years, the Tuileries have been extensively restored, a project due for completion in 1997.*

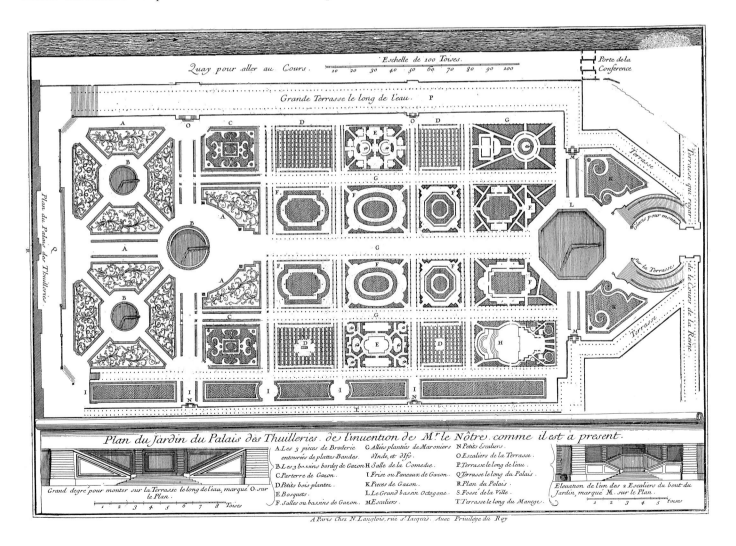

Plan du Jardin du Palais des Thuilleries, de l'invention de Mr le Nôtre, comme il est à present.

A. Les 3 pieces de Broderie entourées de plattes-Bandes.
B. Les 3 bassins bordes de Gazon.
C. Parterre de Gazon.
D. Petits bois plantez.
E. Bosquets.
F. Salles ou bassins de Gazon.
G. Allées plantées de Maroniers d'Inde, et d'Ifs.
H. Salle de la Comedie.
I. Frise ou Paneaux de Gazon.
K. Pieces de Gazon.
L. Le Grand bassin Octogone.
M. Escaliers.
N. Petits Escaliers.
O. Escaliers de la Terrasse.
P. Terrasse le long de l'eau.
Q. Terrasse le long du Palais.
R. Plan du Palais.
S. Fossé de la Ville.
T. Terrasse le long du Manege.

Grand degré pour monter sur la Terrasse le long de l'eau, marqué O. sur le Plan.

Elevation de l'un des 2 Escaliers du bout du Jardin, marqué M. sur le Plan.

A Paris Chez N. Langlois, rüe s.t Iacques. Avec Priuilege du Roy.

A statue of La Seine et la Marne *by Nicolas Coustou, originally made for Marly but moved to the Tuileries in 1720.*

Leopold I included a cascade with seven streams, but cost prohibited its construction. In Germany, the immensely long cascade at Wilhelmshöhe near Kassel, dating from the first years of the 18th century, is French in its emphasis on the main axis, Italianate in detail, and Germanic in the considerable Baroque building at its head. In Russia, Peter the Great's cascade at Peterhof, *c.* 1720, remains a tribute to Marly.

As well as being few and far between, English cascades were understated in their plainness compared with their continental counterparts. A long water staircase was made in 1694 at Chatsworth by Grillet, a pupil of Le Nôtre; statuary and fountains adorn the upper basin, and by 1711 Thomas Archer had added the temple. In Gloucestershire a simple cascade was made at Stanway, and *c.* 1698 George London made a cascade for William Blathwayt at Dyrham Park; sited on a steep hillside, it dropped down some 224 narrow steps. There were cascades at Powis Castle, in Powys, Stainborough in Yorkshire, and Drumlanrig in Dumfriesshire, but, with the exception of Chatsworth, all these have long since gone.

In Spain, the cascade, by the architect René Carlier, of white

marble and coloured jasper at La Granja de San Ildefonso, near Segovia, was built for the first Bourbon king, Philip V, to remind him of the gardens of his grandfather, Louis XIV. This is an original design, majestic and refreshing in the heat of a Spanish summer, and, as at Chatsworth, it has a small pavilion at its head.

This cascade was the inspiration for what must be the most celebrated Italian cascade of the 18th century. It is at La Reggia at Caserta near Naples, built for Charles III, King of Naples and son of Philip V of Spain. The gardens were designed by Luigi Vanvitelli, who, despite his Italian sounding name, was a Dutchman. Although the cascade was old-fashioned for its time, for it was constructed from the 1750s onwards in the Rococo era, it is firmly Baroque in its majestic proportions and the mythological statues that embellish it.

Cascades were so expensive that few could afford them; these examples were the exception rather than the rule; they were the icing on the Baroque garden design cake. The essentials for a garden of importance were a geometric plan with a strong axis over a large area, good proportions and as many fountains as resources could

Dezallier d'Argenville's plans for parterres from La Théorie et la Pratique du Jardinage, 1709. Whereas parterres de broderie *were full of movement, (see Boyceau's designs on p.68), a* parterre à l'anglaise *was a more peaceful backdrop for a display of sculpture. The* parterre de pièces coupées pour des fleurs *is more lavish than the earlier version by de Vries, (p.55), while the* parterre d'orangerie, *the orange garden, has a simple design that will not detract from the carefully shaped citrus trees.*

Parterre a l'Angloise

Parterre de pièces, coupées pour des fleurs

Parterre d'Orangerie

Planche 6.ᵉᴮ
Mariette excud.

One of several designs by Le Blond (1679–1719)
(Misc.3 M38–69) for pavilions with water and
sculpture. Since he was trained as an architect,
Le Blond's work is often profoundly architectural
but he also had a good understanding of garden
design and the ability to make even town gardens
seem spacious.

le Blond. Avec Privilens

supply. It was the entirety of French design, and especially of Le Nôtre's designs, that captured the imagination of garden designers throughout Europe, not necessarily and not only the individual features.

Le Nôtre did not himself publish any of his thoughts or designs, but such was his towering influence that others illustrated and published his creations for him. It fell to Antoine-Joseph Dezallier d'Argenville, nine years after Le Nôtre's death, to codify Le Nôtre's ideas on paper, and in 1709 he published in Paris the most influential book about French gardens, *La Théorie et la Pratique du Jardinage*, an analysis of both the art and the science of gardening. Its publishing history records its importance: it was reprinted in 1711, expanded in 1713, and reprinted six more times up to 1760. It was translated into English by John James in 1712, and reprinted in 1728 and 1743. A French pirated edition appeared three times at The Hague, and German editions came out in Augsburg in 1731 and 1741, and in Leipzig in 1767. D'Argenville acknowledged the assistance he had received from architect and garden designer, Jean-Baptiste le Blond, a former pupil of Le Nôtre, in compiling the book.

D'Argenville's book describes the main principles of French taste, in which fountains were the most important features. *Les Fontaines et les Eaux sont l'âme du Jardin; ce sont elles qui font le principal ornement.*[11] Ponds and canals should have small gilt gondolas and pleasure boats for aesthetic charm and entertainment; they should be well stocked with fish. A cascade was desirable, and two were illustrated, one on a gentle slope with small waterfalls, the other a water staircase with larger steps.

Two items were currently out of fashion. Grottoes, said d'Argenville in 1709, deteriorated rapidly without maintenance, however, in the 1713 edition, the grotto section was much expanded, suggesting that d'Argenville had underestimated their popularity and was responding to demand. Hydraulic systems were explained in detail, with illustrations of the mechanisms involved, and the edition of 1739 had a picture of a Neptune grotto similar to that which first appeared in 1615 in Salomon de Caus's *Les Raisons des Forces Mouvantes*.

Treillage had lost favour too, although d'Argenville thought it could *raise and improve the natural beauty of the Gardens extremely*.[12] The advantage of treillage was that it could be made up with all the architectural detail that the finest building in stone could boast, but with far more delicacy and for a smaller sum of money. But they were still expensive, *as they are very chargeable to make and keep up, and continually liable to decay, most people are out of conceit with them*.[13] They have been in and out of fashion ever since for the same reason.

D'Argenville also elaborated on the construction of treillage by explaining that instead of being entirely made of wood, it should be composed of lattice-work panels supported on an iron framework. This allowed easier and cheaper maintenance, as one damaged panel could be removed and replaced without affecting the structure as a whole. The great curved treillage tunnels or pergolas at Schwetzingen in the Palatine remain as an example of this principle of construction.

Two types of garden building were advocated by the author. Louis XIV's great Orangery had left its mark, for the author proposed stately buildings *like Galleries, which, by their fronts, add to the Beauty of Gardens*.[14] These greenhouses, as they were called in English, were an absolute necessity for orange trees, and served a dual purpose as a gallery or banqueting house in the summer. Then came a belvedere, which was to be placed at extremities of the garden, both for repose after a long walk and for the prospect of the countryside beyond.

The Theory and Practice of Gardening *is esteemed in its way, the best that has appeared in this or any other Language, and seems to be the best-laid Design, and carried on with the most Judgment*,[15] wrote Stephen Switzer about the English translation, in the preface to his 1715 publication, *The Nobleman, Gentleman, and Gardener's Recreation*. As Switzer's praise shows, Dézallier d'Argenville's expression of Le Nôtre's style of garden design was vital in spreading his ideas abroad.

But it is not only Le Nôtre's artistic genius that has given him a hallowed place in the history of design, for his genius was enhanced by his personality: *He had an integrity, a scrupulosity, an uprightness which made him respected and loved by every one and an artless simplicity and truth that were charming*, wrote Saint-Simon.[16] The great Sun King walked by his side round Versailles as the aged designer, too old to walk, was pushed in a wheeled chair. Louis treated Le Nôtre not as a servant, but as a friend.

The French Style in Italy

The amphitheatre in the gardens of the Villa Doria Pamphili in Rome has a spacious grandeur reminiscent of French Baroque, and may have been the work of Le Nôtre. It was illustrated by Perelle in Vues des Belles Maisons de France in 1685.

When Le Nôtre died in 1700, the Duc de Saint-Simon described the great designer as *illustrious as being the first to give designs for those fine gardens which decorate all France, and have so effaced the reputation of the gardens of Italy – which are, in fact, nothing by comparison – that the most famous masters of this art now come from Italy to learn and admire here.*[17]

Knowledge of Le Nôtre's works travelled abroad through published descriptions and engravings of Versailles and other gardens, through travellers who spread abroad the glories of French gardens, and through Dézallier d'Argenville's book and its many translations. And although the French thought their gardens vastly superior, they did join other Europeans in journeying to Venice, Florence and Rome to view Italian gardens of earlier days.

Bishop Gilbert Burnet thought there was yet much to admire in Italian villas and gardens in 1685. He was deeply impressed by, among others, the Villa Aldobrandini, the Villa Borghese, the Viceroy's palace in Naples, and the diversity of the villas on the Brenta Canal, although he did temper his enthusiasm by adding that *there are none that lay out so much Wealth all at once, as the Italians do upon their building and finishing of their Palaces and Gardens, and that afterwards bestow so little on the preserving of them.*[18]

Veue de l'Amphiteatre de la Vigne Pamphile
A Paris chez N. Langlois rue St. Iacques a la Victoire auec Priuilege du Roy

He was very taken with the automatic watering system used in many of the gardens he visited:

There went a Course of Water round about the Walls, about a Foot from the Ground in a Channel of stone that went along the side of the Wall; and in this there were Holes so made, that a pipe of white Iron or Wood put to them, conveyed the Water to such plants, as in a dry Season, needed watring; and a Cock set the Water a running in this Course, so that without the Trouble of carrying Water, one Person could easily manage the watering of a great Garden.[19]

Despite eulogies on Italian gardens recorded by travellers like Bishop Burnet, there is no doubt that Le Nôtre's were the best new gardens at the end of the 17th century. He was invited to work in other countries, but his proven handiwork is all in France. It was not until 1679, when he was 66, that he first set foot in Italy, his one expedition abroad – and that, according to Saint-Simon, only after the Pope had pestered Louis XIV to lend him Le Nôtre for a few months.

Le Nôtre's name is associated with two gardens in Italy, the Villa Doria Pamphili and the Ludovisi gardens, both in Rome, although there is no proof of his activities at either place, and only part of the Villa Doria Pamphili garden has survived. The great park of the castle at Racconigi, an amalgam of the French and Italian Baroque tradition, is attributed to Le Nôtre in conjunction with Guarino Gaurini.

Saint-Simon's assertion that Italians were flocking to France for inspiration may have been true, but it did not result in many copies in Italy. The reason is partly topographical, since most villas were still built on hillsides, gentle or steep, and therefore had to be divided into level terraces; the Villa Garzoni near Lucca, *c.* 1652, and the Villa Carlotta on Lake Como, *c.* 1690, are two such examples. Both followed the Italian Baroque tradition but with the addition of a parterre in the French style on the lowest level. The Villa Cetinale near Siena, designed by Carlo Fontana in 1680, also remained loyal to the Italian tradition.

The Italian garden closest to French principles is at the Villa Barbarigo near Valsansibio, in the Veneto. Begun in 1689, it bears the French stamp in its mainly flat site, its ground-plan and its size. It still has a most remarkable water gate, at which visitors would arrive by boat from Venice. Other individual features in Italian gardens might echo French ideas – for instance, the avenue of fountains at Pratolino, where a spacious walk led up to the villa, with low walls on either side from which arose a line of vertical jets.

The Villa Pisani at Stra near Padua is a garden with a partly French flavour mixed with ancient and Italian traditions. It was created for Alvise Pisani, Venetian ambassador to Paris from 1699 to 1704, who was elected Doge of Venice in 1735, and for his brother Almoro. The villa and gardens were built on the banks of the Brenta Canal near Venice, whence affluent Venetians escaped by gondola from the heat of the city in summer. Of all the grand houses that line

The Villa Carlotta on the shores of Lake Como, c. 1690, has a terraced garden with a small parterre with fountains on the lowest level near the lake. The walls of the terraces are covered with climbing plants and shrubs, which, combined with the pale façade of the villa, give it a unique character.

the canal near Stra, the Villa Pisani is by far the largest and the most
imposing. Designed by Girolamo Frigimelica, the gardens were laid
out first, beginning in 1719, while the house was designed later, by
Francesco Maria Petra, and completed in 1756.

The French elements in the composition were the strong central
axis dividing *parterres de broderie*, with groves of trees beyond them on
either side, and all within a grandiose geometric plan. The ancient
element lay in the semicircular end to this immense parterre, which
was framed by the curved wings of a handsome Classical stable
block. The precedent for curving the far end of the parterre rather
than leaving it straight lay in the hippodromes of ancient Rome, for
instance the Circus Maximus, still extant. Raphael had included a
hippodrome with one curved end in his design for the Villa
Madama, and the Duca Mattei had laid out his garden in Rome with
a long rectangle and a curved wall at the end. Publication in 1670 of
an engraving of the Villa Mattei in G.B. Falda's *Li Giardini di Roma*
would have helped to promote this handsome device for enhancing
the far boundary of a garden, and the Villa Mattei design may have
inspired the curved shapes at Zeist, Driemonds and Het Loo in
the Netherlands, and later at Chiswick House in London. But there
were French precedents, too, in the Tuileries by 1570 and the
vertugadin at Chantilly, post 1663.

The design of the Villa Pisani may also have been influenced by
the publication in 1699 in Amsterdam and Paris of a book by
André Félibien des Avaux on the gardens of Pliny: *Les Plans et les
Déscriptions de deux des plus belles maisons de campagne de Pline le Consul*.

Publication and reprints in 1706, 1707 and 1736 of Félibien's
work point to the continued quest for knowledge about Roman
civilisation, including gardens, a search that had continued from the
time of Alberti. Although the natural philosopher's garden created
by John Evelyn at Albury Park in Surrey from 1677 showed that
Alberti's ideals were still admired and that the concept of the
idealised Arcadian scene was known to some, the general preference
had drifted from the pastoral purity and simplicity of Arcadia to the
more sophisticated gardens of ancient Rome.

Supposed replicas of Roman garden features had been made
during the 16th century – for example the busts of Roman emperors
at the Villa Brenzone in the Veneto. Ovid and Virgil were studied
in Latin and in translations, and Claude, the French artist, was
commissioned by Roman patrons to paint scenes from classical
history or mythology. His landscapes and seaports revel in
architecture, whether entire temples or ruined fragments, and in
mythology. Understanding how the Romans lived and thought was
a preoccupation of educated circles throughout Europe, circles in
which Alvise Pisani moved while he lived in Paris as well as in
Venice. It is not surprising, therefore, that his new garden should
reflect not only current tastes but also show Pisani's familiarity with
classical humanism.

In their gardens the Pisani included free-standing buildings, for these were rooted in Italian custom. Four still exist; all by Frigimelica, they are the round tower in the centre of the labyrinth, the *esedra*, the *testate* and the coffee house. Each was originally framed by its setting within a precise ground-plan, although with the removal of the geometric layout of paths, some of their logic has been lost.

The *esedra*, a hexagonal structure with generous concave scoops on each of its six sides and six pairs of statues above on the balustrade, was at the centre of six radiating paths. The term itself is Greek in origin, but was also used by the ancient Romans to describe an open structure, usually independent of the villa, and suitable for leisure, for seating was often included. But the term no longer implies a precise form, and has subsequently come to mean an open semicircle without seating, such as at Chiswick House, *c.* 1730; this latter exedra, a type of hippodrome, is formed by a semicircle of statues and urns backed by a yew hedge.

The *testate delle cedraie* was the winter home of citrus trees, and its design was based on a model by Sebastiano Serlio. The coffee house on the mount might have been inspired by Francis Bacon's combina-

tion of mount with banqueting house, although Frigimelica's coffee house is Baroque.

While absorbing some aspects of French design, Villa Pisani, like many Italian gardens of the 18th century, retained the spice of its native traditions. It is this mixture of traditions that gives Italian gardens their special character, just as the gardens of the other countries in Europe stamped their own mark on French theory.

James Stuart's sketch (L3/4 f.9) of the belvedere at the Villa Pisani. It was designed by Frigimelica as one of the entrances to the gardens, and was much admired by Président de Brosses on his travels in Italy, 1739–40. It is still intact.

Franco – Dutch Gardens of the Netherlands

A design for a treillage arbour or bower from
Van der Groen's Den Nederlantsen Hovenier, *1669.*

A view of the garden of Mr. Huigens on the River
Vecht, by Daniel Stoopendael, 1719. (Maps C.9.e.11.)
The Vecht was lined with country houses of varying
sizes, and most had a koepel on the riverbank, serving as
gazebo, belvedere, tea house, boat house or fishing pavilion.

In the 17th century, the United Provinces, which comprised the northern Netherlands and the province of Holland, became, through astute commercial trade, one of the major European states. Its importance increased as the century progressed and the great riches amassed by its inhabitants were spent on architecture, art, furnishings and gardens.

Much of the emphasis in gardens was on the cultivation of flowers and fruit, for the Dutch have always been exceptional horticulturists. Lilac, laburnum, jasmine, clematis, lavender, carnations, roses, hellebores, peonies, aconites, and gentians were just some of the many shrubs and plants available to them, as shown in the many meticulous still lifes painted by artists such as Jan Davidsz. de Heem, Willem van Aelst and Rachel Ruysch.

OVERHOLLAND, *de Buiten-plaets van den H.^r Theod: Huigens, Schepen van Amsterd: Heere van Honkoop.* ‖ OVERHOLLAND: *la place du Sr Theodore Huigens, Eschevin d'Amsterd: Seigneur de Honkoop.* 42

Bulbs were even then a major export industry for the Dutch and it was with great reluctance that Louis XIV reduced his purchase of bulbs when he was at war with the Netherlands. Their propagation was a matter of skill and investment, and when 'tulipomania' gripped the country in the 1630s, collectors paid absurd sums for the most unusual 'sport' varieties, until, eventually, the market collapsed and the speculators went bankrupt.

Apart from their enthusiasm for flowers, Dutch gardens also had another characteristic that set them apart from the French tradition. This was the custom of dividing the garden into separate compart ments with high hedges. Whereas in France the main vista was wide and long and edged by high hedges, in the Netherlands the entire area was subdivided by high hedges into separate sections, in which either a basin, fountain or flower parterre would predominate. The reason for this compartment principle was probably to disguise the fact that most Dutch gardens were limited in size by the cost of land in this small, populous country.

Generally, large structural embellishments were limited by lack of space and the flatness of the countryside. The terraces and long cascades of Italian and French gardens were simply not feasible, and usually there was inadequate water pressure for powerful jets. Moreover, the more flamboyant aspects of Baroque architecture that could have been incorporated, elaborate fountains and statuary, for example, were rejected by the Protestant Dutch, who shrank from such displays of wealth. Altogether, the scale of Dutch gardens was smaller and embellishment restrained; nature was far more important. Statuary, for instance, only became more popular in the latter part of the 18th century and then mainly in the gardens of the *nouveaux riches*.

Given these limitations on the application of French design, towards the end of the century the Dutch embraced other garden features; *parterres de broderie*, bosquets similar to those of Le Nôtre at Versailles, labyrinths, trellis arbours and pavilions were all typical features of these Dutch gardens.

A useful book on horticulture, garden design and decoration by Jan van der Groen was published in 1669. *Den Nederlandtsen Hovenier* had been reprinted several times by 1721 and the fact that it was published simultaneously in French and German gave a clue to the international reputation of the Dutch in garden skills. For van der Groen, horticulture was paramount, although the flower parterre could be complemented by a variety of carpentry structures, such as tunnels and pavilions. The Dutch were particularly noted for their carpentry, and craftsmen skilled in this technique were in demand abroad.

Town gardens in the Netherlands assumed a greater importance than those in other major European cities. Enclosed for privacy and small by necessity, they were usually laid out within a rectangle edged with trees and often backed on to a canal or river which would have been part of a network of waterways. Excess water was always a

problem, so most included an internal canal, long and narrow, reflecting the shape of the garden. These canals were essentially drainage ditches turned to advantage, and they were more often than not at either side of the garden. No centrally positioned canals had been shown by de Vries in *Hortorum Viridario ...* the bible of design published in 1583, and canals were kept relegated to the side by custom. By the later 17th century, however, the canal often lay along the central axis of the garden, which could have been the result of a natural decision to turn it into a feature in the French manner.

Towards the end of the century, the French artist Daniel Marot, a Huguenot who left France following the Revocation of the Edict of Nantes in 1685, was primarily responsible for disseminating French ideas on garden design and for influencing the emergence of the Franco–Dutch style. He settled in the Netherlands, became designer to the Stadtholder, William of Orange and his wife Mary, and was soon the arbiter of taste in design, in the garden and as well as in interior decoration.

In addition to the emphasis on flowers and hedging, Dutch gardens had another characteristic that give them a distinct identity, a *koepel* or pavilion overlooking the canal, frequently used as a retreat for drinking tea, occasionally doubling as a boathouse. While the idea was Dutch, these were often French in their architectural detail. The view of the pavilion in Mr Huigens's garden at Overholland is grander than most, but there were smaller versions in other gardens, including Ouderhoek, Middelhoek and Driemond, and trellis versions at Hofwerk and Rupelmonde, all on the River Vecht. Even modest houses often had a small *koepel* by the water's edge. Their profusion struck William Beckford when he visited the Netherlands in 1780: *numerous banquetting rooms and pleasure houses which hang directly above the surface* [of the canal] *and seem calculated on purpose to enjoy them.*[20]

The most important residences of nobles and rich burghers were to be found on the principal waterways, and of these none was more prestigious than the River Vecht, which flows for over twenty miles from Utrecht to the Zuyder Zee and can be said to be the Dutch equivalent to the Brenta Canal near Venice. The many gardens on the banks of the Vecht were recorded for posterity by Daniel Stoopendael in *De Zegepraalende Vecht*, which was published in 1719

Modellen van Luft-priëlen.

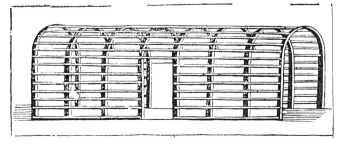

One of several gardens at Enghien enclosed by high hedges in the Dutch manner, engraved by Romain de Hooghe, c. 1687. (157*.a.17.) This is a topiary garden, dominated by exceptionally tall, tapering, tiered estrades, clipped trees in pots and a fountain in the centre. A cloister-like tunnel arbour around the edge gives a medieval touch.

in Amsterdam. This is an outstanding illustrated record not only of the great gardens of the nobility but also, interestingly, of the smaller gardens of the affluent middle class, for the latter properties are usually unrecorded. All the illustrations are in watercolour.

In a charming series of pictures, Stoopendael depicts an occasional antique temple or Dutch gabled gazebo, but the majority show pavilions in the French style favoured by Marot. Most of the pavilions were separated only from the Vecht by a road, or by a road and boundary canal. They were square, hexagonal or octagonal, built in stone or brick with sash windows and had a domed roof painted blue, often crowned with a small lantern. The design was easy to emulate and comparatively inexpensive, so it is hardly surprising that these French-inspired pavilions were found not only in the Netherlands, but also later in England. In *Britannia Illustrata*, published in 1720, Kip showed them at Grimthorp in Lincolnshire and at Longleat in Wiltshire.

Designé et gravé par Romain de Hooghe.

With such a combination of horticultural skills and aesthetic charms, it is not surprising that the Netherlands made a favourable impression on foreigners. In August 1716, Lady Mary Wortley Montagu wrote that *nothing can be more agreeable than travelling in Holland. The whole country appears a large garden.*[21]

In 1780, the young William Beckford gave a description of the Vecht that showed that it had changed little over the decades, since formal gardens had stayed in fashion throughout the 18th century. Beckford aspired to lead taste, not to follow it, and scorned the bourgeousie, but here his comments are quite complimentary:

Both sides of the way are lined with country-houses and gardens of opulent citizens, as fine as gilt statues and clipped hedges can make them. Their number is quite astonishing: from Amsterdam to Utrecht, full thirty miles, we beheld no other objects than endless avenues and stiff parterres like the embroidery of an old maid's work-bag. Notwithstanding this formal taste, I could not help admiring the neatness and arrangement of every inclosure, enlivened by a profusion of flowers, and decked with arbours, beneath which a vast number of consequential personages were solacing themselves after the heat of the day. Each 'lusthuys' we passed contained some comfortable party dozing over their pipes, or angling in the muddy fishponds below.[22]

The 18th century saw a newcomer to the range of garden structures in the Netherlands, the Turkish tent. They are first mentioned in William of Orange's accounts in 1693, and two were illustrated in prints in the late 1720s.[23] They seem to have had one central pole from which the fabric walls were suspended. In fact, the exotic term was something of a misnomer in the early days, for the tents were Turkish in name only; in reality they were in the French style advocated by Daniel Marot. The name may have been a clever sales initiative, tempting customers to purchase something with an exciting oriental flavour at a time when silks, brocades and porcelain from China were snapped up as soon as they reached the European market. These early designs gave birth to several generations of tents during the 18th century. Their form varied from Marot's fabric pavilion to complex wooden buildings on two or three floors, decorated with Turkish crescents and moons; but they could also have touches of chinoiserie, in which case they were called Chinese or Tartar tents. It was enough that they were exotic, and no one was fussy about accuracy because no one knew exactly what Turkish, Chinese or Tartar architecture was like.

The concept of the Turkish tent was exported to other European countries in due course, and resulted in many examples appearing later on in the 18th century. Two fine examples can be seen at the Désert de Retz near Paris and at Painshill in Surrey, both recently recreated. In the Netherlands, tents survived well into the 19th century, but with the advent of the landscape movement and the destruction of formal gardens, later there than in other countries, the tents, like many other garden features, were pulled down.

As well as grand gardens on canals and rivers, the Dutch built impressive houses in the country, and the important country houses and gardens of the second half of the century included Zorgvliet, Huis ten Bosch, Clingendael, Rosendael, Heemstede, de Voorst, Driemond, Het Loo and Zeist.

In the former southern Netherlands, now Belgium, the magnificent garden of Enghien was created over many years in the middle of the century by an aesthetic Capucin monk, Charles d'Arenberg, for his brother Philippe. In 1671, when Louis XIV visited Enghien, one of the ladies of his Court, Mademoiselle de Montpensier, wrote that it was the most beautiful and extraordinary place in the world. It clearly outshone not only Versailles, which had been started only a few years before, but also the older royal gardens of the Tuileries and Fontainebleau.

Enghien had one long vista, although the gardens were hidden behind high hedges. A maze was laid out in a pattern of circles, a parterre was enlivened by a pair of pavilions built into the high perimeter walls, and berceaux separated several garden rooms. The water garden, with its rectangular lake on which a splendid classical pavilion seemed to float, was also screened from other areas by walls or hedges. The practice of concealing special features was apparent in the bosquets at Versailles, but in the Low Countries it was followed throughout the entire garden, even up to the house, so Marot's influence was clearly seen when he opened up the parterre to view, as he did at Zeist, de Voorst and Het Loo, and pushed the secret rooms further away from the house.

All the Dutch gardens so far discussed were altered or destroyed in the later 18th or early 19th centuries, but they were recorded by many artists and engravers of their day, including Daniel Stoopendael, Romain de Hooghe and Daniel Marot himself. It is thanks to such detailed records, as well as to contemporary descriptions and garden archaeology, that it has been possible to recreate one of them, the royal gardens at Het Loo. This ambitious and ultimately successful project began in 1980. Gone are the acres of grass and irregular clumps of trees planted c. 1810 for Louis Napoleon, and the house now has its proper partner, a Baroque garden in the Franco – Dutch style.

Stadtholder William of Orange bought the old castle of Het Loo in 1684. The surrounding countryside had a rare advantage in this part of the Netherlands: it was well watered with streams and underground springs that could provide good water pressure for fountains, a crucial ingredient for William. In 1685, he and Mary engaged Jacob Roman to design the new palace, and Mary laid the foundation stone soon after; at some later date, perhaps the following year, Daniel Marot was involved with the layout and decoration of the gardens and interior of the house, and was also responsible for the water supply. There is no doubt that Marot, with this overall view, achieved a unity of composition in the gardens, and a harmony between house, garden and the wider landscape, in the same way as Le Nôtre had done at Vaux-le-Vicomte.

The design of the Lower Garden immediately north of the palace is based on eight huge square beds in the parterre, which is surrounded by a raised terrace running in front of the house and along either side of the parterre. On the main axis is the Fountain of Venus and on either side one of the original delights of Het Loo, the great globe fountains. At either end of the parterre's cross-axis are Baroque cascades adorned with statues and built into the sloping grassy bank of the terrace, some five metres high. The cascades are identical and, in both, water slips from basin to basin in three separate streams.

Another masterpiece at Het Loo is the mighty plume of the fountain in the Upper Garden, which rises to nearly 15 metres. The two colonnades in the Upper Garden were, in fact, a clever afterthought, for they were originally attached to the palace before it was extended sometime between 1691 and 1694. Eventually they will only be glimpsed from the palace when the trees on the cross-axis have grown. This second cross-axis, called the *Middendwarslaan*, followed the contemporary practice of compartmentalising gardens, thus putting another Dutch stamp on the garden, for Marot's French instincts might have preferred a wider view to the colonnades.

The main parterre is vivid with flowers in the border strips, or *plates-bandes*, around the edges of each section of the parterre. These *plates-bandes* are further accentuated with conical yew trees, which in Dutch gardens were often cut to a slender, more tapering height than those in French gardens. The *broderie* pattern within the border is made in outline with box hedge, with a background of red-and

cream-coloured gravel and grass. All the elements of William and Mary's garden have been painstakingly renewed, acquired, or copied in meticulous detail, in order to give a true impression of the original.

Beyond the Lower and Upper Gardens and the King's and Queen's Gardens were other extensive areas, some for practical use like vegetable cultivation, and others for pleasure, with features including a maze and an aviary. In addition, there was a feature unique to Het Loo, the intertwined initials of William and Mary made in narrow, twisting channels of water only inches wide. While visitors were admiring this sentimental emblem, they could be jerked backed to reality by a sudden spray from water jets concealed in pebbles surrounding the monogram.

In its time, Het Loo was famous and much visited, as indeed were most important gardens, by observers. The most comprehensive account was written in 1693 or 1694 by Walter Harris at the request of Queen Mary, who returned to England in 1689 with William on their accession to the English throne; she did not see Het Loo again before her sudden death from smallpox in 1694. Mary wanted to know exactly how the gardens were developing and what was growing, and Harris, her physician, complied by providing his impressions as well as precise, measured descriptions. His account was published in 1699 under the title *A Description of the King's Royal Palace and Gardens at Loo. In the Upper Garden we behold a most Noble Fountain, with a Basin of a vast extent, and with three and thirty spouts, that in the middle of all throwing up the water five and forty foot high*,[24] wrote

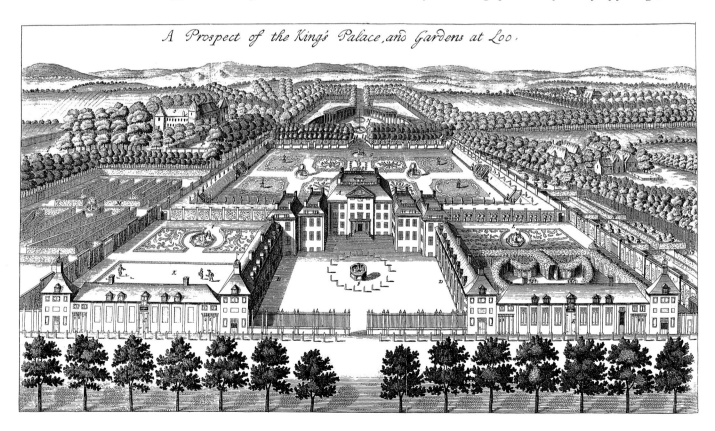

A Prospect of the King's Palace, and Gardens at Loo.

Harris. He also describes the impressive automatic watering system built into the slopes of the terrace in the Lower Garden. *At the upper part of the* Green Slopes *there are abundance of little Pipes of Water, about a foot distance one from the other. Each of them hath a copper head, wherein there are four small holes, through which the water is made to play, in order to water the* Slopes, *and to preserve them always* Green.[25] He also noted that the terraces were edged with pyramidal junipers at regular intervals. Again on the question of water, Harris wrote that because the water was supplied from natural springs, it was always sweet-smelling, unlike at Versailles.

Harris also testified to the importance of Het Loo and its influence abroad. *The Gardens of Loo are become so famous and remarkable to all the Provinces near them, that Curious Persons from divers Parts of Germany, as well as out of all the United Provinces, do frequently resort thither to satisfy their Curiosity.*[26]

Finally, Harris added a further thought just before his description went to the printers in 1699. *These Gardens in the whole are a Work of wonderful Magnificence, most worthy of so Great a Monarch; a Work of prodigious expense, infinite variety and curiosity; and after nine years labour by abundance of Workmen they were some years ago intirely finished, and brought to perfection in all respects.*[27]

Although its size, statuary and water effects were limited by comparison with Versailles, Het Loo was the Dutch response to Louis' creation – not that anything anywhere could compare with either Versailles or Louis. It was, however, the single most influential Dutch garden and not only because it belonged to the monarch, for it set a style that others were to emulate.

In the surrounding countries of northern Europe, Germany, Denmark, Sweden, Scotland and England, Dutch gardens were highly regarded. They were associated with the economic and cultural prestige of the Netherlands, which was at its peak in the late 17th century. In addition to travel in France and Italy, part of a young man's education was a visit to the Netherlands, with perhaps some months' study at the prestigious University of Leiden. Links across the Channel, in particular, were intensified when William and Mary succeeded to the English throne, and aspects of Dutch culture, including garden designs, were introduced into England.

An engraving of Het Loo from A Description of the King's Royal Palace and Gardens at Loo *by Walter Harris, 1699. Eventually, the Upper Garden and the Colonnades would be obscured by a screen of trees, whereas in a French garden the view would be kept open.*

Het Loo and its Lower Garden, designed by Marot in the 1680s and restored in the 1980s. The arrangement of yew trees, box hedges, flowers, and coloured stones is best appreciated from the piano nobile *of the house or from the terraces on either side of the Lower Garden.*

Let us divide our labours, thou where choice,
Leads thee, or where most needs, whether to wind
The Woodbine round this Arbour, or direct
The clasping Ivie where to climb, while I
In yonder Spring of Roses intermixt
With Myrtle, find what to redress till Noon.

John Milton, *Paradise Lost*, 1667

Il Mercurio Italico. 147

A. Virgills Tombe
B. The entrance into the Grotte.
C. a litle chappell taken for
Virgills Tombe, but falsely.

This Tombe of the Prince of
Poets is built in a *Rotunda*, or
Cupola, about five paces long,
within, the walls are of Bricke,
in square after the Roman way,
H 2   the

In the time of King Charles II, *Gardening was much improved and became common: I doe beleeve, I may modestly affirm, that there is now* [1691] *ten times as much gardening about London as there was in Anno 1660.*[28] So wrote John Aubrey in his life of Sir John Danvers. Gardening and garden creation are fairly low priorities after a period of political upheaval like the Civil War, and it took some time for momentum to gather. After the restoration of the monarchy in 1660 the impetus was stimulated by the expansion of trade, not only with Europe but also with southern Africa, India, China, and the West Indies, bringing with it money to be spent on building houses and gardens, and plants to enhance them.

Hardy trees, shrubs and flowers were planted out, but the tender plants from warmer climes gave rise to two new types of buildings for the garden, the greenhouse and the hot house or stove. Architecturally unimportant, the hot house was hidden in the kitchen garden, while the greenhouse was often a stone or brick building forming a handsome backdrop to the parterre.

Just as Louis XIV was building his vast Orangery at Versailles, so country gentlemen in England were putting up handsome greenhouses in their formal gardens, and by the early 1700s hardly a great garden existed that did not boast a greenhouse with five or seven huge south-facing windows, and housing orange trees and other plants from the Mediterranean and South Africa in winter.

Apart from a delight in collecting new plants, there was also great curiosity about the gardens of the ancients among the intellectual elite in England. The natural philosopher's garden, designed by John Evelyn at Albury Park in 1677 for Henry Howard, Duke of Norfolk, was modelled on the gardens of ancient Rome, with a niched alcove or nymphaeum in the centre of a noble terrace, canals, and a tunnel reminiscent of one near Virgil's tomb.

But this Roman influence was an exception, whereas French influence became the norm. In Europe, France was the undisputed leader of fashionable taste in gardens as in the *beaux-arts* and one of the leading English experts on French gardens was John Evelyn. Having lived in Paris as well as Italy during the Civil War, Evelyn was a great authority on countless matters of learning. He was consulted by friends about laying out their new gardens in the French style, at Euston Hall in Suffolk, Cassiobury Park in Hertfordshire and Cornbury House in Oxfordshire. He made a point of visiting other gardens too, like Ham House in Surrey, laid out in 1671, now carefully restored by the National Trust.

Of French gardens known in England in 1660, St Germain-en-Laye was probably the most famous, since Charles II had lived there before his restoration to the throne. Perceived as a French garden, it was, of course, Italianate in its series of great architectural terraces, and is considered to have influenced two gardens in Britain, the first in Scotland at Drummond Castle, *c.* 1630, and the second in Wales at Powis Castle, *c.* 1685. Powis is distinguished by its four terraces embellished with niched walls, an aviary, and a greenhouse. Once there was a great parterre on the floor of the valley and, rising up the opposite slope, an architectural response to the terraces in the form of a cascade crowned by a *tempietto*.

But, once again, it was Le Nôtre whose influence was all pervasive. Thanks to his exile in France, Charles II would have known Le Nôtre and his work, at least by reputation. After his accession, Charles sent a request to his cousin Louis XIV for Le Nôtre to visit London and draw up plans for the gardens of St James's Palace. Although there is no proof that Le Nôtre ever came to England, he did draw up a plan for the Queen's House at Greenwich, *c.* 1662. His detailed proposals for basins and fountains were never realised, but the parterre and walks on either side of it were planted by 1665. In his French gardens, his majestic vistas, cascades, enchanting fountains, expansive sheets of water, clever management of changing levels, and dramatic contrast between light and shade, all added up to a breathtaking ensemble, elements of which were eventually imitated not only by his pupils but also by his English admirers.

One such pupil of Le Nôtre was Grillet, who had been employed by the Duke of Devonshire to build the cascade at Chatsworth in Derbyshire in the 1690s, and was then taken on by a Derbyshire neighbour, Philip Stanhope, 2nd Earl of Chesterfield, to assist in the completion of the garden at Bretby.

Bretby was said to have been inspired by Versailles, and to be the grandest garden in England. The laying out of the gardens had been started in 1669, presumably with the parterres nearest to the house, and it is likely that Grillet's contribution was the area to the left in Kip's engraving, where the terraces drop to three assorted basins. Had Grillet been involved at the start, he would surely have emphasised this axis from the house with greater width and an unbroken view to the semicircular *vertugadin*, so reminiscent of Chantilly.

Celia Fiennes, a traveller of insatiable curiosity, took a detour in order to visit Bretby in 1698, when the gardens were not quite finished. *But that which is most admired – and justly so to be – by all persons and excite their curiosity to come and see is the Gardens and Waterworks.*[29] At Bretby there were fountains of great beauty and variety, including one that struck the hours, chimed the quarters and played a tune too.

The master of the French style of garden design in England was George London, the foremost professional garden designer at the end of the 17th century, with his partner, Henry Wise. London had been schooled in the French tradition by visits to Paris, and was the designer in the London and Wise enterprise. He travelled round the country from one great estate to another on horseback, while Wise ran the nursery at Brompton in Kensington and cherished potential clients in the capital. Together they were given commissions for some of the foremost gardens in England, including Chatsworth in Derbyshire from 1685, Longleat House in Wiltshire, Wanstead in Essex, Canons in London, Castle Howard in Yorkshire and Melbourne Hall in Derbyshire. Apart from Melbourne Hall, all have disappeared or been altered to varying degrees, Melbourne Hall

John Raymond's drawing of Virgil's supposed tomb, much visited by 17th-century tourists, from Voyage Made Through Italy, *1648.*

The lake and the birdcage at Melbourne Hall, a garden laid out by George London in 1704. The birdcage, built in 1706 by Robert Bakewell, has recently been painted in colours favoured by Bakewell; most of the ironwork is smolt blue, while repoussé *leaves are picked out in green and berries in red.*

A statue of putti *in the wilderness at Melbourne Hall.*

being one of the few gardens of this period to emerge unscathed when the pendulum of fashion swung from formal to landscaped gardens later in the 18th century.

The gardens at Melbourne Hall were designed by London in 1704 for Thomas Coke, Vice-Chamberlain to Queen Anne. They retain their original layout, with wide grassed terraces leading down to an octagonal lake known as the Great Basin, a tunnel of yew trees, straight allées, and on one side a bosquet or wilderness with straight radiating paths. The term wilderness is misleading, for it was not an area where trees were allowed to grow untamed, but rather a series of orderly plantations contained by hedges. The view from the house is open, reflecting the French ideal that beauty lay in breadth as well as length of vision. In spite of its age, the garden at Melbourne Hall has kept its formal spirit, even though the yew tunnel has been allowed to billow and bulge in a fashion that would never have been permitted by George London.

The tunnel, some ninety metres long, is one of the great features of the garden. The birdcage is another, and forms the focal point on the main axis, beyond the basin and near the perimeter of the garden. The bosquet, a regular feature of gardens of this period too often abandoned elsewhere, has straight walks lined with beech hedges, behind which grows a variety of trees. The trees are trimmed above the hedges to prevent them from obscuring the vista, but they still provide summer shade, an important requirement in gardens in the French style. For contrast of colour and form and at the intersections of the walks are fountains, single jets in a round pool, or statues, ranging from embracing *putti* to a large Baroque urn.

Like the gardens at Melbourne Hall, Wrest Park in Bedfordshire was also French inspired, and has partly survived. Its principal feature is a stretch of water known as the Long Canal, at the end of which, in 1711, Thomas Archer completed a beautiful pavilion, known as the Banqueting House.

Bretby, Melbourne Hall, Wrest Park and Canons were all noble gardens, although they hardly merit mention in the same breath as Versailles. There were no equivalents to Versailles, or St Cloud, or Chantilly in England. Although many fine English gardens were recorded for posterity in bird's-eye views, principally those published in two volumes in *Britannia Illustrata* and in *Vitruvius Britannicus*, none had majestic French proportions. Versailles was the great yardstick to which pretentious owners liked to compare their properties, although often such comparisons were slightly absurd.

If one could not emulate a Versailles, the alternative was to imitate the Franco–Dutch style that had evolved in the Netherlands through the work of Daniel Marot. The accession of William and Mary to the British throne, and the arrival of Dutch courtiers in England meant that many Dutch customs were adopted after 1688, though of course earlier Dutch practices, especially in horticulture, had percolated across the Channel throughout the 17th century.

With the experience of Het Loo fresh in their minds, William and Mary wished to bring the old Tudor palace at Hampton Court up to date, and the result was the grandest gardens in England in the Franco–Dutch style. While Sir Christopher Wren was rebuilding the east front of the palace, Daniel Marot was commissioned to redesign the gardens from 1689 onwards. The result was the Great Parterre, or Fountain Garden as it became later, an immense semicircle within which radiated a *patte d'oie*, or goose foot, of three avenues. A long canal continued on the line of the central avenue beyond the semicircle.

But the life of this garden was remarkably short. Queen Mary's sister Anne, who succeeded when William died in 1702, loathed the smell of box and heartily disliked her Dutch brother-in-law and, *ergo*, his Fountain Garden. Most of the fountains were soon removed, probably because water pressure was insufficient to guarantee a good display, and grass replaced the box-edged beds. The outline of the semicircular garden and the goose foot avenues remain, as do many of the original yew trees, which have been allowed to grow into dark green cones of giant size.

Hampton Court Palace and its gardens in a painting by Leonard Knyff (OM 423) at the beginning of the 18th century. It shows the broderie parterres *in the semicircular Fountain Garden and, with considerable artistic licence, all the fountains in full flow. To the left of the Palace is the Privy Garden, which looks now, after reconstruction, just as it does in Knyff's painting. Tijou's screen is on the extreme left, between the large round basin and the River Thames.*

The Privy Garden at Hampton Court Palace in 1995, when the carpentry tunnel called Queen Mary's Bower was yet to be covered by its hornbeam hedge. It has been constructed following the form shown by Van der Groen in Den Nederlantsen Hovenier *on p.129, and will eventually look like the tunnel arbour at Het Loo, to the left of the photograph on p.133. The orange trees in tubs and the agave in a lead urn have been positioned according to old records.*

On the south front of the palace and adjacent to the Fountain Garden was the Privy Garden dating from the time of Henry VIII. In 1691, the garden was widened, and a single terrace made on either side, as at Het Loo, from which the gardens could be admired. On the west terrace, a pergola of wych elm was built; called Queen Mary's Bower, it was probably of a similar construction to those in the Queen's Garden at Het Loo. The parterre was divided into four beds with grass cut into patterns known as cutwork or *gazon coupé*.

However, this plan failed to satisfy William, who decided in 1700 to increase the size of the Privy Garden and open up the view to the Thames by demolishing the Water Gallery. The Tudor mount, that had stood beyond the old garden near the river, had already been razed to the ground in 1697. In the new design, by an unidentified hand, both terraces were extended, stepped in two levels and edged with pyramidal yews. The parterres were laid out with *plates-bandes* round the edge, and *broderie* designs in box, grass and sand. At the river end, a new round basin was made and beyond it the garden's most original feature was erected, a magnificent wrought iron screen. Jean Tijou was the designer of this masterpiece of concave and

convex curves and exquisitely intricate panels and he completed it in the autumn of 1702, some months after William's death. Through this *clairvoyée* is the view to the Thames.

Over the centuries, the hollies and yews in the Privy Garden grew rampant and were bolstered by new trees and shrubs which totally altered the the character of the garden. It became a Victorian shrubbery, smothering all visible traces of William's garden except for the basins and the outlines of the beds.

Thanks to the recent revival of interest in formal gardens, it was decided to restore the Privy Garden to its 1701 design. Archaeology has played a vital part in determining the precise levels and measurements of all the beds, and supplemented by many illustrations and records, a clear picture has emerged to allow a very accurate recreation. The Privy Garden of 1701 was recreated in 1995.

Following William and Mary's accession, contacts between England and the Netherlands were numerous. English politicians, nobles, and merchant traders travelled to The Hague, Amsterdam and Leiden, and their Dutch counterparts came to England in William's wake, and stayed. Some of William's closest Dutch advisers, William Bentinck and Arnold Joost van Keppel for instance, were given English titles and estates, and settled in their new country.

This friendly invasion strengthened the existing Franco–Dutch influences on English gardens. Topography, frequently similar, made Dutch gardens an appropriate model, and their cost, too, made them additionally attractive, for they were smaller and required less reshaping of the landscape than French equivalents. Many of the favourite Dutch features were included: narrow vistas over long canals, flower borders, slim cones of yew and balls of holly, fountains and basins, and high hedges that divided the garden into a series of rooms.

A Franco–Dutch garden was made at Bulstrode in Buckinghamshire for William Bentinck, newly Earl of Portland. The design included a hippodrome that seems to have been inspired by the Daniel Marot garden at Zeist in the Netherlands. Other gardens were planted with high hedges, like those at Waddesdon Manor in Buckinghamshire, or with the emphasis on flowers planted in narrow beds, such as at Dyrham Park in Gloucestershire. At Wimpole in Cambridgeshire, the pair of trellis pavilions in the hedged bosquets could have been copied from van der Groen's *Den Nederlandtsen Hovenier*.

The best surviving example in England of a garden in the Franco–Dutch style is at Westbury Court in Gloucestershire, rescued from near dereliction by the National Trust in 1967 and since restored. The Dutch influence is seen in the absence of a grand vista, in the architecture of the Tall Pavilion, in the walls and hedges that subdivide the garden into separate compartments, in the dominant role played by water, and in the emphasis on flowers and fruit trees. The gardens were laid out between 1696 and 1705 by Maynard Colchester on a site adjacent but unrelated to an older house.

The Baroque Tall Pavilion in the Dutch style at Westbury Court, 1703. It is at the south end of a long canal that is bordered by yew hedges, and it has been much restored by the National Trust.

Although the Franco–Dutch taste was popular, it never replaced the French influence; the London and Wise interpretation of Le Nôtre was still in demand, too, even north of the border, and they are credited with commissions in Scotland, notably at Hatton, the seat of the Duke of Lauderdale. But, forever asserting independence from their larger neighbour, the Scots generally preferred to take their inspiration directly from France, rather than filtered through England. Between Scotland and France, political and intellectual contacts had been strong for centuries, and besides, France was the great old ally against the traditional enemy, England.

One of the principal bearers of new ideas from the Continent was Sir William Bruce, born *c.* 1630, who, after an early career in politics, turned himself into a gentleman architect. It was his exposure to foreign influences that gave Bruce the impetus to create, for he had been a confidential messenger between the Scottish lords and the future Charles II while he was in exile in the Netherlands; he had also travelled in France in 1663 and had visited London on several occasions. This widened vision, combined with his interest in architecture, made him the founder of Classical architecture in Scotland; indeed he has been called both the Inigo Jones and the Christopher Wren of Scotland. He also brought the French concept of garden design north of the border.

Bruce's main achievements included the rebuilding for Charles II in the 1670s of the Palace of Holyroodhouse in Edinburgh in the French style complete with new gardens. He also built some fine country houses, but it was the design of his own property, Kinross House, built between 1686 and 1693 that shows his adherence to the principle of house and garden as a single composition. The proportions between the stately mansion and its vast rectangular walled garden are in total harmony, but they are dramatised by the wider landscape they grace; the gardens stretch down to the shores of Loch Leven, and the main axis of the house looks through the Baroque Fish Gate towards a ruined castle on an island, just as Vaux-le-Vicomte focused on the grotto and the distant skyline statue. Bruce's choice of site was exceptional, for this is a magnificent view, and one that Claude, with a little exaggeration, might have framed in one of his paintings of imaginary landscapes.

Since Scotland was further from the Continent, books were an even more vital source of knowledge on both architecture and gardening. In 1683 Bruce subscribed to the Edinburgh Botanic Garden Catalogue, and his library would certainly have contained a copy of the first book on gardening to be published in Scotland, *The Scots Gard'ner* by John Reid, which appeared in 1683. Consistent with Bruce's approach, Reid advised that a house and its garden should be fully integrated in design. Bruce's library is thought to have been extensive, and included a copy of Palladio's *Quattro Libri dell'Architettura* and William Hughes' *The Flower Garden*, which he bought in 1676. He probably also possessed Sebastian Serlio's *Architettura* and Androuet du Cerceau's *Les Plus Excellents*

Bastiments de France, since elements in his work bear traces from illustrations in these books, while the design of the Fish Gate suggests he may also have had a copy of Francini's *Livre d'Architecture*.

At Kinross, the knowledge acquired from books as well as from observation was put into practice. The walled garden on the loch front was laid out with square beds leading on to orchards, an elaborate plan for Scotland in 1700, and one that cost £400 per annum to maintain, much to Sir William's chagrin. Now the garden has extensive lawns, rhododendrons and herbaceous borders all enclosed by the original garden wall.

Auchendinny, Mertoun and Balcaskie and Hopetoun House were also designed by Sir William Bruce in the French manner, and of these probably the greatest was Hopetoun House near Edinburgh. Bruce built the house and laid out the gardens between 1699 and 1703, working with the architect and landscape gardener, Alexander Edward. The two men were responsible for centring the view from the east front on a faraway feature, North Berwick Law, reminiscent of the island focus from Kinross House; perhaps they also designed the terrace walk overlooking the River Forth, but William Adam's subsequent alterations in the 1720s obscured much of their work.

At Hopetoun a large parterre adorned with statues reminded the traveller John Macky of Canons in London, but it was the view that was and is the most spectacular aspect, and it was extolled by Macky when he visited the house in the early 1720s: *From the Terras to the North of this Parterre is the finest View I ever saw anywhere; far beyond Frescati near Rome.*[30] From North Berwick Law in the east, over the Firth of Forth to the towns of Fife and then to the north-west to Stirling Castle and the mountains of Perthshire, Macky delighted in it all.

There were other remarkable gardens in Scotland in the early 18th century, but all have been altered or ruined. Two of these, Drumlanrig Castle in Dumfriesshire and Arniston House in Midlothian, had one special feature, a cascade, which seems to have been rare in Scotland at this time. Arniston House was designed for Robert Dundas in 1726 by William Adam, who may also have been responsible for the cascade. It was fed by burns transported by aqueduct to a holding pond, and gushed frothily for a hour when the tap was turned on, long enough to impress Dundas's dinner guests. Unfortunately, no records remains of its appearance, and it was demolished in 1764 when more natural cascades came into fashion. In Scotland, as in England, too few of the old gardens have escaped the swinging pendulum of fashion.

The Fish Gate, with its stone basket laden with fish from the loch, is one of the principal features of the gardens of Kinross House. On the main axis, the view through the gate is to the ruined castle on an island in Loch Leven.

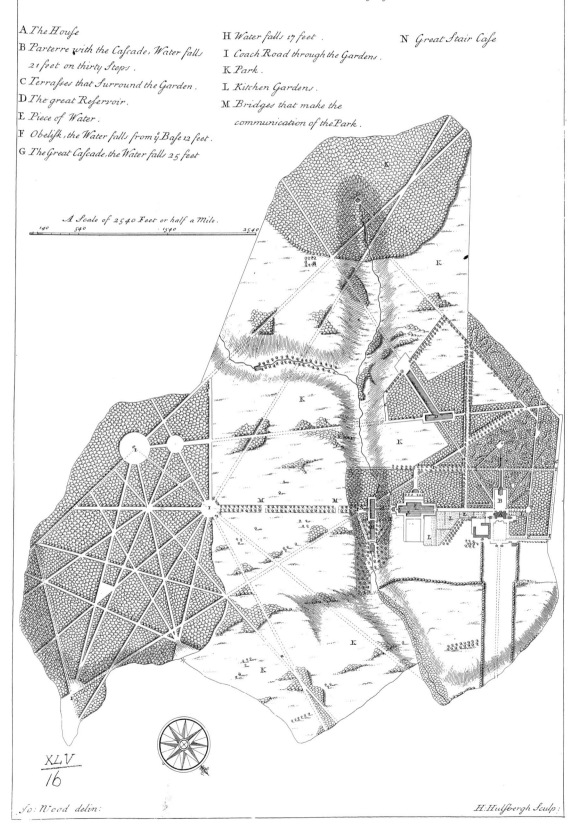

The Plan of Bramham Park, In the County of York
the Seat of the R.t Hon.ble the Lord Bingley.

A The House
B Parterre with the Cascade, Water falls
   21 feet on thirty Steps.
C Terrasses that Surround the Garden.
D The great Reservoir.
E Piece of Water.
F Obelisk, the Water falls from y.e Base 12 feet.
G The Great Cascade, the Water falls 25 feet

H Water falls 17 feet.
I Coach Road through the Gardens.
K Park.
L Kitchen Gardens.
M Bridges that make the
   communication of the Park.

N Great Stair Case

A Scale of 2540 Feet or half a Mile.
140   540   1540   2540

XLV
16

Jo: Wood delin: H. Hulsbergh Sculp:

Bramham Park in Yorkshire is the last of the French gardens in England to have survived with little alteration. Started at the beginning of the 18th century, by Robert Benson, 1st Lord Bingley, it is laid out in the grand manner with a parterre in front of the house and an extensive series of straight, criss-crossing allées lined with high beech hedges enclosing groves of trees. These beech hedges are one of the most significant features of Bramham, especially when the young leaves flutter like slips of silk in a spring breeze.

The vistas framed by the hedges stretch over the countryside and often terminate in a stone trophy or building, of which Bramham has a rich collection. Bingley could have been reading from the pages of *The Nobleman, Gentleman, and Gardener's Recreation*, Switzer's invaluable book on the principles of designing a garden published in 1715. *A statue, banqueting house, obelisk, or whatever the designer pleases* should be placed at the end of a long view or vista, *quite a cross the Valleys up the rising Hills on each side.* He also like to include a cascade *rowling down* the hillside.[31] Bramham has a cascade, an obelisk, and various temples added at intervals until 1760 by Batty Langley and the renowned architect James Paine.

The overall design of Bramham is French, but it has a puckish humour which shows that its creator could toss Gallic logic away at times in favour of a whimsical approach. French gardens were laid out with absolute precision, while at Bramham, although the pattern of allées seems orthodox at first, there are unexpected departures from geometry and symmetry not caused by topography. Few of the allées are parallel, and the intersections are almost always at odd angles. The allées vary in width too, for no very obvious reason.

Furthermore, the bar of the T in the T-canal is neither in the middle of the downstroke nor at 90 degrees, but tilted at an angle. Daniel Defoe's comments on the place were apt: *It is a fine, new built, beautiful House, with very curious Gardens.*[32]

All this must have been intentional, for Bingley was an amateur architect of skill and good taste and was both owner and designer. Had he generally been so careless of geometry he could hardly have put up such a well-proportioned house nor been admired for his understanding of architecture. Perhaps he saw in the French style, to which there was little alternative in 1700, a wearisome pomposity that he sought to avoid by devising these subtle variations. As for the curious T-canal, dug out in 1728, it anticipates the teasing English version of Rococo.

Bramham is also unusual in overlapping with the change in taste from formal gardens to landscaped parks, and provides a rare opportunity to see the garden buildings of Batty Langley and James Paine in a formal context. This blend of exceptional features makes Bramham unique.

Fortunately Bramham Park escaped the destruction that overtook so many formal gardens. In England, the first whiff of change was already in the air while Bingley was at work, but he and his heirs resisted what became a national scramble to destroy and start again. Other gardens, such as Chiswick House, ended up as hybrids, part formal and part landscaped, and belong therefore to a later part of the design saga. Meanwhile, in Continental Europe, yet more gardens of Le Nôtre proportions were being laid out.

The plan of Bramham Park (Maps K.45.16) ignores the customary plan of arranging allées and paths at 45° or 90° or radiating from the centre of a circle, and results in an unusual and whimsical arrangement unrelated to topography. It bears a distinct resemblance to Switzer's garden plan on p.165.

German gardens are Germany's best kept secret. They are little known beyond the frontiers of their own country, perhaps because, like Spanish and Portuguese gardens, they have not given birth to any revolutionary ideas or major changes in gardening design. Through originality in geometric design and a particular brand of Baroque and Rococo opulence, German gardens have a character quite distinct from those of neighbouring countries like Italy, France, the Netherlands and Britain.

With the outbreak of the Thirty Years' War, German gardens entered a bleak period and then took years to revive after the war ended in 1648. Gardens are always a barometer of affluence, and it was not until the end of the 17th century that there was sufficient economic activity for resources to be spent on creating new ones. Fortunately the War of the Spanish Succession (1701–14) had a far less devastating effect on the economic life of the states than the previous war, and recovery was swift and widespread.

In the 18th century a host of German gardens were created in the formal tradition still seen as the epitome of perfection. Those of Bavaria were modelled closely on Versailles, while northern gardens were likely to borrow ideas from their neighbours in the Netherlands. Viennese gardens were Italianate in origin, and during the course of the century they influenced others, such as Pommersfelden, Seehof and Gaibach.

The Wittelsbach Elector of Bavaria, Max Emanuel, had lived in the Spanish Netherlands and visited Paris. After his accession, he

This Baroque floating saloon was moored on the River Oder at Pleniz near Breslau in Poland. A ballroom-cum-concert hall, its interior was as ornate as any reception room and illuminated with many lights for high society parties and special concerts.

The plan of the gardens at Nymphenburg near Munich (Maps 28650.(4)). The gardens were designed by Effner and reveal a French influence in the extent of the grand canal. The Badenburg is to the left and the Pagodenburg to the right, both near the canal.

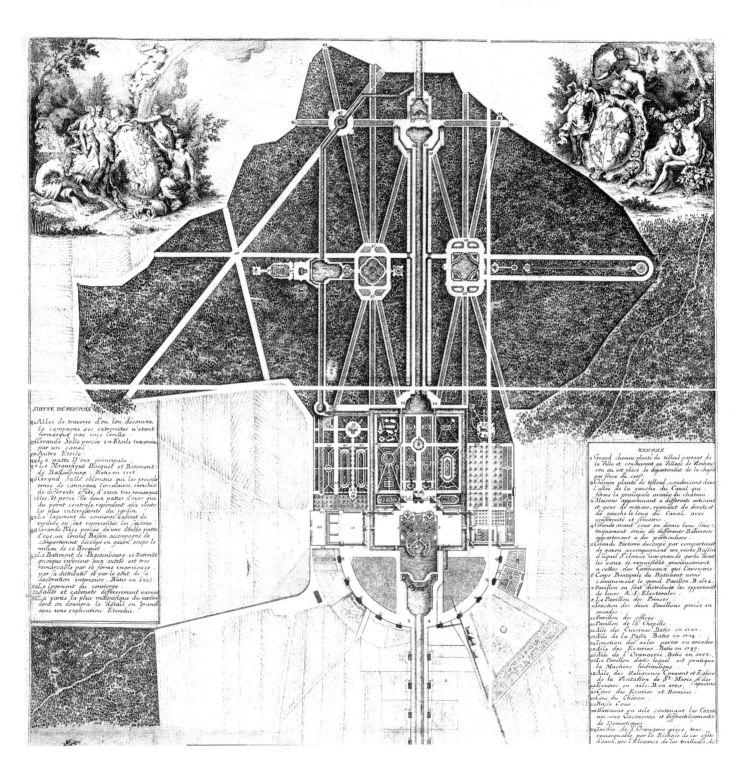

started planning a summer residence at Schleissheim, now on the outskirts of Munich. The concept was immensely grand, for Max Emanuel cherished hopes that his son would succeed to the Spanish throne and therefore would require a residence of appropriate importance. The result was a composition of three palaces, the old and the new, and Lustheim, a schloss for private entertainments.

Zuccalli was commissioned to plan the gardens between Lustheim and the two schlosses, but his design was not up to expectations, and a Frenchman, Dominique Girard, was employed instead. The finished plan included a grand parterre, a marble cascade by Joseph Effner, then a canal some 600 metres long, with Lustheim and its reflection shimmering in the distance. In fact the canal stops short of Lustheim and splits into a circle, turning this retreat into an island sanctuary, like the Hermitage of St Anthony in the Buen Retiro gardens in Madrid. Now grassed with some simple flower borders, the garden was originally laid out as one large round parterre with a complicated pattern of beds. Lustheim retains an element of its original frame, thanks to the circular canal, assisted by subsequent plantations of trees. Following the Dutch custom, another canal was made around the entire perimeter of the gardens.

A view of the schloss at Nymphenburg, taken from the bridge that crosses the grand canal.

Another feature of Schleissheim that is still as designed are the bosquets or wildernesses on either side of the central canal. As in gardens from Versailles to Melbourne Hall, these are hedged and laid out with great precision, the pattern on one side of the canal being mirrored on the other. Straight and curving walks lead to green rooms, *salles de verdure*, of varying shapes and sizes, in which entertainments could be staged.

Nymphenburg was Max Emanuel's other great project near Munich, and here the Versailles influence is also powerful, although there are elements of Franco–Dutch design, too. This garden has been altered more than Schleissheim, but its grand vista along a 900-metre canal on the garden side is distinctly French. At its far end a pink marble cascade by Effner is a lively variation on his earlier version at Schleissheim.

But it is the canals at Nymphenburg that hark back to the Netherlands, in a joyful celebration of water. The main canal is continued on the Munich side of the schloss on the same axis, having divided in two to run on either side of the large parterre and the schloss and reunite in elegant basins before the *cour d'honneur*. Crossed continually by bridges with headroom only for ducks, these canals, and others leading off them, were for visual pleasure and effect, not for boats.

The garden buildings of Nymphenburg, the Badenburg, the Pagodenburg, the Magadelenklause and the Amalienburg, are its chief features. The Pagodenburg, or pagoda house, was designed by Joseph Effner and completed in 1719, and the Badenburg, a bath house, also by Effner, was finished in 1721. The Magdalenenklause was Effner's last project for Max Emanuel, a genuine contemplative retreat with a chapel only finished in 1728 after the Elector's death. The Amalienburg, the most glorious gem of German Rococo, was designed by François Cuvilliés the elder, and was completed in 1739.

Three of the buildings, the Pagodenburg, Badenburg and Amelienburg, were once surrounded by their own Baroque gardens, framing them like pictures and completing the architectural composition. But parterres were costly to maintain, which was probably why they were so readily torn up and replaced with grass when gardens were remodelled to look like scenes from an idyllic landscape. The pity of destruction is more acute in the case of the Badenburg and Pagodenburg than in most other instances, for with their exquisite interiors and handsome façades, these supremely sophisticated buildings now look ill at ease surrounded simply by rough grass. The Amalienburg, built as a hunting lodge for refreshments during the chase, is more fortunate in still having a framework of trees.

In spite of the loss of their contemporary gardens, Nymphenburg's garden buildings are a delight, and a good reflection of the spirit of their age. The fashion for exoticism was manifested in the Pagodenburg; its Classical exterior belies the *chinoiserie* decoration

The Amalienburg was added to the gardens at Nymphenburg in 1739 by the elder Cuvilliés. Decorated within and without in spirited Rococo mood, it was built as a hunting lodge, and approached up a wide avenue lined with fountains and hedges. Above the door, a group of figures surrounds Diana, goddess of the chase.

inside, one of the earliest examples in the garden of the growing enthusiasm for all things oriental. The earlier *Trianon de Porcelaine* at Versailles had only pretended to an impression of oriental exoticism; the Pagodenburg was one step closer to the true mysteries of China.

The Badenburg, with its marble bathing pool and splendid banqueting hall, served a double purpose in the scheme of things. Not only were the pool and hall used as a means of reviving jaded courtiers, but the building itself enhanced the gardens with a structure of architectural importance. Such buildings were rarely on the main axis, and were either a feature in a cross-axis, as at Nymphenburg, or the centre of a smaller design, as at the Villa Pisani in Italy. A garden building could be used for any number of purposes, from eating, bathing, protecting tender evergreens or viewing the countryside, or it could be dedicated to heroes, gods or ideal values. Its existence was more important than its purpose.

A glance at some of the other significant German gardens of the late 17th and early 18th centuries shows a variety of characters. The vast square Herrenhausen in Lower Saxony had a profoundly Dutch atmosphere, complete with its perimeter canal; La Favorite on the Rhine near Mainz was a tribute to Marly; and Wilhelmshöhe near Kassel was loosely modelled on the Villa Aldobrandini.

The scale at Wilhelmshöhe is immense, and the cascade, which drops 200 metres, is the most amazing feature. At its head the massive octagonal building, the Wasserschloss, is more German than Italianate in aspect, and is topped by a bronze copy of the Farnese Hercules.

In considering what sort of style to choose, German garden owners could read the German version of Dezallier d'Argenville's *La Théorie et la Pratique du Jardinage,* published in German in 1731, and they could turn to pattern books produced by architects for plans for buildings. The Austrian J.B. Fischer von Erlach, one of the most important Baroque architects of the early 18th century, published designs of buildings from many countries in *Entwurf einer historischen Architektur.* It was first published in Vienna and Leipzig in 1721, appearing in French in 1725, and in English in 1730 and 1737, and was the first architectural treatise to illustrate Egyptian and Chinese

buildings, hence its popularity in Germany and abroad. The book subsequently became a source of inspiration, direct or indirect, to the Rococo designers of the later 18th century. In addition to pyramids, the Acropolis in Athens, Roman triumphal arches and obelisks, pagodas, and a Turkish mosque that was probably Sir William Chambers' inspiration for the mosque at Kew, Fischer von Erlach included a view of the Italian Isola Bella. International in both inspiration and readership, his book demonstrated the demand for knowledge and ideas shared by creative people in most countries of Europe.

German gardens of this period display an interesting mixture of ideas, borrowed and adapted from a variety of sources. Since their owners seem to have resisted following every turn of fashion and they have been moderately well maintained, more have survived intact than in other European countries.

This considerable Baroque pleasure pavilion is a design by Fischer von Erlach from Entwurf einer historischen Architektur, *1721. Large and elaborate garden buildings enjoyed more success in 18th-century Germany and Austria than in Italy, France or Great Britain. In this composition, the figures straining so convincingly to drag a sea creature from the basin are pulling at a copper net.*

A view of the Fountain of Neptune and Thetis taken from Résidences Memorables *by Kleiner, 1731. Behind the fountain is a stilt hedge, commonly known as a* palissade à l'Italienne. *Its simplicity anticipates the stark outlines of 20th-century Bauhaus architecture.*

VII.

<small>Salomon Kleiner Ing. Elect. Mog. del.</small>

<small>Iacob Gottlieb Thelott sculpsit.</small>

<small>7.</small>

Spanish and Portuguese Baroque

French influence in garden design rippled in every direction, including as far as the royal palace of La Granja de San Ildefonso in Spain. Situated near Segovia on the north slope of the Sierra de Guadarrama, on a gentle hillside above the intense heat of the plains, the property was bought in 1720 by Philip V, grandson of Louis XIV, who planned to develop it as a country retreat.

Philip's intention was to create a French garden that would be a nostalgic reminder of the illustrious gardens of his grandfather, but the site, chosen for its climate, was not intended as a grandiose stage for the Court in the French manner. This garden was to be more private and more reflective, with neither wide vistas nor vast parterres. Only certain elements derive from French sources – the Great Cascade on the main axis, the hedged bosquets, the iconography and a preponderance of fountains, while the system of water flowing in channels along the sides of the alleys was current in Italy. Thanks to centuries of experience in designing villas and gardens as cool summer retreats, the Italian influence could also be seen in appropriate touches of intimacy, and in the shading trees as backdrops to many fountains, for the Queen, Isabella Farnese, daughter of the Duke of Parma, was also Italian.

Several of the hands that created La Granja, however, were French. While Teodoro Ardemans was building the palace in 1721–3, René Carlier started work in the gardens. He had been invited to Madrid in about 1712 to impose some French logic on the gardens of Buen Retiro, and appears to have stayed on afterwards. Carlier was the architect of La Granja's Great Cascade, which falls down 11 steps of white marble, edged in red marble and coloured jasper and decorated with alternating circles and diamonds. At the top of the cascade is an elegant pavilion in pink stone with delicately chiselled decoration, by Procaccini in the style of the early years of the reign of Louis XV. Before it in the basin is the fountain of the Three Graces by René Frémin.

Fountains are by far the most spectacular feature of this garden. Inspired by drawings by Le Brun for Versailles, but never executed there, they cool and refresh even on the hottest of days. To appreciate La Granja in all its 18th-century splendour, by far the best time for a visit is on an important feast day, for then all the fountains are sure to play. Unlike Versailles and Marly, water was, and is, in abundant supply here, stored in an artificial lake higher up the hillside.

One of the fountains in The Horse Race
at La Granja de San Ildefonso.

The fountains were mainly created by the leading sculptors of the day and their pupils, including René Frémin and Jean Thierry, who created the dramatic series of figures known as The Horse Race. From the Fountain of Neptune and the Fountain of Apollo, the culmination of the race is Frémin's Fountain of Andromeda, where a dragon spouts a mighty plume of water some 37 metres high.

Mythological subjects abound. The Fountain of Pomona was created by Thierry, assisted by Doubou, Lagru, Cousac and Lebasseau. The figures of Mercury carrying Psyche at the Plaza de las Ocho Calles, where eight avenues meet, is by Frémin, as are the eight gods around the circle between the avenues, each in a Rococo frame. The Fountain of the Frogs, by Hubert Dumandré, represents the goddess Latona, mother of Apollo and Diana, one of the most obvious reminders of Versailles; its 50-metre jet was the highest in Europe at the time, and clearly visible from Segovia. Another reflection of Versailles was the Fountain of Fame and the Parterre of La Fama, both truly French in design.

The Fountain of Diana is La Granja's greatest achievement. A great Baroque extravaganza, it was designed by Bousseau and built

The cascade at La Granja rises up 11 marble steps to a fountain in front of Procaccini's pavilion. It is on the main axis that runs through the palace, and is best viewed from the first floor apartments that overlook it.

by Antoine Dumandré and Pierre Pitué as a gift from the Queen to the King, and was completed in 1742. Water gushes from lions' mouths and urns on the top, ripples over basins, and sprays from one attendant nymph to another in the surrounding pool, while Diana prepares to bathe. Philip V was far from grateful: *It has cost me three millions and amused me three minutes,*[33] he is said to have sighed gloomily.

Of course, iconography was important too, and the identification of the House of Bourbon with Apollo and Diana was well understood. Philip and Isabella were glorified not only by their supposed relationship with the great gods of mythology, but also by association with Louis XIV. It was a mighty combination.

La Granja was not, however, much observed by curious travellers, being some distance from Madrid and intended as a private rather than a public palace. Lady Holland, whose husband was a diplomat in Madrid, went there in July 1803, but was less than enchanted:

The gardens are reckoned among the finest in Europe; they are in the old French style of high clipped hedges, salons de verdure, *alleys, &c. Tho' that is the style I prefer far beyond any other, yet these gardens are* sombre, *and only striking from the number of their fountains, which stand unrivalled. We obtained permission from the* Intendente *to have the fountains play for us, a request usually complied with upon paying two ounces of gold.*[34]

After Carlier's death in 1722, others took over the design, possibly with guidance from Ardemans, the architect, while Esteban Boutelou from France, the brothers Basani and Salvador Lemmi from Florence, Esteban Marchand and Enrique Joly were responsible for construction, hydraulics and horticulture. The design departed from the current European practice of geometric plans and level alleys and where a French hand might have controlled the landscape with precision, an Italian might have made more use of terraces. It may be that because there was no great figure of authority heading the plan, and because of the gradual acquisition of extra ground, the result is a design that lacks cohesion. The consequence, however, is a garden with individual character and the promise of surprise, thus adding piquancy to exploration. Lady Holland's description of La Granja as sombre is unjust, for it has a unique vitality born of its dazzling fountains, and supplemented by the wider setting, mountains snowcapped till early summer and a great plain disappearing into a haze.

The Portuguese, too, put their individual stamp on their gardens, benefiting from a wide variety of influences. Their cultural history evolves from Roman and Moorish occupation, from their extensive trading interests and colonies in South America and the East, as well as from European neighbours. Like the Dutch and the British, the Portuguese having always been sea-faring and outward looking.

In architectural terms, there is a certain spirit of adventure in Portuguese decoration, demonstrated most visibly in the early 16th century by the style known as Manueline gothic, which takes its name from Manuel I. A flamboyant variation of gothic decoration, it is full of motion and reminders of the great Portuguese maritime tradition. Ribs of vaulting carved like ropes, twisted columns, coral, anchors, knots, sails and sea-horses embellish façades and interiors. Examples can be seen in churches and royal palaces, but not in major gardens of the 16th century, although there are legacies from this period to be seen in the gardens of the 19th century.

It is this love of decoration and freedom to experiment that stimulated a Portuguese tradition that did flourish in gardens: the use of painted and glazed tiles. Earlier, this tradition was shared with southern Spain, where the *azulejos* of the Moors were decorated with geometric patterns, like those on the Charles V pavilion in the Alcazar of Seville. As a result of Italian influence during the Renaissance, the Portuguese discarded the old patterns in favour of free-flowing scrolls surrounding images of plants and landscapes, cherubs and the human form. Tiles were applied to walls, benches and staircases as an alternative, or a supplement, to architectural decoration, and could be treated as frescoed pictures too, using the luxury of a palette of colours.

A factory near Lisbon supplied tiles to central and southern Portugal; further north, gardens relied more on carved stone rather than tiles for their decoration. Granite and skilled craftsmen were plentiful around the northern city of Oporto, so here stone was used in preference to tiles, and today the gentle wet winter climate of the area has enriched the stonework with an enviable patina.

The other outstanding feature in Portuguese gardens is the *estanque*, or water tank, another relic from Mudéjar days. The Moors rejoiced in the extra dimension of reflections and would site a water tank in a strategic place for the double appreciation of a building, trees or sky. The best-known example is in fact in Spain at the Alhambra in Granada, where the Torre de las Damas, a tower with a slender-columned loggia, is reflected in the pool at its feet, as illustrated on p.94. The *estanque* also serves the purpose of water storage to ensure supplies in hot dry summers, and could be used for bathing, boating and water fowl too. Traditionally straight-sided, it was sometimes sunk into the ground, but could also be raised with retaining walls.

The combination of tiles and tank, together with Renaissance tradition, has given the gardens of Portugal a unique character. The Renaissance principle of house and garden designed as a single concept was adopted in the 16th century for the country house, or *quinta*, an early example being the Quinta da Bacalhoa, c. 1550, followed by the Quinta das Torres towards the end of the century. Both are near Setubal and both have their *estanque*. At Bacalhoa, the tank lies beside an arcaded loggia, an idyllic composition and one bearing a distinct similarity to the Torre de las Damas at the Alhambra. The Quinta das Torres is modelled on an Italian villa, and in the garden the unique feature is the Italianate stone rotunda in the centre of the tank, a circle of columns supporting a dome and tall finial. It has two tiny landing stages, inviting those who need refreshing shade to come and relax in this island bower.

The churches and palaces of the Manueline gothic age and the later 1500s had been financed through trade and through discoveries in Brazil, at a time when the Portuguese economy was expanding and confident. But there followed many lean decades. The monarchy passed to Philip 11 of Spain in 1580, and thereafter Portugal limped through the 17th century, often at war with Spain.

By the end of the 1600s, prosperity returned and rekindled the creative urge, and in gardens various aspects of Italian and French design were soon adopted. The vast panoramas of Le Nôtre were too grand and too expensive, but bosquets of shading trees and trimmed or pleached hedges from France were eagerly copied. The hilly terrain of the country dictated terracing and small parterres in the Italian mode, with statuary to decorate them, and as water was usually at a premium, fountains relied for their attractions more on sculpture and less on abundant sprays.

The 1690s saw the start of one of the great palaces of Portugal, the Palácio dos Marqueses de Fronteira, now in a suburb of Lisbon. The house, built for the Marquis of Fronteira, derives from Italian villa designs of the 16th century. The garden has four distinct areas, the parterre, the water tank, the woodland garden and the tiled terrace, called the Chapel Promenade. The parterre is a green carpet of box, with precision-cut hedges separating the narrowest of beds. Yews, domes of box, statues and an imposing fountain in the centre provide vertical tension.

At one end is the *estanque*, the finest in Portugal. A large rectangle, it is edged beside the parterre with a balustrade. Twin flights of steps rise on either side, leading to a pair of square pavilions with steeply pitched roofs, and in between an upper terrace whose rear wall is articulated with niches displaying the busts of Portugal's monarchs. This is the Gallery of Kings.

All the walls are decorated with painted tiles. Around the tank set into arches are blue and white panels depicting cavaliers in feathered hats on prancing horses, while the central arch reveals a grotto. Above, the gallery wall is tiled a brilliant blue, the piercing colour dominating the entire architectural composition. The arrangement is offset by a frieze of patterned tiles running along the base and top of the wall and bordering the niches in a pattern of exceptional beauty and originality; pine cones in relief are alternately white and coloured with a coppery lustre.

The water tank, the estanque, *at the Palácio de Fronteira is a remarkable structure, theatrical in its composition and glorious in its tiled decoration. Seen from across the box parterre, the vibrant blue of the Gallery of Kings and the terracotta rooftiles of the twin pavilions provide a stimulating contrast of colours.*

A side wall of the estanque at Fronteira

The interior of the grotto at Fronteira, in which fragments of pottery are used to add colour to patterns of shells.

Next to the *estanque* is the woodland garden, which would originally have been laid out symmetrically but was planted informally in the 19th century. This contains an exquisite shellwork fountain and an equally remarkable grotto decorated with shells, pebbles and china mosaics. Doubtless inspired by the mainstream European fashion developed by Salomon and Isaac de Caus, it has qualities of fantasy and humour in the occasional tile pictures set in its richly decorated walls.

Beyond this lies another great extravaganza, the tiled Chapel Promenade. While the *estanque* is pure Portuguese, this terrace is Italianate in spirit, a theatrical experience in the manner of the Water Theatre at the Villa Aldobrandini. Painted tiles must have offered exciting possibilities to a Baroque designer, and here they have been seized with relish. Again, the colour scheme is blue and white. Heroic statues of gods are set in arched recesses, and in between are arched panels painted with the Muses. Above the statues are bas-relief busts of warriors, encircled by relief wreaths of green leaves and lemons and other yellow fruit, reminiscent of the bas-reliefs produced by Della Robbia at the end of the 15th century in Italy. At the far end is the blue- and white-tiled chapel, whose arched entrance and square upper windows have been edged with more 'Della Robbia' leaves and lemons.

In 1699, the ruler of Florence, Duke Cosimo de' Medici, came to see the Marquis' palace, which was not yet complete, although the garden was already laid out. *The villa, at present under construction, is being built with economy and taste and has a garden with parterres, statues and bas-reliefs. There are five great fountains and others, smaller but of differing heights, on differing levels in the garden.*[35] Even before completion, the gardens had a reputation that attracted this important visitor, and they remain today a prime example of the essential elements of Portuguese taste.

Early in the 18th century, the arrival of gold from Brazil brought fabulous wealth to Portugal, wealth that found its way to architecture and gardens from the Quinta da Palmeira north of Braga to the Palácio de Bélem in Lisbon, now the residence of the President of Portugal. The next generation of gardens, from the northern borders with Spain to the southern coast of the Algarve, would revel in the fashion that followed Baroque – Rococo.

The theme of ceramic decoration is repeated again in the Chapel Promenade, where all the architectural details are enhanced by painted tiles. Raised flower beds are encased in tiles, too, and built into the niched wall in one of the most comprehensive of tiled compositions in a garden.

The Birth of Rococo in France

Rococo is the final flourish of Baroque in architecture and design. Its roots are planted in Baroque, yet at the same time it is a reaction to it, a reaction, in general, to ponderous grandeur and in particular to the pomp of Versailles and Louis XIV.

Rococo sparkles with frivolity, intimacy and variety. In art, it is epitomised by the gaiety of Watteau, Boucher and Fragonard, contrasting with the gravity of Baroque artists like Algardi, Le Brun and Rembrandt. In art, architecture and design, Baroque is controlled, conformist, and prompts an emotional response, whereas Rococo arouses little more than a smile from the beholder. Rococo is carefree, pleasure-seeking, and feminine, while Baroque is profoundly masculine. In music, Bach's great organ works are Baroque, while Mozart's spirited sonatas and divertimenti are typical of Rococo.

Rococo thrived in the comparative peace of 18th-century Europe, which between 1715 and the French Revolution was troubled only by the War of the Austrian Succession in the 1740s and the Seven Years' War between 1756 and 1763. The term itself derives from the French word *rocaille*, meaning rockwork ornament, and the style, originated in France in the early 1700s, was developed by Meissonier, Oppenord and others in the 1720s, and spread in varying degrees to other countries in Europe.

Rockwork ornament had decorated grottoes from the Renaissance onward; coloured stones, fossils, tufa, coral and shells had been arranged in patterns for centuries, with pride of place in design often given to the fan-shaped shell, either real or carved in stone. Shells were placed over an arch or upturned into a basin and filled with water. The shell had been the symbol of pilgrims since the Middle Ages, and was generally an important motif in Baroque times, but with its curving shape and absence of straight lines, it came to personify the Rococo movement. Straight lines were anathema to the Rococo designer, so anything as naturally curvaceous as a shell was the perfect motif.

Scrolls, too, became an integral part of Rococo decoration, delicately chiselled and curled into the letters C and S, or turned into *rinceaux* of vine stems flowing like waves. Plaster, wood and stone could seem like putty in the hands of skilled craftsmen, and the effect was light and playful.

These essentials of Rococo decoration dominated interiors in France until the middle of the century, from furniture and fabrics to panelling and paintings. However, they were not transferred into French gardens with the same enthusiasm. The great era of innovative garden design had waned, and new gardens tended to follow in the safe footsteps of Le Nôtre and Dezallier d'Argenville till late in the 18th century, rather than experiment wholesale with adventurous Rococo ideas, which were thought better kept indoors. New gardens, like La Motte-Tilly in Aube, continued with established

Fragonard's painting of The Lover Crowned, *c. 1770, is in playful Rococo spirit and shows a relaxed, romantic view of nature associated with late Rococo.*

This plan for the Jardin du Tillet, from
Détails des nouveaux jardins, Cahier VI,
by Le Rouge, c. 1778, is a rare example of a
Rococo parterre. There were others, for example
by Bélanger at Bagatelle, but this one is exceptional
in its combination of regularity and asymmetry.
The designer could not destroy the central axis, yet
needed to throw off all other shackles of formality.
The curiously irregular shapes near the fountain
are neither water nor grass, and may have been
formed in stones.

This, the most Rococo of Blondel's garden
structures, he described as a belvedere in Maisons
de Plaisance, *1737. Ideally it should be built on*
a slight eminence like the belvedere at Sceaux.
To lighten the mood of the façade, he drew little
figures sporting on the roof.

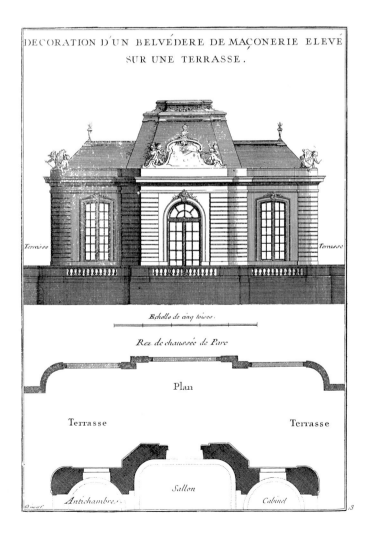

DECORATION D'UN BELVÉDERE DE MAÇONERIE ELEVÉ
SUR UNE TERRASSE.

Echelle de cinq toises.

Rez de chaussée de Parc

Plan

Terrasse   Terrasse

Sallon

Antichambre   *Cabinet*

traditions, while older gardens, like Chantilly and Versailles, were modified from time to time to incorporate some Rococo elements.

Books were available to give people ideas. Apart from d'Argenville's bible of design, of which there were nine editions between 1709 and 1760, two more French books appeared. The first, by Jacques-François Blondel, *De la Distribution des Maisons de Plaisance*, was published in two volumes in 1737 and 1738. Designs for parterres, pavilions, trellised berceaux, fountains, vases, and urns followed in succeeding pages, but they are largely in a restrained Baroque mood. It is only in interior design that Blondel romps off to Rococo.

For the garden, Blondel illustrated a belvedere, which, he said, should be sited so that it could be admired from a distance, like the example in the gardens at Sceaux. With a playful hand, he garlanded the solemn Egyptian sphinx with flowers and ribbons and drew a child astride her back.

The second book was by a former pupil of Blondel's, François Cuvilliés, together with his son. *Oeuvres*, published in Paris between 1738 and 1773, leans more to Rococo decoration than Blondel's book, and includes some massive garden ornaments, such as pyramids, urns and statues, fountains, and two sphinxes. Although some of them followed Baroque taste, the very range of subject matter points to the freedom of Rococo. Like many a designer in the past, Cuvilliés was more appreciated abroad than at home; he worked extensively in Munich, where his talents matched the tastes of the Elector of Bavaria.

Apart from the light-heartedness of Rococo following the heaviness of Baroque, other changes were in the air. Gardens of immense size had gone out of fashion, not just because they were reminiscent of Versailles but also because of sheer cost. To sink a fortune into landscape domination was no longer essential; the new garden could instead be smaller and more intimate, while the older garden could be modified to make more private spaces. The mood was for privacy, for lovers' rendezvous, for amusing picnics and musical entertainments for a few friends, accompanied by mischievous little cherubs in stone. The garden was still vitally important as a space in which to receive guests, it was just that the type of entertainments offered had changed.

Elements of Rococo in French gardens are seen in ground-plans, statuary, trelliswork, and in decoration applied to buildings. As far as ground-plans were concerned, the change was perceptible but not revolutionary. In the parterre, the principal beds still had straight sides, but the ends might be shaped in asymmetrical curves. The overall plan was still dominated by straight walks, although regularly twisting paths could be found within a square or rectangle. Blondel showed several designs where the outlines of the beds were all strictly geometrical, but internally each one had a different, intricate pattern of paths.

As far as the parterre itself was concerned, in addition to the typical *broderie* design, the cut-work style of the late 16th century

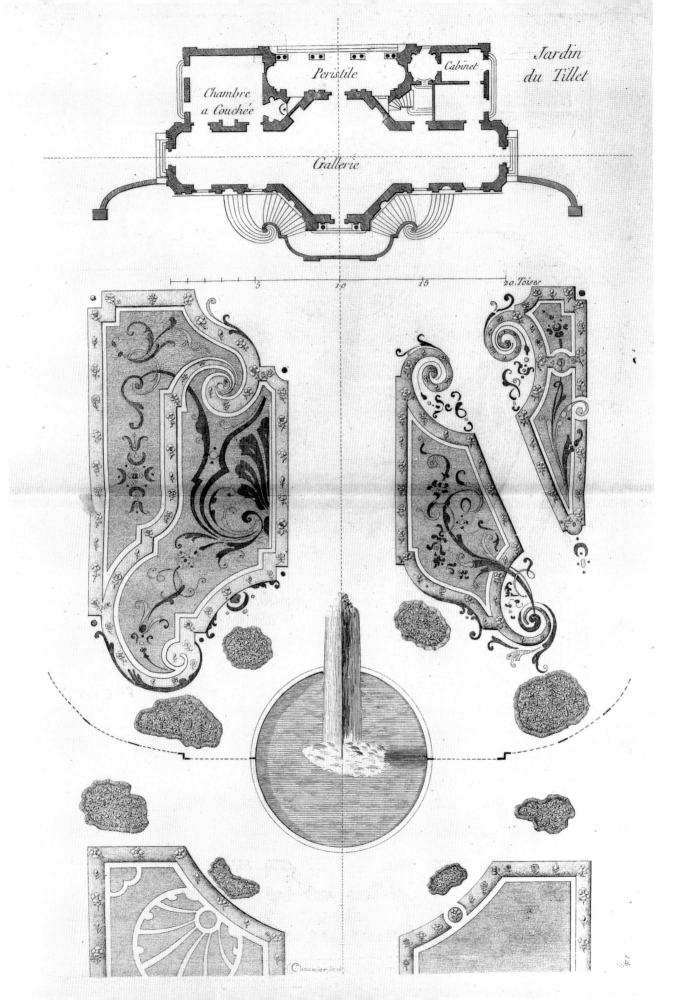

Chambre
a Couchée

Peristile

Cabinet

Jardin
du Tillet

Gallerie

5   10   15   20. Toises

Chaumier Scul

Four drawings from Blondel's Maisons de Plaisance, *1737, all of which have been softened from Baroque versions by the addition of fabric or delicate garlands of flowers.*

became increasingly popular and was renamed a *parterre à l'anglaise*, known as a *plat* in England. The design was shaped simply in cut turf, often with a statue placed in the middle. A more elaborate cut-work version was also current, a *parterre de pièces coupées pour des fleurs*, which had the bonus of some flowers to give it colour, while a plain ground-plan was appropriate for the display of orange trees.

Both *parterres de broderie* and *parterres à l'anglaise* were included when royal architect Ange-Jacques Gabriel was given one of the major commissions of the middle of the century, to rebuild the château of Compiègne in Oise for Louis XV. The gardens were designed on five levels, and included grand staircases, balustrades, statues, and two *pièces d'eau*. This garden, however, was a casualty of the Seven Years' War, for although started in 1756, it was never fully realised according to Gabriel's plan, and was altered later by Napoleon.

An example of a *parterre à l'anglaise* was at the Comte d'Artois' garden at Bagatelle, in the Bois de Boulogne, Paris. It was designed by François-Joseph Bélanger in 1775, when Rococo had given way to Neoclassicism in architecture, and to the landscape movement in garden design. Bélanger is far better known for his *jardins irréguliers* at Bagatelle and elsewhere, but for the area in front of the house, Bélanger, or his client, preferred the formality of a parterre. The entire layout has since been destroyed.

With statuary, the Rococo influence is more obvious. Heroic gods were replaced by elegant ladies and gentlemen, shepherds and shepherdesses, or peasants romanticised in pretty costumes, all alive with movement and gaiety. These figures often adorned the smaller spaces, the paths and green rooms or *cabinets de verdure*, and stood on curving plinths. Gone were massive Baroque fountains and stiff, straight-sided Roman vases; instead stonemasons chiselled statues and objects on a smaller scale – cherubs, sphinxes or waisted baskets brimming with fruit or trailing flowers.

Trelliswork was reproduced as a finer version of sturdy Baroque carpentry, with a flowing silhouette of concave and convex curves, and sometimes without symmetry. It was used as a screen, or took the place of buildings when a vertical feature was required. Treillage was back in fashion again since beauty was preferable to economy, wrote Blondel. Buildings are largely absent from his book, but he did include one *petit Bâtiment champêtre* to adorn the garden.

Buildings rely on decoration for the Rococo touch. A rich and complex vocabulary of concave and convex curves had been developed by Baroque architects; it was for Rococo successors to lighten the form and apply more delicate ornamentation. But buildings themselves are solid affairs, and even small pavilions are serious structures; so in the Rococo age the garden building was erected if there was a purpose for its use, rather than simply as an enhancing feature. Ruins were thought more appealing, as tastes moved towards Romanticism.

DESSEIN DE SPHINX GROUPÉ D'UN ENFANT AVEC GUIRLANDES DE FLEURS

DESSIN DE SPHINX POSÉ SUR SON SOCLE POUR LA DECORATION DES TERASSES

Echelle de 5 pieds.

A Rococo building that still exists is the Pavillon Français at the Petit Trianon at Versailles; designed by Gabriel in 1750, it is an octagonal rotunda of exquisite proportions with a balustrade decorated with *putti* and is the focal point of the garden. Originally known as the *Salon de Compagnie et de Jeux*, it was presented by Louis XV to the Marquise de Pompadour. The intimate gardens that surround it are a perfect example of the desire for privacy, in sharp contrast to the ostentatious gardens of Versailles or Marly.

Antique temples were by now too serious and grand cascades too heavy; if a cascade was required, it was a smaller more delicate affair than its Baroque predecessor. Water features were still important, thought Blondel, because they added life to the garden, but new cascades were the exception rather than the rule, on grounds of cost and formality. However, in one place where the site provided both abundant water and natural slopes, a cascade of great refinement was built. This was at the Château du Touvet in Isère near Grenoble, constructed for Comte Pierre de Marcieu between 1753 and 1762, when the château was also restored. The garden, on several terraces, is remarkable for its water staircases, the intricate stonework surrounding them and the basins on each level. In the 19th century, trees and shrubs replaced the formal layout on the terraces, but recently all has been restored in the 18th-century spirit.

In addition to these structural signs, Rococo could also be seen in a more relaxed attitude to nature. Jacques Boyceau in his *Traité du Jardinage* of 1638 had mentioned the wisdom of circles and curves in the ground-plan, since they allowed the variety that nature demanded. He would never have permitted nature to develop unchallenged, but he did foresee that straight lines, whether on the edge of a path or the outline of a hedge, could become tedious. In a Rococo garden, nature was allowed to follow some of its instincts to make the prettiest possible picture. The gardeners' pruning shears spent more time in the tool shed, as trees and shrubs were free to throw out graceful branches, and the old clipped hedges and *palissades* were softened by benign neglect. With the change of emphasis from stone construction towards trellis and small picturesque scenes, gardens became the province of the aesthetic designer rather than the trained architect.

Just as the Italian gardens of the Renaissance had been emulated in varying ways from one country to another, so the physical signs of French Rococo spread to the neighbouring countries of Europe. Travelling architects, word of mouth, books and engravings were still the main means for the transfer of information from one country to another, but there was no overall plan that was universally adopted. Rococo in all its aspects was modified, developed or ignored according to national preferences, since this was still an era when each country stamped its own character on the current fashions. The English teased some strands of frivolity, intimacy and variety from the French tradition, and added their own interpretations, with relish.

The English Version of Rococo

Thou who shalt stop, where *Thames'* translucent wave
Shines a broad Mirror thro' the shadowy Cave;
Where ling'ring drops from min'ral Roofs destill,
And pointed Crystals break the sparkling Rill,
Unpolish'd Gems no ray on Pride bestow,
And latent metals innocently glow.

From 'On His Grotto at Twickenham' by Alexander Pope,
1688–1744

Switzer's plan for a garden, published in Ichnographia, *1718, has a strong central axis and pockets of symmetry elsewhere in between serpentine and curiously angled paths.*

A cascade by William Wrighte from Grotesque Architecture, *1767. Like most of Wrighte's designs, it was copied by Le Rouge in* Détails des nouveaux jardins.

In England, Rococo never established itself as the major style in architecture, nor in interior or garden design, for several reasons.

The leading architects looked for inspiration to Italy and not to France. Whereas the French reacted to Baroque by inventing Rococo, the English sought the fundamentals of Classical architecture. They craved the simplicity and purity of Palladio, not the variations of Baroque, which many thought corrupt and vulgar, nor its more frivolous deviation to Rococo. Lady Mary Wortley Montagu was not alone in finding in French royal gardens *an excessive prodigality of ornaments and decorations, that is just the opposite extreme to what appears in our royal gardens.* This, she wrote to Alexander Pope in 1717, was due to French taste, *which always pants after something new, and thus heaps ornament upon ornament without end or measure.*[2]

Whereas in France Rococo remained unchallenged as the fashionable taste in garden design, in England it was competing with a totally new concept, the landscape garden. After centuries of formality, the English were reacting to geometric plans and, from the 1720s, were moving perceptibly towards making the garden look like a picture of a landscape. For many, Rococo was inadequate as a pausing place on the route to change. It was seen as a side-track with a doubtful destination and did not tempt those set on a revolutionary course. The fact that in England from the 1720s to the 1750s there were two parallel approaches to garden design makes the garden history of the period confusing at times, especially when buildings, such as pavilions, were common to both approaches. The geometric ground-plans and parterres of the Renaissance were waning, while

Romantic Arches, with Cascades.

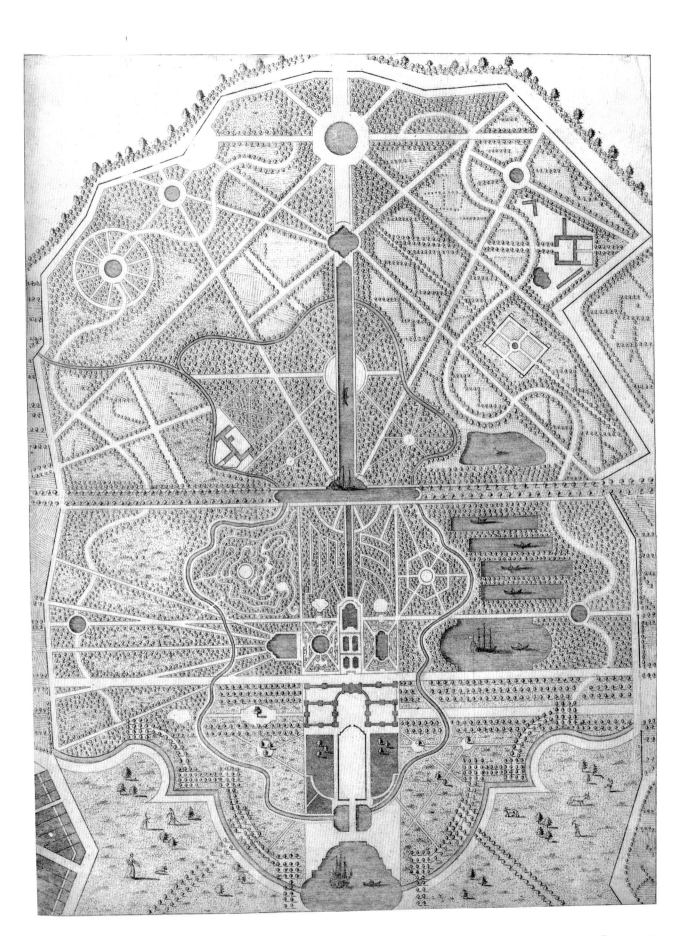

The gardens of Marston were another very rare version of a transitional phase between formal and landscape gardens. In two areas, irregular paths are carved through groves of trees, while in the third area on the left, a grid of hedges has been planted like a lopsided board for noughts and crosses. This was illustrated by Badeslade and Rocque in Vitruvius Britannicus, Volume the Fourth, *1739. While the owner of Marston, John Boyle, 5th Earl of Cork and Orrery, was experimenting with new ideas in garden design, his cousin Richard Boyle, 3rd Earl of Burlington, was also gradually changing his garden at Chiswick into a more natural form, and with lasting impact.*

the irregular gardens of William Kent and the Earl of Burlington, Lord Temple and Capability Brown were in the ascendancy.

Rococo had a third disadvantage for the English; it had no intellectual message of its own to consolidate its visual display. It had to be taken purely for its visual attraction, rather than for its ideals and associations. This lack of intellectual authority did, however, have a benefit in that Rococo was adaptable and could borrow with equanimity ideas, such as chinoiserie, from other traditions.

How much did Rococo express itself in England? In the strict French sense of asymmetry within formal ground-plans and trellis-work, if Rococo gardens existed in England, they are currently lost in obscurity.

In recent years, however, garden historians have taken a wider view of Rococo, and shown how the English interpreted French essentials of frivolity, intimacy and variety using different means and often in an informal setting. Rococo was a mood, an atmosphere, a way of treating, placing and mixing features in a garden, and a way of using a garden. Its essence is subtle, so subtle that sometimes it

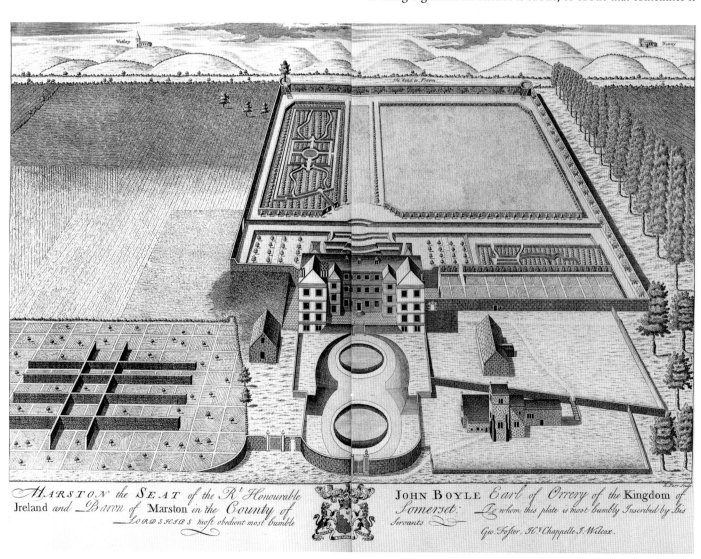

MARSTON the SEAT of the Rt Honourable Jreland *and Baron of* Marston *in the County of* Lordships *most obedient most humble* JOHN BOYLE *Earl of Orrery of the Kingdom of* Somerset: *To whom this plate is most humbly Jnscribed by his* Servants Geo Foster, He. Chappelle J. Wilcox.

can almost be confused with the landscape style, but it is in this comprehensive sense that some English gardens are Rococo.

Of course, there were differences in emphasis. Frivolity was taken further in England by the addition of the bizarre and the whimsical. As far as intimacy is concerned, French gardens tended to develop private spaces within the larger garden, whereas English Rococo gardens are all comparatively small or even modest. As for variety, the quest for it in England coincided with a resurgence of interest in medieval gothic and the opening up of trade relations with the East in general and with China in particular. These factors made it easy to expand the architectural horizon by adding to the classical tradition the whimsy of a whole new range of types and styles of buildings. But aside from these novel introductions, the features that had decorated gardens for centuries showed signs of change, too.

Statuary was treated in a similar fashion in both France and England. Antique sculpture was generally considered too solemn, and the gods of war fell slightly out of favour and were replaced by elegant courtiers and dancing peasants, or by characters from pastoral mythology, such as Ceres and Pomona, Diana the Huntress and the Seasons, reflecting a rekindled yearning for the fresh innocence of pastoral Arcadia. These carefree creatures were commercially cast in lead or carved in stone, and their principal supplier in England was John Cheere, a sculptor and caster who had taken over the business and the moulds belonging previously to John Van Nost. These rustic figures, which Van Nost had supplied for gardens such as Powis Castle in the 17th century, were now sold in quantity by Cheere, from his yard at Hyde Park Corner in London.

Grottoes, too, were liberated by the Rococo mood, and decorated with stones and shells in a more delicate manner than their predecessors. They were made at Oatlands and Hampton Court House, both in Surrey, at Goldney near Bristol, and at Goodwood in Sussex, where the Duchess of Richmond and her daughters created a sumptuous grotto in shells. And because of the ever-pressing search for variety, there was great freedom to experiment with designs and materials, with some startling results.

The most dramatic grotto is at Painshill in Surrey, where in the 1750s Charles Hamilton employed professional grotto makers, Joseph and Josiah Lane, for his island grotto. The exterior is faced with tufa-like limestone, which has a delicate, lacy look, while inside all the passages, antechambers and the main chamber are hung with spar to look like stalactites. *In the interior of the grotto . . . water trickles like a gentle rain from the strainers concealed in the vaults of the niches, and all this water finally runs down irregular little falls and cascades into the nearby artificial lake, from which the sunbeams are reflected . . .*[3] was the description in the 1770s by Fredrik Piper, garden designer to Gustav III of Sweden. After a lengthy restoration by Diana Reynell, it glows and sparkles again when candles flicker in the gloom.

The cascade was reappraised, and changed both character and location. Whereas before it had been a grandiose Baroque affair running down a hillside for all to see from the house or the parterre, a Rococo cascade was far more likely to be much reduced in length and built into the dam that held the lake, as at Wroxton Abbey in Oxfordshire and West Wycombe Park in Buckinghamshire. Usually, the water flowed down a short gentle slope and then dashed down a waterfall into a meandering stream or river. Or it could be built just above the lake, with water tumbling down over rough stones, as designed by William Kent at Chiswick House and at Claremont, in Surrey, both *c.* 1740.

Then some new ideas started appearing in English gardens. Whimsy had surfaced early at Bramham Park in Yorkshire. As already described, in the early years of the 18th century the garden was laid out like a formal French garden by the amateur but competent architect and owner, Lord Bingley. The novelty is that the geometry of the walks is imperfect, and the T-canal, completed by 1728, is a very odd shape, with the bar of the T both angled and lopsided. Both exhibit a refreshing and droll sense of humour.

As far as garden buildings were concerned, the English did not follow the Blondel patterns, but instead developed a more playful approach. A whole range of buildings that were not quite what they pretended to be started to appear, among them the mock medieval castles of Sanderson Miller, sham bridges at Carshalton, Surrey and Kenwood in London, and Thomas Wright's Ruin at Shugborough in Staffordshire.

This was an age when eccentricity burst like an exploding firework, and sprinkled absurdities in gardens, parks and in the countryside all over Britain. Ruined arches, bathhouses, dog kennels, gazebos, ice houses, menageries, obelisks, pyramids and towers, and more besides, sprang up in the gardens and estates of the mighty and of the middle classes. Far too numerous to describe here, they have been revealed in all their glorious irrationality by Barbara Jones in *Follies and Grottoes*, by Gwyn Headley and Wim Meulenkamp in *Follies*, and in the journal of The Folly Fellowship.

Many are wonderful oddities, follies in the truest spirit in that they have little or no function other than to improve the view, or to amuse. William Kent's eyecatcher at Rousham in Oxfordshire, *c.* 1740, was constructed in the fields beyond the park purely to add interest to the Cherwell valley. Others had some notional ancient purpose, such as Druids' rings and stone circles.

Yet other follies were for hermits, built in a rustic style, decorated either with rough stones or with gnarled old tree-trunks and contorted roots, and thatched with straw and overgrown with moss; they might even have had a resident hermit paid to act the part, complete with books on philosophy and mathematics, a shaggy beard and probably an illicit gin bottle nestling amongst the branches. But hermits and their like were notoriously unreliable, so model figures were sometimes used instead; at Kew, Merlin's Cave was occupied by a waxwork figure, to avoid the embarrassment of a magician unable to realise his spells.

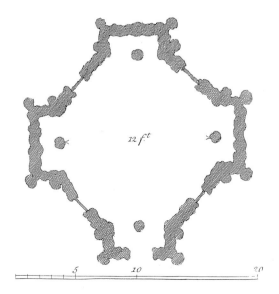

Hermitages, inhabited or otherwise, were popular features and, among many others, Kent designed one for Henry Pelham at Esher Place in Surrey in the 1730s, Thomas Wright drew another for the Duchess of Beaufort at Badminton, *c.* 1750, and several designs appeared in pattern books by Thomas Wright, Charles Over, Paul Decker and William Wrighte. All were frivolous, functionless items and were created with imagination for decoration and amusement.

Of all the bizarre buildings that remain from this period, the Red House at Painswick in Gloucestershire has to be the most Rococo. Its lack of symmetry, its slightly angled twin facades and its Gothick details all display the whimsical approach, and the rest of Painswick is Rococo too. There is a classical pigeon house, a pedimented Doric seat, a Gothick exedra in the form of a semicircle of columns around a circular pool, a Gothick alcove at the end of a long walk, and the Gothick Eagle House, which has recently been rebuilt. The old hermitage is scheduled for reconstruction when funds are available. The gardens were laid out in the 1740s for Benjamin Hyett by an unknown designer, perhaps the owner himself. In a naturally irregular valley the layout was as straight and geometric as possible, although no attempt was made to level the ground. However, the paths to the Red House were allowed to twist naturally along the sides of the valley, as is shown by Thomas Robbins in an aerial view of 1748, and it is thanks to his paintings that an exact recreation of the garden has been possible.

Painswick is currently England's best-known Rococo garden, and it exemplifies the spirit of whimsy and the love of variety within an intimate setting that are such important features of these gardens; although it covers six acres, it feels smaller because of the wooded, secluded atmosphere.

A few other Rococo gardens have survived; Belcombe Court in Wiltshire has a classical rotunda with a deep dome, a pool, a heap of boulders with a grotto underneath, and a Gothick cottage, all set in a sloping hillside behind the house. Also still fairly intact is Hampton Court House in Surrey, where the garden was made in the late 1760s by Thomas Wright, the foremost Rococo designer in England. While 'Capability' Brown was tearing up parterres and remoulding the countryside, Wright was designing smaller gardens for private enjoyments. Hampton Court House was one of his later works, and into this limited space he set a range of buildings to surprise and delight, including a pool, a fountain arch, a grotto, an exedra, and an ice house. The last three buildings were all given an irregular surface by a facing of burnt clinker and stone, which provides a unity in their variety, as well as reflecting the compulsive desire for decoration as a contrast to the austerity of Classicism.

The search for English Rococo leads on to a garden now gone, Grove House at Old Windsor in Berkshire, a property that Mr Dickie Bateman acquired in 1730. The house was a four-bedroomed villa with a Gothick front and a garden, also of a limited size but stocked with the full range of architectural styles. *Half-gothic, half attick, half chinese, and completely fribble*[4] were George Lyttleton's derisive comments in 1760. The 'chinese' reference was doubtless an allusion to the Chinese farm that, John Harris argues, was probably built *c.* 1735.[5] In fact, the farm was a confusion of Chinese, Indian and Dutch styles, with a pair of Classical alcoves inserted in one of the building's façades.

But that was not all. There was also a small Ionic temple in a grove of trees, a swing and a hammock in which to relax, and nearby a flowerbed set in a lawn. Dr Pococke also described *a grotto of grotesque shell-work with a summer house over it, and beyond that a Chinese alcove-seat, near which there is a Chinese covered bridge to an island, and another uncovered beyond it to another island*, and he concluded that the bridges, the islands, and the swans on the river made it *a most delightful piece of scenery.*[6]

All these gardens are imprinted with the hallmark of English Rococo, which relied essentially on whimsy, intimacy and variety, often arranged in an irregular manner rather than in old-fashioned formality. But Rococo was always a minority movement, suited to smaller gardens and not for the rolling acres being reshaped around country mansions. The main arbiters of garden taste in the middle of the century were men like William Kent, Lord Burlington at Chiswick House in London, Lord Temple at Stowe in Buckinghamshire, Charles Hamilton of Painshill, Lord Lyttleton of Hagley Hall in Worcestershire, William Shenstone of The Leasowes in Warwickshire, Henry Hoare of Stourhead in Wiltshire, and Sir William Chambers. They were designing on a grand scale in which English Rococo was irrelevant.

Stowe, Kew, Painshill, Hagley and Stourhead were the famous gardens that were visited by the French architect François-Joseph Bélanger when he came to England in 1763 and in the 1770s, and they were the gardens that influenced his later work in France. To Continental eyes, what was interesting was not the English version of Rococo, but the landscape garden and its many decorative buildings.

The Red House at Painswick, both whimsical and asymmetrical, was painted by John Piper c. 1985. Since the artist completed this work, the house has been painted red.

The Gothick Taste in England

*The Gothick Temple at Bramham Park,
as illustrated by Batty Langley in* Gothic
Architecture, *1742, and opposite, as copied
from Langley's book. It stands in a long rectangular
sward of grass, part of which was once a
bowling green.*

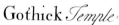

Gothick was, in part, the English response to French Rococo. Medieval gothic architecture had its own native version in each European country and therefore in England it had a known pedigree. Whereas Classicism, Rococo and chinoiserie were foreign styles, its pointed and ogee arches, lancet and rose windows, trefoils, quatrefoils and buttresses were familiar in parish church and cathedral, manor house and castle. This made the Gothick revival easily acceptable to those of a conservative bent who were suspicious of things foreign.

To distinguish it from medieval gothic and later Georgian and Victorian Gothic, the Rococo version is often spelt with the extra letter 'k', although the Gothick of Horace Walpole and Sanderson Miller were faithful reproductions of genuine gothic architecture and decoration.

Gothick was also an alternative to the grandeur of Classicism which, especially for smaller buildings, could be overpowering. Although frequently used for temples in landscaped gardens, Gothick was also popular for the smaller Rococo setting, such as Painswick. It falls loosely under the Rococo heading because of its light-heartedness, and also for its association with chivalry and pageantry and the achievements of England's medieval kings, for the Middle Ages and its buildings were heavily romanticised in the 18th century.

The Gothick revival started slowly, with the 'castle' that Sir John Vanbrugh designed for himself at Greenwich in 1718, followed by the belvedere he built at Claremont in Surrey for the Duke of Newcastle. William Kent, the artist turned architect, who led the change from formal to landscape in garden design, followed with a crenellated Gothick façade at Esher Place in Surrey in 1733 and two years later built the thatched Merlin's Cave at Kew. Sanderson Miller produced sham castles in the 1740s, and the revival was boosted by Horace Walpole when he rebuilt his cottage at Strawberry Hill, Surrey, in 1750. Interiors were fitted up in the new style, too, with panelling and furniture in the medieval manner.

In 1742, Batty and Thomas Langley published the first book on the subject, *Ancient Architecture, Restored and Improved by a Great Variety of Grand and Usefull Designs, entirely new in the Gothick Mode for the Ornamentation of Buildings and Gardens.* It was reissued in 1747 under the sensibly revised title *Gothic Architecture Improved by Rules and Proportions.* The book was an attempt to explain and classify medieval gothic architecture, and it contains some forty designs for buildings both elegant and imaginative and mostly of a size appropriate for gardens, ranging from porticoes to pavilions to temples.

The Langleys' book was obviously a most valuable contribution to the architectural debate. Exact replicas of two of its designs are still to be seen, the octagonal Gothick Temple at Bramham Park in Yorkshire, and the wonderful ogee windows with their distinctive glazing bars in the greenhouse at Frampton Court in Gloucestershire, built in the 1740s.

Other books illustrating Gothick designs followed. In 1751

A hexagonal Gothick temple from Overton's
Original Designs of Temples, 1766, and
closely resembling one by Charles Over in
Ornamental Architecture, 1758. It shares
similarities, too, with buildings designed by Batty
Langley. In an age when there was no copyright on
designs, Overton's temple was reproduced by
Le Rouge in Détails des nouveaux jardins.

Robert Morris published *The Architectural Remembrancer*, followed in 1752 by W. and J. Halfpenny's *Rural Architecture in the Gothick Taste*, one of a series of pattern books for a variety of styles. Gothick was covered, along with other styles, by Thomas Wright in *Universal Architecture*, published in 1755 and 1758. Charles Over's book of 1758, *Ornamental Architecture in the Gothic, Chinese and Modern Taste*, included Gothick temples, gates and seats of pleasing proportions. One was an octagonal *Cupulo Garden Seat, raised on* Gothic *Columns, being roomy, genteel and not expensive.*[7]

Paul Decker's slim contribution of 1759, *Gothic Architecture Decorated*, was followed in 1766 by T.C. Overton's *Original Designs of Temples and other ornamental Buildings for Parks and Gardens in the Greek, Roman and Gothic Taste*, also published under an alternative title, *The Temple Builder's Most Useful Companion*. Most useful it was, and influential, too, packed with designs that were well proportioned, interesting but not too outrageous. A book for the establishment, it had an impressive list of subscribers, including Richard and Henry Hoare and three notable architects, George Dance, Francis Hiron and Henry Holland. A Mr Richards of Spittle Croft near Devizes, Wiltshire, was a client with a small Gothick temple in his gardens, *a room 10 feet square within, with the addition of a wing on each side to enlarge the front for shew only; the raking battlements and pinnacles at the angles give it the appearance of a small chapel.*[8] Overton borrowed patterns from Batty Langley, Robert Morris and Charles Over, and years later designs by all four were reproduced by George-Louis Le Rouge in his masterpiece on European gardens, *Détails des nouveaux jardins à la mode*, published between 1776 and 1787 in 21 booklets or *cahiers*.

The final great contribution to the stylistic debate in the mid-century came from William Wrighte in 1767 in *Grotesque Architecture, or Rural Amusement*. This is aptly titled as it contains 28 designs both bizarre and amusing in true Rococo spirit. There is glorious confusion in the *Gothic Grotto*, and charming whimsicality in the final entry, *a Green-house, of the Grotesque Kind, faced with Flints and irregular Stones.*[9]

Pattern books have always been a fascinating source of information on current tastes, and their influence in the 18th century was enormous. Authors were only too pleased to be able to write proudly in captions to their plans that such and such a temple had been built for so and so at whatever country seat, and as there was no copyright on plans, there was no reason why authors could not reproduce the designs of others, with or without attribution. Le Rouge borrowed extensively from Overton and Wrighte, as did the author of the most important book about garden design in German, C.C.L. Hirschfeld, in *Theorie der Gartenkunst*, published in five volumes between 1779 and 1785. Hirschfeld used illustrations from Halfpenny, too, but the Gothick taste was less to his liking than the Classical, and he did not care for chinoiserie at all.

Gothick architecture did not seize the continental imagination as vigorously as it did the English in the 18th century. There were examples in France, such as at Betz in Oise, a landscape garden created c. 1781 by the artist Hubert Robert and the Duc d'Harcourt. One spectacular building that still remains in Germany is the Gothick House at Wörlitz, in Halle, a remarkable building erected in 1773 in north Italian gothic, then extended in the English Gothick style between 1785 and 1790. It is in a landscaped park laid out to emulate those in England, so, logically, it required a Gothick structure to complete the range of buildings.

In England, medieval gothic ruins were the height of fashion. Some were genuine, such as the magnificent Fountains Abbey, which John Aislabie incorporated into his landscaped garden at Studley Royal in Yorkshire in the 1730s, but most were fake versions, designed by architects like Sanderson Miller. Miller, a country gentleman, became an expert in Gothick architecture, and a specialist in ruined towers. He built them at Ingestre, in Staffordshire and at Wimpole in Cambridgeshire, but his most famous version was at Hagley Hall in Worcestershire. It was planned like a medieval fortress with an inner courtyard and a tower at each corner, but only one tower was built, and the rest of the structure resembles a decaying keep. Horace Walpole must have gratified the owner, Lord Lyttleton, when he wrote that he could see in it the true rust of the Barons' Wars.

Of the plethora of Gothick temples, one of the most Rococo is at Painshill, built c. 1760. Sited at the brow of a hill from which there is a fine view over the lake, the temple has a particular delicacy, thanks to being made of wood painted to look like stone. The movement knew no bounds. Gothick seats proliferated – for example, at Painswick – and in the craze to gothicise, even some Classical buildings were altered, as was the Octagon Tower at Studley Royal, built in 1728 and remodelled some ten years later.

Gothick was an extremely popular style for garden structures, outnumbered only by the Classical form, and became so popular that it transferred into mainstream architecture as Georgian Gothic. Never derided as was the Chinese taste, it had started out as an alternative to French Rococo mainly for the garden, battled with chinoiserie and won, then turned into a serious style for country mansions and, like the gothic of the great cathedrals, finally possessed the gravitas appropriate for the rebuilding of the Houses of Parliament in the 1830s.

The ruined castle at Hagley Hall, designed by Sanderson Miller to add interest to the natural landscape and built c. 1750.

Exoticism

Exoticism is the fashion for a range of ornate oriental architecture and artefacts, from Turkish to Indian to Chinese. In Britain it has wavered in and out of fashion over the last three centuries, which makes a purely Rococo association with it somewhat tenuous, but it falls under the Rococo label because the taste for oriental decoration started in the late 17th century, and blossomed in England in the mid-18th century as the fashion for Rococo reached a climax. Exoticism also satisfied the mid-century desire for frivolity and variety.

While the chaste grandeur of Classicism was considered appropriate for church, town hall and mansion house, Gothick had emerged as a minor alternative, to be followed soon after by exoticism. With these three completely different architectural styles to choose from, or to mix together at will, there was an explosion of stylistic anarchy that reached a peak in the decade of the 1750s. Perhaps it was the very severity of Palladianism that encouraged Gothick and exotic tastes, for many fashions stimulate opposing elements as a counterbalance to excess. Gothick and exotic were certainly the foil or the light relief to Classical architecture.

While country gentlemen wanted noble plain façades for their houses, they also wanted sumptuous interiors, including a room or two in the Chinese taste. For their gardens, the same country

A watercolour of a copper tent designed by Louis-Jean Desprez in the park at Haga in Sweden, 1787. A royal park in Stockholm, Haga was laid out by F.M. Piper c. 1785; the copper tent was built for the corps de garde.

gentlemen desired not only Roman temples, as mini versions of the mansion, but also the richness that came with diversity. So pavilions in the garden could be austerely Classical, wildly rustic, elaborately Gothick or whimsically Chinese, all in the same landscape. Few people had the discipline to maintain strict Classicism when all around were having fun with ogee arches and chinoiserie.

What was it all about? The exotic Orient, stretching all the way from the eastern shores of the Mediterranean to Japan and China in the Pacific Ocean, had developed riches in architecture and design that fascinated Europeans. The Dutch had flirted with the idea of a Turkish tent from 1693, albeit a structure that no Turk would have recognised. The theme was resurrected in England at Painshill in Surrey, when Charles Hamilton commissioned a splendid Turkish tent in the late 1750s, and there were others later at Stourhead in Wiltshire, *such as Sultans take out when they go to war*,[10] thought Fanny Burney in 1773. Still extant is a very large tent of sheet metal on a wooden frame designed by Adelcrantz, and built in 1781 in the royal garden at Drottningholm, Sweden; two copper tents were put up at Haga, as well as a Turkish pavilion complete with a crescent finial. In France, Turkish tents could be found at Groussay and at the Désert de Retz.

Also influential were the mosques of Turkey, Arabia and India. Their domes and minarets were powerfully exotic, and versions were built in royal gardens, including Kew *c.* 1750, copied later at Steinfort in Germany and, on a much larger scale, at Schwetzingen in 1780, the latter by Nicolas de Pigage. Designs for mosques were included in some pattern books, for example by William Wrighte in his *Grotesque Architecture, or Rural Amusement*, and by Le Rouge in his *Détails des nouveaux jardins à la mode*. Although the religious and political symbolism of a mosque is not mentioned in contemporary writings, the threatening Ottoman Empire was too close for comfort to Vienna, a factor that may explain why built examples of mosques were very rare compared with the number of Chinese pavilions. This makes the surviving mosque at Schwetzingen, with its pink walls, its domes, its soaring minarets and great rectangular courtyard, all the more significant.

Hindu architecture was a curiosity rather than a major fashion. In terms of garden design, the Moguls had always followed geometric plans, so there was nothing dramatically new to learn from them, although their skill with water was greatly admired. However, there were some occasional examples of the Indian style, most notably the Indianhaus at Augustusburg, Brühl, North Rhine – Westphalia, built sometime between 1745 and 1750. It followed the typical German outline for a greenhouse, having a long single-storey façade with a large central pavilion and two more pavilions at either end, all three on two floors. The fenestration and the roof design made a confused gesture towards Indian decoration, hence the name, but the Indianhaus is now known only through a painting by F.J. Rousseau, as the building was later demolished. But mock Indian garden

The Moorish Temple in the Royal Botanic Gardens at Kew built in the 1750s by Sir William Chambers, and illustrated by Le Rouge in Détails des nouveaux jardins, *Cahier II, 1776. At this time, Kew was famous for its garden buildings but not for its plants, since the botanical collection was not started until 1759.*

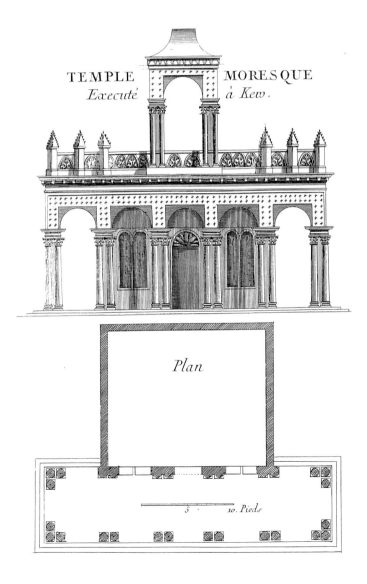

buildings were few and far between compared with the popularity of chinoiserie.

Chinese decoration and architecture were first discussed by Sir William Temple in an essay entitled 'Upon the Gardens of Epicurus', published in 1685. It was the irregularity of their gardens that most surprised the European mind, contrasting with the formal ground-plans that had been the ideal of beauty for so long. This irregularity was primarily a curiosity, but it may also have permeated the subconscious of those who were ready for change. From the 1720s onwards, in England, boredom with the status quo grew: twisting paths gradually crept into ground-plans, octagonal basins were extended into natural-looking lakes, and the landscape was moulded into banks and glades. Anything straight was banished. To complete the picture, trees were planted and a temple, column or pavilion was added in a focal spot. Thus evolved the landscape garden, nudged no doubt in its youthful phase by Chinese images.

These buildings were usually Classical in the first decades of landscape gardens in England, but then the Rococo urge for variety took hold, and buildings in the oriental taste also began to appear. Fascination with the Orient was widespread.

In searching for the source of inspiration for designs of Chinese pavilions, John Nieuhoff's detailed descriptions and superb engravings in *An Embassy from the East India Company of the United Provinces to the Grand Tartar Cham, Emperor of China* was the first and most informative. The visits took place in 1655 and 1663, and the account was published in the Netherlands, then in English in London, with a second edition in 1673. Nieuhoff's illustrations of buildings are exceedingly detailed, far more so than those published in 1735 by Jean-Baptiste du Halde in *Description géographique, historique, chronologique, politique et physique de l'Empire de la Chine*, the latter published in English in 1736 and 1741. An Italian priest, Matteo Ripa, made a series of 36 drawings of the Emperor's Gardens at the summer palace of Jehol, which, although they have never been published, circulated in London *c.* 1724. An account of the Emperor's Gardens in Peking, was published by Father Jean-Denis Attiret in Paris, later translated into English by Joseph Spence in 1752 under the title *A Particular Account of the Emperor of China's Gardens near Pekin*; it was attributed to 'Sir Harry Beaumont'. All these accounts fed the curiosity that was raging on both sides of the Channel.

What made chinoiserie so attractive? There was the obvious

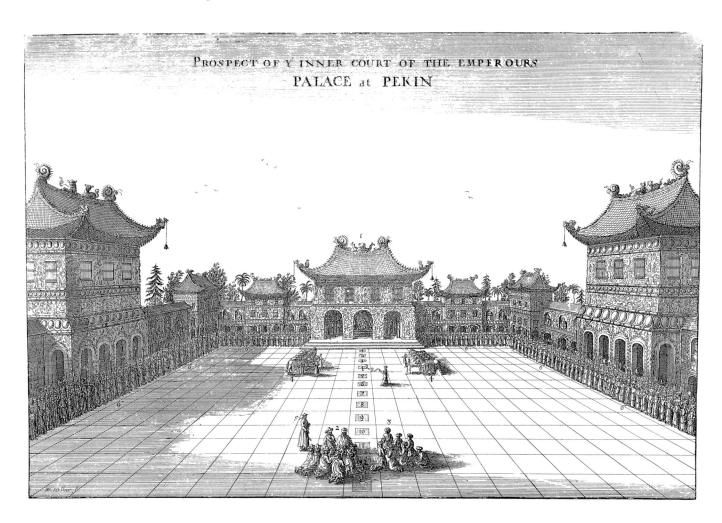

intellectual fascination with tales of a vast, distant Chinese Empire, its autocratic ruler and his magnificent Court, the customs, clothes and architecture. Then there were Chinese products to buy, such as lacquerware, porcelain, wallpaper, silks and spices.

Apart from books, lacquerware may also have been a prime source of ideas as it showed scenes from China of houses, gardens and the countryside. Porcelain made for the domestic market in China regularly depicted pavilions and pagodas in gardens but this domestic range was rarely exported to Europe. The great majority of items made for the export market in the early 18th century were blue and white and painted with flowers. Chinese porcelain is hard to date precisely, but it seems that the many items decorated with enchanting garden scenes did not reach Europe in any quantity until the 1750s, just when the frenzy for chinoiserie was at its height in England.

The fact that knowledge of Chinese architecture was hazy never stopped its growing popularity. Far from exact copies, European chinoiserie was often hopelessly inaccurate, and architects would mix European and Chinese styles with equanimity. But fretwork screens, bells, dragons, and the famous curling roofs were enough to satisfy the equally ignorant customer.

If the designs were far from authentic, at least construction methods were closer to the original. Nieuhoff had noted that *they use no stone for their buildings* and that *the walls are made last of all of clay or mortar*, the reason being that *the Chinese . . . build according to Man's life, and (as they say) onely for themselves and not for others; whereas we on the contrary build for future Ages*.[11] Chinese houses in Europe were usually built in timber and rendered, or the timber was covered with canvas; both finishes were painted in strong lacquer colours. They were clearly very fragile structures and needed constant maintenance, while some were made to be erected in summer and stored away in winter, like the pavilion now indoors at Boughton House, Northamptonshire. If neglected, they disintegrated, hence the disappearance of so many.

The first pavilion with an oriental name was the Pagodenburg of 1721 at Nymphenburg, followed by the Trèfle at Lunéville, Meurthe-et-Moselle, c. 1741, in an oriental spirit. In England, the Hon. Richard Bateman was an early pioneer of chinoiserie, and may have built the first Chinese bridges in the country at Grove House, Old Windsor, as well as other partly oriental structures, c. 1735. All have long gone, but were recorded by Thomas Robins in the 1750s and by earlier anonymous artists. Bateman's enthusiasm for the Orient is proved conclusively by his portrait painted in 1741, in which he wore Chinese robes with a Chinese pavilion in the background.

Stowe in Buckinghamshire has an early Chinese building of proven date, commissioned by Lord Cobham, cousin to Sir William Temple. It was in existence by 1738 and erected near the Elysian Fields on stilts over a formal lake according to Chinese custom. Rectangular in shape, the wooden structure had four lattice windows, and was approached over a small bridge. The exterior walls were painted, while the interior was decorated in the Chinese manner, a treatment commonly and curiously called 'japanning'. The designer is unknown.

Another early example was at Studley Royal in Yorkshire, completed by 1745, and the next example was probably Thomas Anson's Chinese House at Shugborough, Staffordshire, completed in 1747. It was probably the most authentic in its time, based as it was on the drawing of an actual building in Canton, and it has survived intact. A visitor in 1782 thought it *a true pattern of architecture of that nation, taken in the country by the true hand of Sir Piercy Brett: not a mongrel invention of British carpenters*.[12] The House of Confucius at Kew followed in 1749.

The Emperor's palace at Peking, illustrated by John Nieuhoff in An Embassy from the East India Company, *1673. This book must have been referred to by William Kent for his drawings of Chinese pavilions, as reproduced by John Dixon Hunt in* William Kent: Landscape Garden Designer, *1987, for Kent's rooflines are very similar, but he resisted adding the menagerie of animals along the ridge at the top.*

An illustration from Views at the Summer Palace at Jehol *by Matteo Ripa, c. 1724. (1955.2-12 01.) This series of copper engravings was never published at the time, for although they reveal the relationships between a Chinese house, its gardens and the landscape, the buildings themselves are far less decorated and exotic than those drawn by Nieuhoff, and may have been of insufficient interest to merit publication.*

There followed a rash of Chinese buildings in the 1750s. To put this explosion in its context, it should be borne in mind that there was a general building boom in England from about 1748, after the War of the Austrian Succession was concluded with the Treaty of Aix-la-Chapelle. The decade or so before 1748 had been lean for landowners, through war, taxes, disastrous harvests in 1740 and 1741, successive severe winters and low grain prices. After the Treaty, a reduction in taxes and interest rates and a rise in grain prices put money back in private pockets to the benefit of the building industry in general, and to country houses and their gardens in particular. Not even the Seven Years' War from 1756 to 1763 was able to dampen enthusiasm for improvements and new developments.

The Chinese taste was by then the height of fashion, having overtaken Gothick. *A few years ago every thing was Gothic; our houses, our beds, our book-cases, and our couches, were all copied from some parts or other of our old cathedrals . . . According to the present prevailing whim, everything is Chinese, or in the Chinese taste: or, as it is sometimes more modestly expressed, partly after the Chinese manner.* So wrote a contributor to *The World* in March 1753, and he continued . . . *every gate to a cow-yard is in T's and Z's, and every hovel for the cows has bells hanging at the corners.*[13]

Nowhere was there a larger collection of exotic buildings than in the royal gardens at Kew. There was a Turkish mosque and a Moorish temple, a House of Confucius and six more Chinese structures: a temple, a pavilion in the flower garden, another pavilion on a circular lake approached by a zigzag bridge, two more arched bridges and a pagoda. This concentration of buildings in one style in a small area was perhaps the most successful example of chinoiserie in England, although some of the Classical temples that were also packed into the gardens were sufficiently close to cause a clash of cultures. At any rate, Kew was extremely influential, both at home and abroad. The Kew pagoda, built by Chambers in 1757, indirectly inspired the building in 1775 of a stately, partly Classical pagoda at Chanteloup, Indre-et-Loire; and later, the five-storey *Chinesicher Turm* of 1789–90 in the Englischer Garten in Munich.

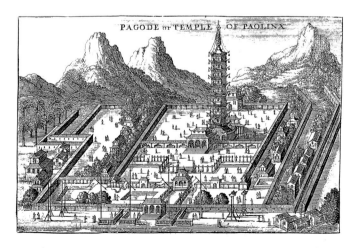

The design for the pagoda at Kew was finalised by Chambers in 1761. Once there were dragon finials at every corner, but these have not survived. Having visited China himself, Chambers was the foremost authority on its architecture, and also designed for Kew a temple, an aviary, a menagerie and a flower garden in the Chinese style.

The pagoda at Paolinx, from An Embassy from the East India Company, *Nieuhoff, 1673. One of several pagodas illustrated by Nieuhoff, this one is 10 storeys high and has bells suspended from ropes at every corner.*

An Umbrello'd Seat, *as shown by Charles*
Over in Ornamental Architecture, *1758.*
The circular bench has a pattern of Chinese
fretwork that was equally fashionable for
indoor furniture.

Chambers' elevation of a temple that he saw
in the middle of a small lake in Canton, from
Designs of Chinese Buildings, *1757.*

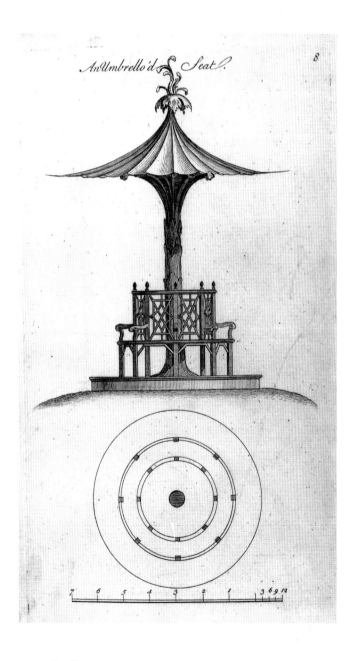

Pattern books of Chinese designs now started to appear. William Halfpenny produced *New Designs for Chinese Temples* in 1750, followed in 1752 by two books written with his son John, *Chinese and Gothic Architecture properly ornamented and Rural Architecture in the Chinese Taste*. The latter was reprinted in 1755 and included many whimsical designs. George Edwards and Matthew Darley offered *A New Book of Chinese Designs* in 1754. Other authors drew garden buildings in many different styles, including oriental, although not all were in favour of the new fashion. Robert Morris, a relation of the architect Roger Morris, published *The Architectural Remembrancer* in 1751. He thought the Chinese taste a *far fetch'd Fashion*, but felt obliged to include one example of a seat in the oriental taste. In a scathing postscript to his book he attacked chinoiserie:

> … *it consists in mere* Whim *and* Chimera, *without Rules or* Order, *it requires no Fertility of Genius to put in Execution; the Principals are a good choice of* Chains *and* Bells, *and different colours of* Paint. *As to the* Serpents, Dragons *and* Monkeys, *&c. they, like the rest of the Beauties, may be cut in Paper, and pasted on any where, or in any Manner: A few* Laths *nailed across each other, and made Black, Red, Blue, Yellow, or any other Colour, or mix'd with any Sort of Chequer Work, or Impropriety of Ornament, completes the whole.*[14]

For Morris, these were tawdry structures and he did not admire them nor want them to last, and his opinion would have been shared by other leading architects like James Paine and Robert Taylor. The contributor to *The World*, too, was ridiculing the slavish following of fashion rather than praising chinoiserie as an example of good taste. In fact, in the garden, it was considered in poor taste by others besides the leading architects. As early as 1748, William Gilpin, writing in *Dialogue upon the Gardens … at Stow*, expressed his disapproval through the words of an imaginary visitor to Stowe, who considered that the Chinese had *very little of true, manly Taste* and that *their ingenuity lies chiefly in the knick-knack way*.[15] Not surprisingly, the Chinese pavilion at Stowe was removed by 1751, leaving intact the purity of the classical Elysian Fields.

Despite criticism, the public was hungry enough for new designs to stimulate the publication in 1758 of *Ornamental Architecture in the Gothic, Chinese and Modern Taste* by Charles Over. Although this book contained the most elegant published versions of Rococo chinoiserie, it does not appear to have been reprinted.

In 1757, Sir William Chambers had published his *Designs of Chinese Buildings* in a bilingual English/French edition. Before training as an architect in Paris and Rome, Chambers had visited China twice in the early 1740s, which gave him an authority on its architecture unrivalled by others in his profession. Apart from the Chinese buildings at Kew, his commissions included a Chinese temple at Ansley Hall in Warwickshire in 1767, and another at Amesbury House in Wiltshire in 1772. His first book was followed in 1772 by *A Dissertation on Oriental Gardening*, which was published the same year in Paris and again in 1773, and appeared in German in 1775.

2

P. Fourdrinier Sculp.

In the Preface to *A Dissertation on Oriental Gardening*, Chambers also alludes to the low opinion of chinoiserie, admitting that several friends had advised against publication as the book *might hurt my reputation as an Architect*.[16] But, sounding slightly piqued, he considered it unreasonable to suggest that his career should be blighted purely by his knowledge of Chinese buildings, and carried on with publication. One of his designs was slightly adapted for the Drachenhaus or Dragon House at Sanssouci for Frederick the Great, and another was copied by the Prince de Croy at the Hermitage near Condé.

In this second book, Chambers summarised the principles of making a Chinese garden: *The usual method of distributing Gardens in China, is to contrive a great variety of scenes, to be seen from certain points of view; at which are placed seats or buildings, adapted to the different purposes of mental or sensual enjoyments. The perfection of their Gardens consists in the number and diversity of these scenes*.[17] Later, he continued: *The buildings are spacious, splendid and numerous; every scene being marked by one or more* [building]: *some of them contrived for banquets, balls, concerts, learned disputations, plays, rope-dancing and feats of activity; others again for bathing, swimming, reading, sleeping or meditation*.[18]

Unfortunately, Chambers embellished his 30-year-old memories with flights of fancy, and was immediately ridiculed by some critics in England for inaccuracy, but he was accepted on the Continent as a true authority. Part of his dissertation was reproduced again in Le Rouge's *Détails des nouveaux jardins à la mode*, which included not only Chambers' work, but also Attiret's description of the Emperor's garden in Peking and many illustrations of architectural Chinese gardens.

The Chinese taste was also taken up with enthusiasm in Europe. The Germans played with the components of chinoiserie from the 1750s onwards, and between 1781 and 1785 created a complete Chinese garden at Wilhelmshöhe in Hessen, and there are still Chinese bridges, steeply arched, at Schwetzingen and at Fürstenlager in Hessen. But first there was Sanssouci.

Perhaps the finest remaining example of chinoiserie is the Chinese Teahouse at Sanssouci at the royal palace of Potsdam in Germany. It was commissioned by Freidrich II, Frederick the Great, and built by J.G. Büring over three years from 1754. The Teehaus is a circular pavilion, with a sloping roof rising to a drum with a shallow dome, and topped by a figure shaded by a Chinese umbrella. Inside, from the frescoed ceiling, oriental ladies and gentleman and their pet monkeys look down over a balustrade to Rococo furniture and displays of Chinese porcelain. The overall effect is far more exotic than, for example, the Pagodenburg at Nymphenburg of 1719; it is still European Rococo chinoiserie, but under a much stronger Chinese spell.

In England, the passion for chinoiserie faded slowly, while in France, it began to take hold in the late 1760s. Instrumental in provoking the rise of French chinoiserie were Chambers' books, and later, the *cahiers* of Le Rouge. The scene was set for a flurry of ornamental buildings *à la chinoise* in the 1770s and 1780s.

The most noble and elaborate was the Maison Chinoise at the Désert de Retz, Yvelines, which was built in 1776 by the Baron de Monville. Also in the Chinese style, and illustrated by Le Rouge, were a pavilion at Romainville, two bridges at Bonnelles, kiosks at Chaville and Rambouillet amongst many others, as well as a plan for a pigeon house at Attichi. Other examples of chinoiserie were made famous by reputation, such as the kiosk at Chantilly, which was built as the centrepiece to a newly laid out labyrinth. At his estate at Thury-Harcourt near Caen, the Duc d'Harcourt, an amateur landscape gardener of great renown, made an informal Chinese garden with paths winding amongst exotic trees and spectacular rockwork.

As elsewhere, all too many of these delicate Chinese pavilions in France have perished, but a few have survived the centuries, such as the pagoda at Chanteloup, the kiosk in the Parc de Canon in Calvados, and the remarkable Pavillon Chinois at Cassan, Isle d'Adam, in the Val d'Oise. This was rescued from ruin in the early

VÛE DE LA MOSQUÉE DU, KIOSQUE, ET DU PALAIS CHINOIS.

1970s by the architect Olivier Choppin de Janvry (the saviour also of the Désert de Retz) nearly 200 years after its creation, having been built around 1788 for Pierre Jacques Bergeret, and possibly designed by Bergeret himself. It stands in a landscaped park on the edge of an irregular lake and, like pavilions in China, it doubles its impact through reflection.

Chinoiserie spread throughout Europe, from Queluz in Portugal to Drottningholm in Sweden to Fredriksberg in Denmark, as well as to Dunkeld House and Blair Castle in Perthshire, and Penicuik in Midlothian, the latter in Scotland. On the whole, however, the Scots did not succumb to chinoiserie; it seemed too frivolous, and too costly to maintain. Neither had it much success in Italy.

A view of the gardens at Steinfort, Westphalia, published by Le Rouge in Détails des nouveaux jardins, Cahier III, 1776. As at Kew, differing styles of architecture jostled together in close proximity.

The Chinese Teahouse at Sanssouci, designed by Büring and completed by 1757, is yet another whimsical interpretation of Chinese architecture, with much Rococo charm.

The Maison Chinoise, built in 1776 at the Désert
de Retz, as illustrated by Le Rouge in Détails
des nouveaux jardins in Cahier XIII, 1785,
the volume devoted entirely to the fabriques in this
famous garden.

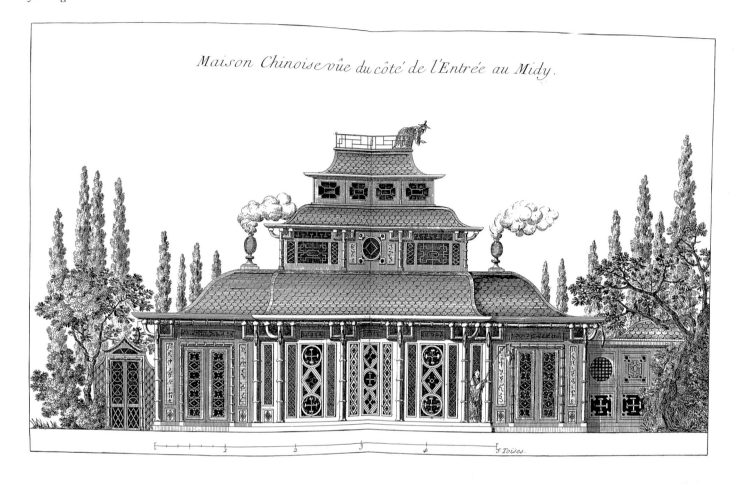

Maison Chinoise vûe du côté de l'Entrée au Midy.

VUË DU PAVILLON CHINOIS ET DE LA MAISON DU PHILOSOPHE A BONNELLES

Had chinoiserie been more robust or less expensive to keep up, it might have lasted longer as an essential element of every fashionable garden. But without regular maintenance, decay was inevitable, and as the process of decay is depressing to watch, so the Chinese pavilions and houses were dismantled.

Yet exoticism in its varying forms has never quite gone out of fashion, being revived from time to time during the 19th century in certain gardens in Europe. The Turkish tent stayed on the list of desirable attractions throughout the 19th century, and to this day advertisements on the streets of Paris are displayed on kiosks topped by Turkish onion domes.

An illustration from Nieuhoff, An Embassy from the East India Company, *1673, and a garden at Bonnelles as shown by Le Rouge in Cahier XII of* Détails des nouveaux jardins, *1784. The Chinese concept of garden design had a major impact in Europe, although, as usual with imported ideas, it was adapted and embellished to reflect European tastes.*

With the freedom to introduce sinuous forms in ground-plans and decoration, came a freedom to experiment with new ideas to please and entertain. Like the Gothick and Chinese tastes, this liberation is associated with Rococo but it lasted longer than the shells and scrolls, playful statues and asymmetrical trellis that are its obvious signs.

If the 18th century was the intellectual Age of Enlightenment, it was also the sensory Age of Amusement, for it abounds with jollity and fun. Pleasure in the garden was nothing new; think of the masques and fêtes of earlier days. But the quest for variety of amusement was an intrinsic part of the Rococo mood, and it combined with a sparkling brand of enthusiasm, an infectious *joie de vivre*. Seen from a viewpoint over two centuries later, these 18th-century pleasures stand out vividly, for the *fêtes galantes* of the French nobility reached peaks of elegance and perfection impossible to surpass; the pastimes of later generations seem dull by comparison.

There is a gaiety and wit in artists' views of Rococo garden scenes; there is also a sense of privacy not reflected in Baroque engravings, which always showed a throng of courtly ladies and gentlemen. Rococo entertainments were more informal, picnics in a trellis bower, intimate dinners with exquisite delicacies and ambrosial wine, and supper parties accompanied by string quartets. The weather was always idyllic, of course, in these pictures.

Leisure was one of the reasons for these lively pastimes, for the upper classes had plenty of it, as well as the desire to amuse themselves and their friends. There was time to plan and enjoy all manner of evening entertainments; as for the daytime, hunting and shooting were for the winter months, but for the summer, diversions were essential to while away the hours.

A boat in the form of a Chinese dragon, complete with oriental passengers, published by Over in Ornamental Architecture, *1758.*

Sailing boats and rowing boats had featured on many a canal or lake, from Buen Retiro in Madrid to Chantilly in France, and mock naval battles had been staged as court entertainments at Fontainebleau as far back as the 1560s. Louis XIV kept a flotilla of model battleships on the canal at Versailles for evening excursions, including one specially designed to accommodate the royal orchestra, and Dezallier d'Argenville had recommended gilt gondolas for canals in 1709. In 1716, Lady Mary Wortley Montagu had marvelled at *two fleets of little gilded vessels, that gave the representation of a naval fight*[19] in the garden of the Favorita in Vienna. Ships and battles seized the 18th-century imagination anew, and graced canals, basins and lakes across Europe. Boats were fun.

The Margravine of Bayreuth described the welcome she and her husband were given on their visit to Brandenburger in April 1732: *The garden, though not large, is pretty: it is bordered by a lake, in the middle of which there is an island where they have constructed a port, in which is seen a flotilla composed of yatchs [sic] and galleys, which have a beautiful appearance. They gave us a triple salute from the port and the vessels.*[20]

Boats were built in a variety of forms, as barges, sloops, cutters, frigates and Venetian gondolas, or like giant swans or Chinese dragons. The Duke of Cumberland had a 'Mandarin Yacht' of 50 tons on Virginia Water in Surrey, as well as a Chinese bridge and pavilion for it to sail past. In the spirit of the age, in 1750 Frederick, Prince of Wales, ordered a chinoiserie Venetian barge rowed by watermen in Chinese costume; this took him on the Thames from London to his palace at Kew in Surrey, where he could continue in Chinese mode by visiting the House of Confucius in his garden.

Of all those who used their gardens as a setting for entertainment, Sir Francis Dashwood probably had the most flamboyant imagination and sense of style. Not only was he the founder of the Dilettanti Society and the notorious Hell-Fire Club, and the builder of the first English version of the Temple of the Winds from Athens, he also set the scene for naval battles in his landscape garden at West Wycombe Park in Buckinghamshire. Here, on a small island, he erected a fort, the Citadel, and built a fleet of four vessels, including a 60-ton frigate, the *Snow*, manned by a professional sailor whose wages appeared regularly in the estate account books. Footmen and gardeners were press-ganged into making up the crew. A diary entry in 1754 by Thomas Phillibrown describes the fleet: *In ye Grand Canal [the lake] are various vessels, one of which is a Snow, Burthen about 60 Tun; it is completely rigg'd and carries several brass carriage guns which were taken out of a French Privateer and a sailor constantly is kept who lives aboard this snow to keep it in proper order.*[21]

The purpose was to stage mock battles, complete with booming cannons and clouds of smoke for authenticity, but realism went a little too far on one occasion when the Captain's blood was drawn: *We were told by ye sailor at one time a battery of guns in form of a fort was erected on ye side of ye canal in order to make a sham-fight between it and ye little fleet but in ye engagement a Capt. who commanded ye Snow comeing to near ye battery, received damage from ye wadding of a gun which occasioned him to spit blood and so put an end to ye battle.*[22]

As is often the case, a good idea spreads around a county. There were ships at Thoresby in Nottinghamshire and Exton Park in nearby Rutland. Another famous fleet in the vicinity was owned by William, 5th Lord Byron and great-uncle of the poet, at Newstead Abbey in Nottinghamshire. By the early 1770s, his navy totalled six vessels, including a 20-gun schooner that is said, incredibly, to have been transported overland on wheels from Hull, a distance of some 70 miles. What dedication to pleasure, regardless of cost! But before many battle seasons had passed, came financial disaster; the contents of Newstead Abbey had to be sold in 1778, and the estate, its lake and fleet were left to ruin.

The citadel at West Wycombe (941/26(47)), built to add authenticity to Sir Francis Dashwood's naval battles on the lake.

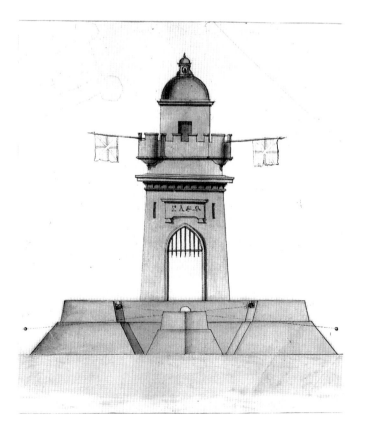

In the late 18th century, water and boats were the elements uniting a vast landscaped garden in Germany, a garden developed in five separate areas. A gondola ride along twisting canals and from lake to lake could quietly reveal the full beauty of an Arcadia bedecked with pavilions, temples, memorials and follies. This was the garden of Prince Franz of Anhalt-Dessau at Wörlitz, Halle, in eastern Germany, developed mainly in the last quarter of the century.

It was obviously more fun as well as more aesthetic to view the unfolding scenery from water; besides, the gondola could be moored in the most bizarre boathouse ever devised, a fake volcano. Known as Vesuv or the Stein, it was completed in 1794 and consists of a massive pile of boulders through which runs a maze of dark passages, leading up to a chamber with a large brazier. Once lit, and constantly stoked, the brazier would send flames and sparks and smoke through the rocky cone on the roof, supposedly just like Vesuvius. Even Sir Francis Dashwood might have envied Prince Franz his talent for dramatic effects.

Paris, too, had an erupting volcano in the Tivoli Gardens, and near Doorn in the Netherlands was a cottage disguised as one huge lump of volcanic rock. In Scotland, a modest replica volcano was made at Cockenhouse in Lothian, but this one was built to look extinct, with tufa simulating the flows of lava.

Naval battles and erupting volcanoes were games for men and boys, whereas swings and roundabouts were for the ladies. In Fragonard's paintings, enchanting *demoiselles* soar through the air on swings entwined with flowers, and in Richard Bateman's garden at Old Windsor, a swing was hung between the trees near a temple. Then there was the fashion for playing at the peasant life, pretending to be shepherdesses tending little lambs, or dairy maids in a beautifully appointed dairy, always, of course, in the most beguiling clothes. Many a cool, marbled dairy was built for ladies to pass the morning separating milk from cream, none more noble than that of Marie-Antoinette at Rambouillet, built by Thévenin in 1787.

These games ostensibly reflected the sophisticated yearning for the simple life, an attempt to recreate Arcadia. But doubtless they were fashionable for another reason, for a clever seamstress could make a dream of a peasant's frock. Dressing up was one of the best games, and the garden could provide the right backdrop for all sorts of different costumes, from pastoral to naval to exotic.

While the aristocracy were dressing up and firing cannons in the privacy of their large estates, the citizens of the capital cities were enjoying the use of royal gardens, such as the Tuileries in Paris, St James's Park in London, and Buen Retiro in Madrid, and, later, public parks like the Prato della Valle in Padua. It was a case of promenading, seeing others and being seen, rather than playing games that relied on expensive equipment, and these public gardens played an important role in the life of the big cities. Some were temporary yet extremely elaborate, like the annual fairs in Paris. A visitor to *la foire de Saint-Laurent* in 1784 described how it was

CHAUMIERE A RAMB[...]

près des deux grands Hetre[...]

PROJET D'UN HERMITAGE A RAMBOUILLET

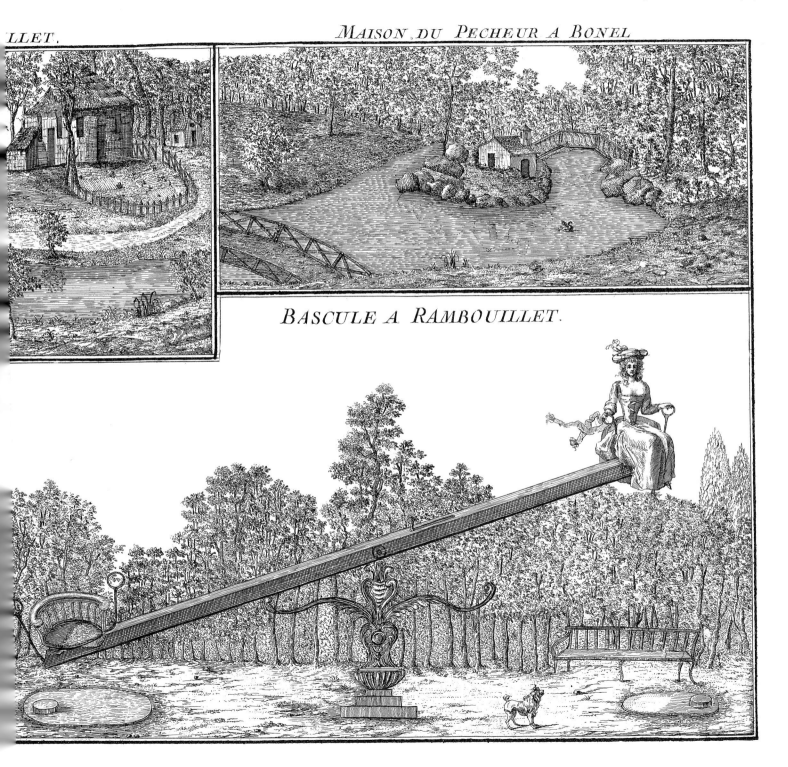

A lady enjoying the pleasures of a see-saw, but one whose airborne position, in the absence of a partner, requires the suspension of disbelief. Perhaps the pug below has frightened her into an advanced state of levitation. Illustration by Le Rouge from Détails des nouveaux jardins, Cahier XI, 1784.

MAISON DU PECHEUR A BONEL

BASCULE A RAMBOUILLET.

decorated as a garden in the Chinese style with amusements ranging from music and dancing to shooting, while another public pleasure garden, the Clos St Lazare, offered dancing and fireworks. In the 18th century, Londoners had two public pleasure gardens to choose from, Ranelagh Gardens and Vauxhall Gardens; the latter, on the south bank of the Thames, became the playground of high society.

Always a commercial venture, Vauxhall Gardens were taken over in 1728 by a new owner who, over the years, spent lavishly on their attractions. A statue of Handel by Roubiliac, a Turkish tent, supper booths in the Gothick or Chinese taste, a bandstand with an organ, walled walks hung with paintings, all were lit by myriad lights, while folk songs or the music of Handel drifted across the gardens in the night air. Frederick, Prince of Wales, was the patron, and the nobility, gentry and middle classes, writers, journalists, politicians, families and friends, thronged through the gates every evening in the summer. In 1739, on evenings when there was a concert, a thousand or more would each pay a shilling for the pleasures within.

The garden in question is the first which had ever been fitted up for this kind of entertainment,[23] wrote Count Kielmansegge, who had come over to London for George III's coronation in 1761. The fame of the gardens was such that, although they were closed for the winter, he was keen enough to arrange a visit. *The garden must be a wonderful sight when the greater part of it is lighted up with nearly 1500 glass lamps*, and he was particularly taken with a clever trick of illusion:

At one end of an avenue, when a curtain is withdrawn, a landscape is to be seen illuminated by hidden lamps, the principal feature being a miller's house, with an artificial cascade. You fancy that you see water driving the mill, and that you hear the rush of the water, though in reality there is none. It is managed just as these things are arranged in theatres and pantomimes, but though it never lasts long, it is supposed to be far better and more cleverly done.[24]

George-Louis Le Rouge enjoyed its many delights in the summer of 1763, and described the two vast paintings by Hayman of British victories at sea and in Canada. He found the gardens *le plus brillant de toute l'Europe*.[25]

Humour was still part of the general garden scene, now expressed in various forms. The old water jokes that had been present in gardens for centuries were still on the accepted list for grottoes, but generally humour became more visual, more subtle, or more absurd. As far as statuary was concerned, heroism was out and humour was in; parodies of real people were much more amusing than Greek or Roman gods. At Weikersheim in Baden-Würtemburg there is an excellent collection of statues representing members of the Court, not pompous figures but gently teasing caricatures. At Queluz near Lisbon, there are enchanting comic monkeys.

Two of the most entertaining garden buildings of the period are the asymmetrical Red House at Painswick in Gloucestershire, already described, and the erotically symbolic Temple of Venus at West Wycombe in Buckinghamshire, where elements of the design are associated with female anatomy. The latter has recently been lovingly restored by the present Sir Francis Dashwood. Both were amusing and fanciful, and as far from pedantic functionalism as imagination could remove them. Since imagination and wit were an intrinsic part of 18th-century life, and since gardens played an important role in social life, it is not surprising that they were handsomely, exotically and amusingly embellished.

The Flyin

One of the members of the court at Weikersheim, depicted as a dwarf. There are 15 others in this humorous series of caricatures, probably the work of Johann Jakob Sommer and his sons.

The Flying Mountains, a perilous big dipper in Catherine the Great's garden at Tsarskoe Selo, as illustrated in Gaudia Poetica by Calvert, 1769. Other gardens had variations on this theme: at Marly there was the Roulette, a royal roller-coaster built for Louis XIV and furnished with gilded cars, and later in the Jardin Baujon a vast circular aerial track was built to thrill Parisians.

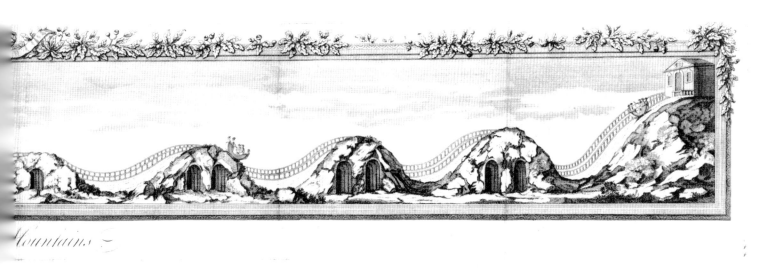

Mountains

VILLA DELIZIOSA DEL SIG.ᵈ D PIETRO VALGUARNERA, E GRAVINA PRINCIPE DI VALGUARNERA, CONTE DI ASSORO &c.
NELLA CAMPAGNA DI PALERMO DETTA VOLGARMENTE DELLA BAGARIA.

I. Strada publica con varie case attinenti
   a detta Villa.
2. Primo Stradone adorno di Statue, Cavalli,
   ed altri ornamenti a Padiglione.
3. Padiglione da Villa.
4. Secondo Stradone.
5. VESTIBOLO, o sia Ingresso al Cortile.

6. Cortile.
7. Palazzo della Villa.
8. Perterra ornato da Vasi di fiori
   e da varie Fonti.
9. Flore adorne di alcune Statue,
   e Fontane.
10. Teatro Scenico.

11. Peschiera.
12. Montagnuola con Barcam.
13. Giardino.
14. Casinetta, che va nominata
    il BUON RITIRO.
15. Gran Fonte presso la stessa.
16. Laberinto d'acqua.

17. Macchine per ascender l'acque.
18. Vedura in parte del resto di Campa-
    gna, che termina al Mare.

Joa.Ant.Bova Sculp

Continental Variations

While Rococo flourished in France for many decades, it also appealed to the Italian taste. Giovanni Ruggeri, a Roman architect, played with the plasticity of scrolls and asymmetry and added a dash of his own inventions. He designed the castle gardens at Brignano d'Adda, now Castello Visconti, including octagonal towers with elaborate, delicate and original ornamentation, which were illustrated by Marc'Antonio dal Re in *Ville di delizia* in 1743.

Dal Re's book is a prime source of information about Italian Rococo gardens, and has detailed bird's-eye views of many that are no longer intact, among them the very intricate gardens of Villa Belgioso at Merate. These were walled and terraced on six levels, and had a different design in each of the five parterres, all fastidiously drawn by dal Re. The entrance gates, a complex and original pattern of piers, statues and wrought iron gates, still herald the refinements that once lay behind them.

The illustrations of these Italian gardens are tantalising, since, bar a few fragments, they are all that is left. Some were never finished, some were neglected, and some were soon demolished when fashions changed.

Where Baroque architecture had attained amazing heights of grandeur and elaboration, as in Germany and Austria with Fischer von Erlach and Pöppelmann, Rococo enjoyed the greatest success. The finest Rococo garden in Germany is at Schwetzingen, in Baden-Würtemburg, the summer residence of the Palatine Elector Carl Theodor. The main parterre in front of the schloss, called the French Garden, is an immense circle, outlined on the side nearest the schloss by a line of curving linked pavilions, known as the Circle Houses, and on the far side by a high pergola in trellis, cut in two to maintain the wide vista.

This circular shape, an echo of Lustheim near Munich, was the result of collaboration between two architects, Alessandro Galli da Bibiena and Nicolas de Pigage, and the court gardener, J. Ludwig Petri. It was laid out in 1753, perhaps a consequence of the Rococo emphasis on curves, when architects and designers would do anything to disguise a straight line. The gardens continue westwards beyond this circle, French in spirit, with a wide view between hedged bosquets towards a once-rectangular lake.

There are other delightful Rococo features in Schwetzingen, such as the waterspouting birds, the curious trellis-worked optical illusion called *The End of the World* and the wriggling streams that lead to the bird bath. There is also the Badenburg by Pigage, a charming bath house whose interior is a triumph of design. All these were created mainly in the 1760s and reflect the extraordinary inventive abilities of German Rococo, which soared to peaks never reached in other countries in Europe.

The Villa Deliziosa, property of the Prince of Valguarnera in Sicily, as illustrated by Leanti in Lo Stato presente della Sicilia, *1761. Like the* Jardin du Tillet *on p.161, it reflects the struggle against conformity in the efforts to alleviate the tedium of a straight approach.*

One of the wriggling streams, rather like a tadpole, that lead to the bird bath in the gardens at Schwetzingen.

Veitshöchheim is another Rococo garden that has remained largely undisturbed by the changes in taste in succeeding centuries. It was laid out by J. Prokop Mayer from 1763 for the Prince Bishop of Würzburg. The house is at one end of the vast rectangular gardens, and looks not down the length but across the breadth of the gardens, a situation quite common in Germany. The rest of the gardens are divided into three lengthwise sections, with the focal point, a vast ornamental lake, the Grosser See, dominating the widest of the three. The lake is edged in stone with a curving outline, and this shape is articulated further by a beech hedge surrounding it that follows a much more complex line of curves and counter curves. An 18th-century version of a Mount Parnassus graces the centre of the lake, a more delicate and tranquil composition than those of the early 1600s. It was carved by Ferdinand Tietz (or Dietz) in 1765–6.

One of the garden's narrower sections has more beech hedging, an ideal background for an enchanting collection of Rococo statues that have a remarkable quality of movement. The sculptures, by Tietz, Johann Wolfgang van der Auvera, and Johann Peter Wagner once totalled about 300, and enough remain to reflect the taste of the era. In the third and narrowest bosquet section, a pair of pavilions, fancifully oriental, nestle in deep shade near two green rooms.

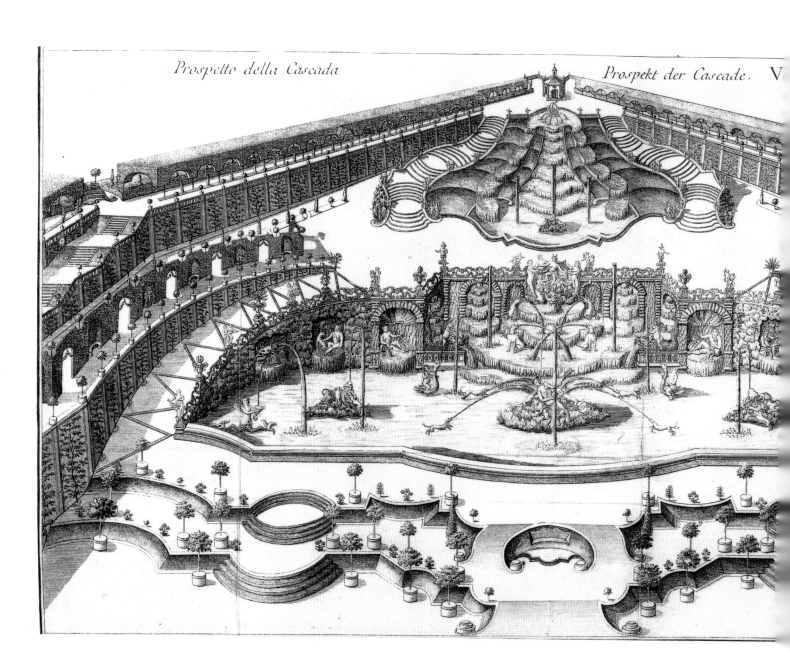

Prospetto della Cascada   *Prospekt der Cascade.* V

One of many dashing figures in the Rococo
garden of Veitshöchheim near Wurzburg.

This plan for the Hofgarten at Wurzburg is
pure Rococo in its flowing pattern of concave and
convex curves. Designed by J. Prokop Mayer in
1774, it was included by Le Rouge in Détails des
nouveaux jardins, Cahier XI, 1784.

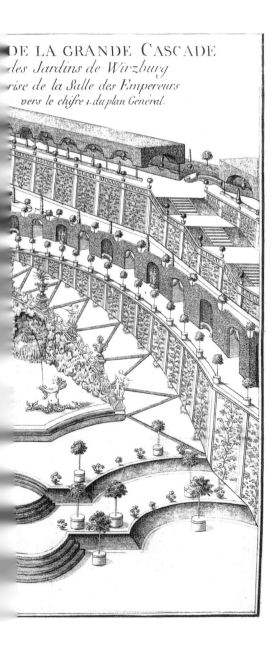

DE LA GRANDE CASCADE
des Jardins de Wirzburg
rise de la Salle des Empereurs
vers le chiffre 1.du plan Général.

But that is not all. There is an open-air theatre, a feature more popular in German and Italian gardens than elsewhere, the ruins of a cascade (damaged in the Second World War), and a grotto house made of rockwork. Completed in 1773, this was the work of Johann Philipp Geigel and Materno Bossi. Protected in little alcoves is a humorous display of animals made of shells, a monkey, a rabbit, a lion, a heron, and inside, a golden dragon. On top, there is a belvedere, a look-out with a view over the gardens and the surrounding countryside, built on the perimeter following Dezallier d' Argenville's advice.

The grotto house at Veitshöchheim was completed by 1773. It is an unusual composition of rockwork with an endearing collection of animals.

A view through a pavilion and a trellis window, one of many special features at Veitshöchheim.

Part of the reason for this Rococo profusion in the German states was thanks to creative talent combined with financial resources, both stimulated by the works of a remarkable family of artistic patrons, Frederick the Great of Prussia and his Hohenzollern siblings, Prince Henry of Prussia, the Margravine of Bayreuth and Queen Louisa Ulrika of Sweden. All four had a passion for building and lavished their aesthetic talents on palaces and gardens at the height of the Rococo age, their talents perhaps sharpened by competition with each other. The results are a delightful series of Rococo gardens of the middle of the 18th century. Frederick's Sanssouci, all laid out to formal plans, has not only the glorious chinoiserie Teehaus of the mid-1750s, the Drachenhaus and a windmill, but also the famous parabolic terraced vineyard built in 1744. The walls ripple along each of the six terraces, facing south and below the summer schloss built for Frederick by Knobelsdorf, the Court architect; schloss and vineyard together make a splendid Rococo composition. There is also the Classical Obelisk Portal of 1747, and the Baroque Neptune Grotto, 1751–7, both by Knobelsdorf.

While Frederick was improving Sanssouci, his elder sister Wilhelmina, Margravine of Bayreuth, was working on the Eremitage near Bayreuth, an 18th-century version of Arcadia of which Alberti would have approved. Schloss and garden were started by the previous Margrave in 1715, and continuously enhanced by Wilhelmina from 1736. She added all manner of attractions, such as a Ruined Theatre. Copied from drawings of ancient Rome and consecrated to the Muses, it was built for open-air opera.

A tinted copper engraving by Johann David Schleuen the Younger, showing the palace of Sanssouci and its parabolic terraces in 1748.

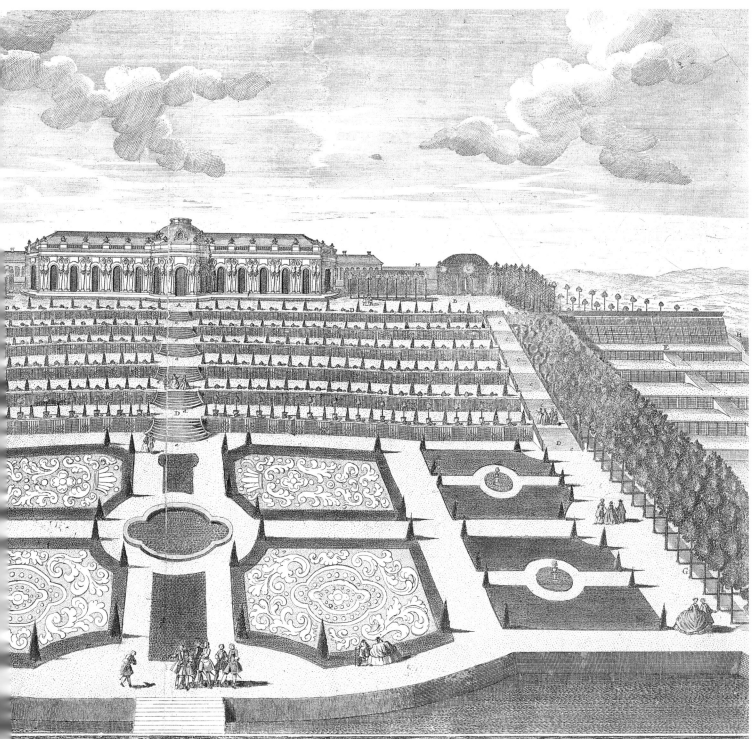

en Lust-Schlosses Sans Souci bei Potsdam.

D. der durch die Kunst sehr magnifique angeordnete Weinberg, bestehet aus 6 Absätzen oder Gängen, zu welchen man in der mitten vermittelst der Stiegen, und an beiden Enden auf denen von Erde gemachten Erholungs Runde, auf und absteiget. Diese Absätze sind mit Mauren eingefasst

The Neues Schloss or New Castle at the Eremitage at Bayreuth was built for the Margravine by Joseph Saint-Pierre and Karl Philipp Christian Gontard, and completed by 1753. An imposing structure, it was an aviary and a greenhouse for orange trees.

The Eremitage was to Wilhelmina what the Petit Trianon was to Madame de Pompadour, a place of escape and retreat from the Court. It was partly for solitude; guests were encouraged to spend part of the day reading or writing in a hermit's cell, and the Margravine would spend her time planning the next developments in the garden, painting the Chinese room in her apartments, composing music or corresponding with her brother. But the so-called hermits forsook their cells in the evening to wine, dine and talk together, in the company of the intellectual Margravine. The garden and its buildings were vital to this literary circle, which Voltaire joined for a while when he visited Bayreuth in 1743, writing to Maupertius in October of that year: *Baireith est une retraite délicieuse où l'on jouit de tout ce qu'une cour a d'agréable sans les incommodités de la grandeur.*[26] Wilhelmina died in 1758, and the gardens were later altered by the removal of the old straight walks and the introduction of serpentine paths, but they retain still the spirit of the Rococo era.

Then there was Drottningholm, the Queen of Sweden's private palace, which she maintained from her own income. In 1753, when Frederick was perhaps thinking of building the Teehaus at Sanssouci, King Adolf Fredrik presented his Queen with an

original birthday present, a Chinese pavilion. For the presentation ceremony, the royal guard were dressed up as Chinese soldiers and taught to march in a supposed Chinese manner; the seven-year-old Crown Prince was disguised as a mandarin and presented his mother with the key on a velvet cushion. According to an eyewitness, the Queen was delighted and deeply grateful, but not exactly surprised, as it was probably her own idea in the first place.

The pavilion was clearly very fragile, for within 10 years it had disintegrated, only to be replaced in 1763 by a new Chinese pavilion designed by Carl Fredrik Adelcrantz. The exterior of the new building is basically European with a nod and a wink at chinoiserie, mainly in the wavy roof line. An Englishman, Nathaniel Wraxall, who saw it on his travels between 1769 and 1772, wrote that it merited *the attention of a traveller above anything in the kingdom*.[27] Named Kina, the pavilion's fame resulted in further exotic buildings in Sweden, including the Chinese pavilions at Värnanäs and Haga.

Another Hohenzollern sibling was Prince Henry of Prussia, Frederick's commander of the army, a dandy and a Francophile. He acquired Rheinsberg, near Potsdam, from Frederick in 1744 and continued to improve it with a variety of garden attractions during the rest of the century. Soon after his sister the Queen of Sweden had commissioned her second Chinese pavilion, Henry built his own version, partly modelled on the earlier Trèfle at Lunéville. He also planted a hedge theatre to rival Wilhelmina's Ruined Theatre at Bayreuth, built hermitages of pine trunks with thatched roofs, made a grotto decorated with mother-of-pearl, shells, coral and feldspar, and constructed a gothic lighthouse. Near the older Rococo parterre, he landscaped a lake, for which the Queen presented him with sumptuously-carved gondolas. In the Classical style, he built an obelisk, the Temple of Friendship, and had mock Greek ruins made out of wood. Finally, he built his mausoleum in the form of an Egyptian pyramid.

Wilhelmina added many features to the Eremitage, including the Untere Grotte, or Lower Grotto, the work of Jospeh Saint-Pierre, which was in existence by 1745. Built to resemble an ancient ruin, it has sculpture in the basin and a total of 25 fountains to spray both statues and water.

In Spain, Rococo made no serious impression on the native version of Baroque, but there is a rare glimpse of it in the Baroque garden of La Granja de San Ildefonso. For much of the 18th century, the emphasis in Spain was on church architecture, and little attention was paid to creating important gardens; an exception was in the province of Galicia in the north-west, where several new houses and gardens were built, including the Baroque terraced gardens of Pazo de Mariñan, and the Pazo de Oca near Santiago de Compostela.

In the garden of the Pazo de Oca is a terracotta-roofed mill house beside two rectangular stone-edged reservoirs. What gives the Pazo de Oca a burst of Rococo is the superb stone boat that floats on the second lake. It is a piece of fantasy that transforms the practical layout of the garden, with its working mill, reservoirs for irrigation, kitchen garden and orchards, into an idyllic place. Around the edge of the reservoir, balls and stubby obelisks in granite take the place of holly and yew, and mature trees overhang it, shading it in summer. From the reservoirs, stone drainage channels transport water around the gardens to keep them fresh.

The gardens of the Pazo de Oca have a magical atmosphere. They date from the middle of the 18th century, probably after the remarkable manor house was completed in 1746. Late in the 19th century, camellias, magnolias and other flowering trees were planted, and have now reached magnificent proportions in this damp and gentle climate.

By contrast with Spain, the architectural history of Portugal in the 18th century abounds with new buildings, religious and secular, and with new gardens. Resources to fund this creativity came from Brazilian gold, imports of which boosted the Portuguese economy massively, reaching a peak in the 1740s. As in the Manueline building boom in the early 1500s, an extra dimension of exuberance

and movement enriches Portuguese decoration. The royal palace-monastery at Mafra near Lisbon is the greatest monument of this period, but it was designed in the mainstream Baroque tradition, and a garden to complement its massive scale was never created. Other gardens in the first half of the 18th century included the bishop's palace at Castelo Branco, the Quinta de Nossa Senhora do Carmo near Estremoz, and the Quinta da Palmeira north of Braga, all following Baroque taste.

The development of a singularly Portuguese Rococo style centred around the northern city of Oporto. The movement was led by Niccolo Nasoni, an Italian by birth, who arrived in Portugal in 1725. Nasoni introduced to northern Portugal the fashion for Italian gardens, already established in the south, with terraces, statues, fountains and belvederes, while in architecture he experimented with asymmetrical ornamentation and Rococo curls and he was

The stone boat at the Pazo de Oca in Galicia. At the bow, a lookout watches for potential dangers, while a sailor catches a fish at the stern. There are cannons to repel enemies on either side of the deck, but they fail to alarm the ducks swimming around on the reservoir.

A 19th-century engraving of Queluz, looking towards the palace through the Portico of Fame to the Garden of Neptune. The pair of sphinxes are behind the equestrian statues of either side.

Jardim, e parte do palacio real de Queluz.

One of many statues of pairs of children that
*adorn balustrades at Queluz. In the background
is the pink façade of the palace.*

commissioned to design country houses at Freixos, Chantre and
Prelada around Oporto. Encouraged by the availability of high-
quality local granite, he and his contemporaries enhanced their
gardens with ornamental stonework and sculpture, as at the Solar de
Mateus and the Casa dos Biscainhos in Braga.

The greatest remaining Rococo garden in western Europe is at the
Palace of Queluz between Lisbon and Sintra. Having decided to
turn an old hunting lodge into a royal summer residence, the Infante,
the future Dom Pedro III, engaged Mateus Vicente de Oliveira as
architect and work started in 1746 in the Rococo spirit. Queluz was
to be the Portuguese equivalent of Louis XIV's Marly, though
happily not in terms of cost. A Dutchman was engaged as
head gardener, and the King's chief engineer was responsible for
organising the water supply for house and gardens.

By 1756, a Frenchman was employed by the Prince at Queluz, not
only to make plated ware in gold and silver but also to draft plans and
to handle the design of the gardens. Little is known about Robillon,
other than that he worked for Thomas Germain, the eminent
Parisian silversmith, and was usually described in France as a
sculptor. Like Daniel Marot, he could turn his eye and his hand
to any aspect of design, both interior and exterior. His ground-plan
is more extensive than that in most Portuguese gardens, showing
French rather than Italian inspiration, but it is a post-Le Nôtre
plan, not majestic, not dominating the countryside but settling
comfortably into it.

A bosquet beyond the parterre had a complex plan of intersect-
ing walks, defined by plantations of lime trees, chestnuts and elms
imported from the Netherlands in 1755 and 1756. On the main axis
through the bosquet, the vista is not open to the countryside beyond
but closed by a huge vertical cascade of rockwork, built in 1772 or
thereafter, reminiscent of the way in which German vistas were
terminated by a greenhouse.

Adjoining the palace are two formal parterres, designed by
Robillon as a setting for Court receptions as well as for private enjoyment. The larger is the Garden of Neptune, named after one of its
principal fountains. This garden once had a Rococo arabesque
parterre, later replaced with a geometric design in box. The statues
and fountains were in place by 1763 and all are enclosed within a
stone balustrade decorated with statues and urns. Next to it is the
Rococo Garden of Malta, a smaller, sunk parterre approached down
a continuous descent of five steps that ripple around the rectangular
garden. In the centre is a fountain of boys with a dolphin, set in a
circular pool the perimeter of which is ruffled with concave and
convex curves.

Among the greatest treasures of Queluz are the countless statues
and fountains carved from stone still crisply detailed while ageing
graciously with a mottled dusting of lichen. The collection is full of
Rococo wit and elegance, ranging from a pair of sphinxes under
feathered headdresses, impish monkeys, guardian hound dogs,

playful children, and, at the Portico of Fame, prancing horses with bugle-blowing cavaliers on enormous plinths, that mark the boundary between the formal garden and the woodland park. Robillon designed the main centrepieces in the gardens, such as the Fountains of Neptune, the Nereid, the Medaillons and also many of the smaller shell-shaped basins. *The swirling outlines of these shallow basins seem to resemble a silver salver by Germain that has been tossed on to the ground*, wrote Angela Delaforce in *Palace of Queluz: the Gardens*.[28]

While the fountains were to Robillon's designs, the sculpture was all imported and listed in an inventory of 1763. From Italy came the boys and dolphins of the Garden of Malta, the statues on the balustrade around the Garden of Neptune, a collection of animals, including the guardian hound, and stone vases and urns. Other Italian figures were added to Robillon's shell basins.

From England came quantities of lead figures from John Cheere's famous workshop at Hyde Park Corner in London. A total of 223 were ordered in 1755 and 1756, and many still adorn the garden. In the same liberal manner with which he added Italian statues to his own designs for basins, so too did Robillon complete his fountains with Cheere's sculptures, incorporating them into the Fountain of

the Nereid, and surrounding the Fountain of Neptune with six statues in lead. Others, like Mars, Minerva and a *Samson slaying a Philistine* copied by Cheere from Giambologna, were placed at strategic places on Rococo stone pedestals.

Unlike great Baroque gardens, there is no single iconographical programme for the statuary at Queluz; the subjects were chosen for aesthetic value rather than mythical association or moral content. And in this they are also Rococo for the love of variety allowed endless freedom of choice. The statues were rearranged after 1763 in order to emphasise certain subjects, but they still encompass gods of mythology, biblical heroes, pastoral characters and mischievous animals.

A shallow basin designed by Robillon for Queluz.

Theatrical and operatic performances were a frequent part of court entertainment at Queluz, and many visitors mention music in their descriptions. Robillon's design for the Stairway of the Lions seems theatrically inspired, like a magnificent stage-set, while underneath he placed cages for wild animals. Exotic birds in aviaries were another entertaining attraction.

Queluz succumbed, too, to the fashion for chinoiserie. A wooden gateway with the outline of a pagoda was made for the Botanic Garden established in 1769 near the cascade. By 1772, a Chinese pavilion had been built there too. But this was following a tradition well established elsewhere in Europe, whereas one other feature at Queluz, the canal, was, and is, totally novel.

The canal predates the bosquet and the parterres, and was made by rerouting the River Jamor into the Lago Grande, a canal 115 metres long. For much of the time, the river trickled along the stone bed, but when the sluice gates at the lower end were closed, the canal filled with water over a metre deep. The sides of the canal above the water level and the steps leading down to it were exquisitely decorated in 1755 with blue-and-white tiles by João Nunes. Polychrome ceramic tiles also decorate the outer walls, the benches and the structure of the bridge that crosses the canal. This bridge once supported a wooden music pavilion, the Casa da Música, attributed to Mateus Vicente and begun in 1760. On each side overlooking the canal it had three French windows, through which music could drift over idle, waterborne courtiers.

The concept of the canal is spellbinding. What could be more idyllic than gliding slowly in a gondola through a panorama of Arcadia on a summer evening, soothed by sarabands and minuets? Perhaps one day the canal will be filled with water again and its music pavilion rebuilt. Apart from those areas closest to the palace, much of the gardens of Queluz, including the Lago Grande, would benefit from restoration.

The Lago Grande, now empty of water, but once the scene of boating parties when an orchestra played on a pavilion on the bridge. The walls were decorated with tiles by João Nunes with scenes from an idyllic Arcadian landscape.

The final words on Queluz must rest with William Beckford, the eccentric young Englishman who visited the royal gardens in the summer of 1787. Beckford recorded his travels in the Netherlands, Germany, Italy, Spain and Portugal in diaries, but he was chiefly interested in people, and gardens receive scant attention on the whole. Some, such as Aranjuez and Nymphenburg, were described scathingly, but his description of Queluz suggests that the dreamlike atmosphere bewitched him. *The evening was now drawing towards its final close, and the groves, pavilions and aviaries sinking apace into shadow: a few wandering lights sparkled amongst the more distant thickets, – fire-flies perhaps – perhaps meteors; but they did not disturb the reveries in which I was wholly absorbed.*

Hopeful of an introduction to the Infanta Dona Carlota Joaquina, he lingered on.

This night I began to perceive, from a bustle of preparation already visible in the distance, that a mysterious kind of fête was going forwards; and whatever may have been the leading cause, the effect promised at least to be highly pleasing. Cascades and fountains were in full play; a thousand sportive jets d'eau were sprinkling the rich masses of bay and citron, and drawing forth all their odours, as well-taught water is certain to do upon all such occasions. Amongst the thickets, some of which received a tender light from tapers placed low on the ground under frosted glasses, the Infanta's nymph-like attendants, all thinly clad after the example of her royal and nimble self, were glancing to and fro, visible one instant, invisible the next, laughing and talking all the while with very musical silvertoned voices.[29]

Such were the pleasures for which these gardens were created.

One of many scenes by João Nunes on the tiled walls of the Lago Grande.

Conclusion

The fashion for Rococo first ebbed away in England. In 1757, a poet called Robert Lloyd lampooned the current taste, or rather lack of it, in *The Cit's Country Box*. This is an account of the imaginary Citizen Thrifty of London who made a fortune and decided to buy a house in the country. Having fitted up the interior with the right furnishings and books, the owner turns to the garden:

> *Now bricklay'rs, carpenters, and joiners*
> *With Chinese artists, and designers,*
> *Produce this scheme of alteration,*
> *To work this wond'rous reformation.*
> *The useful dome, whose secret stood,*
> *Embosom'd in the yew-tree's wood,*
> *The traveller with amazement sees*
> *A temple, Gothic or Chinese,*
> *With many a bell or tawdry rag on,*
> *And crested with a sprawling dragon;*
> *A wooden arch is bent astride*
> *A ditch of water, four foot wide,*
> *With angles, curves and zigzag lines,*
> *From Halfpenny's exact designs.*
> *In front, a level lawn is seen,*
> *Without a shrub upon the green,*
> *Where Taste would want its first great law,*
> *But for the skulking, sly ha-ha,*
> *By whose miraculous assistance*
> *You gain a prospect two fields distance.*
> *And now from Hyde Park Corner come*
> *The Gods of Athens and of Rome.*
> *Here squabby Cupids take their places,*
> *With Venus, and the clumsy Graces:*
> *Apollo there, with aim so clever,*
> *Stretches his leaden bow for ever,*
> *And there, without the power to fly,*
> *Stands fix'd a tip-toe Mercury.*

The mixture of styles and ideas was ridiculed; its adherents might call Rococo an amusing little pot-pourri but its detractors were more numerous and thought it a nightmare of bad taste.

For most of the 18th century, Rococo was in competition with Palladianism, then with the Greek Revival movement that started about 1760, and finally with Neoclassicism and Romanticism. It was no match for these superior styles, and so it dwindled slowly away throughout Europe. The only thread that runs through to the next era of design is the touch of romance, but whereas Rococo romance is the ultimate in prettiness, Romanticism has a brooding and dramatic quality that adds depth to its picturesque scenes. Frivolous and disparate, intimate and exotic, Rococo may be derided, but there is still the hint of a smile on the face of the sphinx at Queluz.

What of these gardens? Were they Arcady? In varying degrees, and through changing fashions, they fulfilled the desire for an idyllic outdoor setting for the pleasures of rest, study, music and entertainment. During these 300 or so years, the setting evolved, just as social requirements and the vision of perfection evolved, for each age had its own Arcadia. Some were profoundly architectural, others gave nature a chance to display its finery, albeit under firm control, while others yet were devoted to the amusement of man. But had the ancient Arcadian shepherds strayed through the gates of the Sacro Bosco of Bomarzo or Hampton Court Palace, they surely would have fled in haste.

This has been a tale of visions and ideals, of artistry and pomp, of creation and decay, and of many pleasures. It has been led by men with towering imaginations who made magic worlds, many of which have disappeared completely. Sadly, most of the old gardens have lost some of their magic through the disappearance of statues and parterres, the downfall of pergolas, the removal of automata, and, most of all, the drying up of fountains. It is near impossible when visiting the Villa d'Este now to envisage it through 16th-century eyes in all its sparkling glory, or to thrill to the splendours of the old Versailles. We are too sated with modern visions of every sort to find it easy to travel back in time, and we judge these old gardens by later concepts of beauty.

Of course, there is a positive aspect to this examination, since a resurgence of interest in formal gardens has developed at the end of the 20th century. Some gardens, like the King's Garden at Aranjuez, Het Loo and the Privy Garden at Hampton Court Palace, have been recreated with painstaking accuracy; others, like Villandry, have been restored with a dash of imagination added to the old style. Far more await the will and the means to bring them back to life.

With the benefit of hindsight, what stands out most from these centuries of history? That gardens are a form of art; that the Italians made the greatest contribution to the evolution of this art, but that many nations have added their own individual interpretations; that, with surprising ease, ideas crossed frontiers, via the printed word and travellers' accounts, especially after 1600; that architects, designers and gardeners travelled around Europe to observe and work; that features, flowers, scents and sounds were always, as now, prized and appreciated; that gardens were a place of escape, a haven for gentle leisure or entertainment and that, as Francis Bacon wrote nearly 400 years ago, gardens were and are to many people, quite simply *the greatest refreshment to the spirits of man*.[30]

The Walk of the Hundred Fountains at the Villa d'Este, completed by 1573, one of many sophisticated water effects in the gardens at Tivoli.

Notes

Introduction

1. Virgil, p.43

Chapter 1:
The Renaissance

1. Alberti, p.100.
2. Ibid., p.104.
3. Ibid., p.189.
4. Ibid., p.190.
5. Ibid., p.193.
6. Ibid., p.192.
7. Jones and Penny, p.247.
8. Ibid.
9. Montaigne, p.111.
10. Masson, p.206.
11. Agnelli, p.54.
12. Ibid., p.21.
13. Montaigne, p.165.
14. Raymond, p.171.
15. Ibid., p.170.
16. Evelyn, 1959, p.202.
17. Evelyn, 1903, p.169.
18. Raymond, p.167.
19. Montaigne, p.166.
20. Ibid., p.270.
21. Williams, p.200.
22. Hentzner, pp.52–3.
23. Ibid., p.52.
24. Ibid., p.78.

Chapter 2:
Baroque Splendour

1. Evelyn, 1903, p.167.
2. Ibid.
3. Raymond, p.117.
4. Burnet, p.262.
5. Wharton, 1988, p.155.
6. Ibid.
7. Jellicoe, 1937, p.126.
8. Evelyn, 1903, p.43.
9. Ibid., p.441.
10. Boyceau, p.71.
11. Metzger, p.81
12. Ibid.
13. Bacon, p.140.
14. Serres, p.602.
15. Evelyn, 1903, p.263.
16. Ibid., p.44.
17. Bacon, p.137.
18. Aubrey, 1982, p.124.
19. Ibid., p.173.
20. Ibid., p.143.
21. Ibid., p.144.
22. Colvin, p.464.
23. Isaac de Caus, *Wilton Garden*, p.3.
24. Bacon, p.144.
25. Aubrey, p.225.
26. Burnet, p.110.
27. Brosses, de, Vol. 1, p.141.
28. Swinburne, p.252.
29. Holland, p.58.
30. Alvarez de Colmenar, Vol. 11, p.341.
31. Casa Valdés, p.129.

Chapter 3:
The Climax of Baroque

1. Nolhac, de, 1925, p.351.
2. Nolhac, de, 1901, p.49.
3. Walter Harris, p.44.
4. Hoog, p.22.
5. Walton, p.50.
6. Saint-Simon, Vol. IV, p.95.
7. Palatine, p.87.
8. Ibid., p.100.
9. Hazlehurst, pp.353–4.
10. Mitford, p.240.
11. Dezallier d'Argenville, 1709, p.192.
12. Dezallier d'Argenville, tr. John James, p.67.
13. Ibid., p.75.
14. Ibid., p.75.
15. Switzer, 1982, p.vii.
16. Saint-Simon, Vol. 1, p.191.
17. Ibid.
18. Burnet, p.240.
19. Ibid., pp.182.
20. Beckford, 1834, Vol. 1, p.30.
21. Montagu, p.5.
22. Beckford, Vol. 1, p.35.
23. Hendrik de Leth, Het Oud Adelyk Huys en Ridderhofstad Ter Meer, *c.* 1725, and Mattheus Brouerius van Nidek, Het Zegepralend Kennemerland, Amsterdam 1729–32.
24. Walter Harris, p.11.
25. Ibid., p.14.
26. Ibid., p.4.
27. Ibid., p.45.
28. Aubrey, p.145.
29. Fiennes, p.173.
30. Macky, p.202.
31. Switzer, pp.104–5.
32. Defoe, Vol. 11, p.616.
33. Jellicoe et al., p.320.
34. Holland, p.77.
35. Bowe, p.59.

Chapter 4:
Rococo

1. Piganiol de la Force, 1736, Vol.11, p.642.
2. Montagu, Vol. 11, p.62.
3. Painshill Scenes.
4. Climenson, p.192.
5. John Harris, 1993, p.227.
6. Pococke, p.64.
7. Over, plate 12.
8. Overton, plate XXX.
9. Wrighte, Plate XXVIII.
10. Burney, Vol. 11, p.322.
11. Nieuhoff, Vol. 1, p.603.
12. Pennant, p.69.
13. Fitz-Adam, 1753, Vol. 1, p.68.
14. Morris, postscript.
15. Jackson-Stops, 1993, p.219.
16. Chambers, 1972, p.1.
17. Ibid., p.19.
18. Ibid., p.25.
19. Montagu, Vol. 1, p.35.
20. Bayreuth, Vol. 11, p.33.
21. Dashwood, p.226.
22. Ibid., p.227.
23. Kielmansegge, p.167.
24. Ibid., p.168.
25. Le Rouge, *Curiosités de Londres*, 1766, p.69.
26. Voltaire, *Lettre No. 115*, LXX 262.
27. Setterwall, Fogelmarck and Gyllensvärd, p.90.
28. Afonso and Delaforce, p.14.
29. Beckford, 1972, pp.203–5.
30. Bacon, p.137.

Glossary

Allée A straight walk or path

Arbour (1) Arbour, berceau, bower and pergola are all similar, being a series of carpentry or trellis arches forming a tunnel and supporting climbing plants such as vines or roses, or a hedge; the curved arch may also be replaced by a squared top (2) A garden shelter or enclosure, associated with gardens of the 18th century or later

Avenue A wide *allée* or road, often lined with trees

Automata Surprise jets to soak the unwary, and hydraulically operated moving figures and accoustic devices

Azulejo Portuguese term for a glazed tile, either polychrome or blue and white

Baroque A style of art and architecture, originating in early 17th-century Italy, characterised by expansive curves and exuberant decoration and, in the garden, large-scale plans and sweeping vistas

Belvedere A tall ornamental building designed to afford views over the gardens and the landscape

Berceau see *Arbour*

Bosquet a grove of trees or shrubs contained within hedges; also known as a wilderness

Boulingrin French phonetic version of English *bowling green*, a lawn for playing bowls

Bower see *Arbour*

Broderie see *parterre de broderie*

Cabinet de verdure A small green space enclosed by clipped hedges within a *bosquet*, a reduced version of a *salle de verdure*

Cascade A construction to enhance a fall of water

Catena d'acqua A type of cascade in the form of a water staircase

Cedraie Italian term for greenhouses built for the winter protection of *cedro* or lemon trees

Chinoiserie The fashion in Europe for Chinese-style architecture and decoration

Clairvoyée or claire-voie A fence, gate or grille designed to permit views to the scenery beyond

classical Relating to the principles of the architecture of ancient Rome

Classical Relating to the revival in the Renaissance of the principles of the architecture of ancient Rome

Cour d'honneur The principal courtyard

Cupola A small dome surmounting a roof or tower

Estanque Portuguese term for a tank, reservoir or pool

Estrade A tree trained to form two or three flat tiers of foliage

Exedra (1) An open structure perhaps with seating, often semicircular and derived from ancient Rome and Greece
(2) A semicircular wall with architectural embellishments
(3) A semicircle of columns, statues or hedging

Exoticism A fashion for non-European architecture and decoration, usually Muslim, Hindu or oriental

Gazebo A tall compact viewing pavilion usually built into the perimeter wall, similar to but smaller than a *belvedere*

Gazon coupé see *parterre à l'anglaise*

Giochi d'aqua Water games, covering not only surprise jets of water but also *automata*

gothic The style of architecture and decoration in Europe from the 12th to 15th centuries

Gothic A revival in the 18th and 19th centuries of medieval gothic

Gothick A light-hearted revival in mid-18th century of medieval gothic

Grotto Either a natural cave, embellished with shells and stones, or an artifical version housed in an architectural structure

Giardino segreto A secret garden, descended from the medieval *Hortus Conclusus*

Hippodrome A course for horse and chariot races, originating in antiquity and reproduced in gardens from the Renaissance onwards

Hortus Conclusus Latin name for a garden enclosed by walls or fencing

Humanism The study of the language, philosophy and literature of classical antiquity

Iconography The symbolic significance of features in a garden

Koepel A Dutch term to describe a pavilion or gazebo positioned on a canal, in which the upper chamber serves as a lookout and as a room for drinking tea

Knot garden A garden planted with low-growing evergreens in an intricate and interlacing pattern

Landscape garden A garden on a grand scale where natural beauty has been enhanced by improving the contours, adding water, and siting trees and garden buildings in strategic positions

Loggia An open gallery or arcade attached to a building

Mannerism A style that evolved in Italy and reached a peak in the second half of the 16th century; a reaction to the harmony and logic of Classical architecture, Mannerism is artificial, discordant and illogical, and full of surprises; in the garden, it is associated with original use of water

Mount A conical mound of earth, sometimes containing a grotto

Mount Parnassus A high mound of boulders embellished with statues of Apollo and the Muses, a symbol of Apollo's abode in ancient Greece, possibly having a grotto within it

Neoclassicism A movement inspired by Greek and Roman remains of the eastern Mediterranean, which started in the 1750s as a reaction against the excesses of late *Baroque* and *Rococo*

Nymphaeum Of Roman origin, a semicircular structure with fountains and statues of nymphs

Orangery A stone or brick building with large windows facing south for winter protection of subtropical plants; known as a greenhouse in English until the 19th century

Palissade A hedge clipped with architectural precision, pierced by arched windows or with the lower stems cleared of foliage to make a stilt hedge

Palladianism A style derived from the buildings and publications of Palladio

Parterre A symmetrical ornamental garden with elaborate flower beds

Parterre à l'anglaise A parterre of grass with patterns cut out and filled with sand, and sometimes edged with a *plate-bande*; a simpler version of a *parterre de broderie*; also known as a *parterre de gazon coupé*

Parterre de broderie A *parterre* with a pattern resembling embroidery, and made in various combinations of box, turf sand, coloured stone, flowers, shrubs

Parterre de gazon coupé Cut-work, or grass with a pattern cut in turf and filled with sand

Parterre de pièces coupées A parterre with many small beds in various geometric shapes

Patte d'oie The meeting point of straight walks, radiating in a semicircle and suggesting the shape of the foot of a goose

Pergola A series of wooden frames forming a tunnel to support climbing plants; also known as an *arbour* or *bower*

Pièce d'eau A circular, square or rectangular sheet of water, usually edged with stone

Plat A parterre of grass with patterns cut out and filled with sand; the English term for *parterre à l'anglaise*

Plate-bande A narrow border edged with box in which flowers, bulbs and shrubs were grown

Portico A roofed structure supported by columns, often forming the entrance to a temple or house

Putti Cherubs

Quinta Portuguese term for a country house

Renaissance Term applied to the reintroduction of Classical architecture all over Europe in the 15th and 16th centuries

Rustication A method of forming stonework with roughened surfaces and recessed joints, principally employed in Renaissance buildings

Rococo A style of art and decoration, originating in France in the 1720s, and personified in the garden by asymmetrical shapes, playful statues, and an emphasis on intimacy; Rococo gardens in England are small, irregular and whimsical, with buildings in a variety of architectural styles. German Rococo relished architectural variety but within a formal groundplan

Salle de verdure A green room or open space within a *bosquet*, in which there might be treillage features or fountains

Tempietto A small temple

Testata Italian term for the façade of a building

Topiary The art of pruning and trimming plants, e.g. box, yew, rosemary, into ornamental shapes

Treillage A trellis structure, elaborate and architectural

Trellis Timber panels with a simple lattice or criss-cross pattern, for supporting climbing plants

Vertugadin A curved grass bank or amphitheatre

Wilderness An area enclosed by clipped hedges in which trees and shrubs are planted

Bibliography

Ackerman, James S., *Palladio*, Penguin Books, Harmondsworth, 1966.

Adams, William H., *The French Garden, 1500–1800*, George Braziller, New York, 1979, and Scolar Press, London, 1979.

Afonso, Simonetta Luz, and Angela Delaforce, *Palace of Queluz: The Gardens*, Quetzal Editores, Lisbon, 1989.

Agnelli, Marella, *Gardens of the Italian Villas*, Weidenfeld & Nicolson, London, 1987.

Alberti, L.B., *The Architecture of Leon Batista Alberti in Ten Books*, tr. by James Leoni, 4 vols., London, 1755.

Alvarez de Colmenar, Don Juan, *Les Délices de l'Espagne et du Portugal*, Leiden, 1707.

Aston, Nigel, 'The Navy Lark', *Country Life*, August 1, 1991.

Aubrey, John, *Aubrey's Brief Lives*, ed. Oliver Lawson Dick, Penguin Books, Harmondsworth, 1982.

Bacon, Francis, *Essays or Counsels, Civil and Moral*, A. Millar, London, 1755.

Badeslade, Thomas, *Thirty six different views of Noblemen and Gentlemen's Seats in the County of Kent*, London, 1750.

Badeslade, Thomas, and J. Rocque, *Vitruvius Britannicus, Volume the Fourth*, London, 1739.

Bayreuth, Frederica Sophia Wilhelmina, Margravine of, *Memoirs*, 2 vols., Henry Colburn, London, 1812.

Bazin, Germain, *Baroque and Rococo*, Thames & Hudson, London, 1977.

Bazin, Germain, *Paradeisos*, Editions du Chêne, Paris, and Cassell Publishers Ltd, London, 1990.

Beckford, William, *Italy, with Sketches of Spain and Portugal*, 2 vols., London, 1834.

Beckford, William, *Recollections of Alcobaca and Batalha*, Centaur Press, Fontwell, 1972.

Binney, Marcus, *Country Manors of Portugal*, Difel, Lisbon, 1987.

Bithell, Jethro, *Germany*, Methuen, 1932.

Blondel, Jacques-François, *De la Distribution des Maisons de Plaisance*, Paris, Vol. I, 1737, Vol. II, 1738.

Bowe, Patrick, *Gardens of Portugal*, Tauris Parke Books, London, 1989.

Boyceau, Jacques, *Traité du Jardinage selon Les Raisons de la Nature et de l'Art*, Paris, 1638.

Brosses, Président Charles de, *Lettres Historiques et Critiques sur l'Italie*, 3 vols., Paris, 1799.

Burnet, Dr Gilbert, *Some Letters containing an account of what seemed most remarkable in Switzerland, Italy*, London, 1724.

Burney, Fanny, *The Early Diary of Fanny Burney*, George Bell, & Sons, London, 1907.

Burrell, The Hon. Mrs, *Thoughts for Enthusiasts at Bayreuth*, 2 vols., Pickering & Chatto, London, 1888.

Calvert, Frederick, Lord Baltimore, *Gaudia Poetica*, London, 1769.

Campbell, Colen, *Vitruvius Britannicus*, London, Vol. I, 1715, Vol. II, 1717, Vol. III, 1725.

Casa Valdés, Marquesa de, *Spanish Gardens*, Antique Collectors' Club, Woodbridge, 1987.

Castell, Robert, *Villas of the Ancients*, London, 1728.

Caus, Isaac de, *Wilton Garden*, London, 1645.

Caus, Isaac de, *New and Rare Inventions of Water-Works*, London, 1659.

Caus, Salomon de, *Les Raisons des Forces Mouvantes*, Frankfurt, 1615 and 1624.

Caus, Salomon de, *Hortus Palatinus*, Frankfurt, 1620.

Cerceau, Jacques Androuet du, *Les Trois Livres d'Architecture*, Paris, 1559, 1561, 1582, republished Gregg Press Inc., Ridgewood, N.J., 1965.

Cerceau, Jacques Androuet du, *Les Plus Excellents Bastiments de la France*, Book I, Paris, 1576, Book II, Paris, 1607.

Chambers, William, *Designs of Chinese Buildings*, London, 1757.

Chambers, William, *A Dissertation on Oriental Gardening*, London, 1772. Facsimile reprint Gregg Int. Publishers, England, 1972.

Climenson, E.J., ed., *Elizabeth Montagu*, 2 vols., John Murray, London, 1906.

Clunas, Craig, ed., *Chinese Export Art and Design*, Victoria and Albert Museum, London, 1987.

Coffin, David R., *The Villa d'Este at Tivoli*, Princeton, N.J., 1960.

Colonna, Francesco, *Hypnerotomachia Poliphili*, Venice, 1499, facs. ed., Methuen and Co., London, 1904; *Le Songe de Poliphile*, Paris, 1546; *Hypnerotomachia, or The Strife of Love in a Dream*, London, 1592.

Colvin, Howard, *A Bibliographical Dictionary of British Architects*, John Murray, London, 1978.

Comito, Terry, *The Idea of the Garden in the Renaissance,* Harvester Press, Sussex, 1979.

Conner, Patrick, 'China and the Landscape Garden', from *Art History*, Vol. II, No. 4, December 1970.

Cowell, F.R., *The Garden as a Fine Art*, London, Weidenfeld & Nicolson, 1978.

Cox, E.H.M., *A History of Gardening in Scotland*, Chatto & Windus, London, 1935.

Craddock, Anna Francesca, *La Vie Française à la Veille de la Révolution*, 1783–6, tr. Odelphin Balleyguier, Perrin et Cie, Paris, 1911.

Crisp, Sir Frank, *Guide for the Use of Visitors to Friar Park*, Part II, 'Mediaeval Gardens', 4th ed., 1914.

Cuvilliés, François de, Père et Fils, *Oeuvres*, Paris, 1738–72.

Dal Re, Marc'Antonio, *Ville di Delizia*, Milan, 1726 and 1743.

Daniels, Margaret H., *The Garden as Illustrated in Prints*, Metropolitan Museum of Art, New York, 1949.

Dashwood, Sir Francis, *The Dashwoods of West Wycombe*, Aurum Press, London, 1990.

Decker, Paul, *Gothic Architecture Decorated*, London, 1759.

Defoe, Daniel, *A Tour thro' the whole Island of Great Britain*, 2 vols., Peter Davies, London, 1927.

Dennerlein, Ingrid, *Die Gartenkunst der Regence und des Rokoko in Frankreich*, Werner'sche Verlagsgesellschaft, Worms, 1981.

Dezallier d'Argenville, A.J., *La Théorie et la Pratique du Jardinage*, Paris, 1709, tr. John James, London, 1712, republished Gregg Int. Publishers, Farnborough, 1969.

Dezallier d'Argenville, A.J., *La Theorie et la Pratique du Jardinage*, 3rd. ed. reprinted 1739.

Dohna, Countess Ursula, Count Philipp Schonborn and Princess Marianne. Sayn-Wittgenstein-Sayn, *Private Gardens of Germany*, Weidenfeld & Nicolson, London, 1986.

Duchêne, Achille, et Georges Gibault, 'Quatres Siècles de Jardins à la Française', *La Vie à la Campagne*, No. 84, Vol. VII, 15 Mars 1910.

Dunbar, John, *Sir William Bruce*, Scottish Arts Council, 1970.

Erdberg, Eleanor von, *The Chinese Influence on European Garden Structures*, Hacker Art Books, New York, 1985.

Evelyn, John, *The Diary of John Evelyn Esquire FRS*, ed. William Bray, George Newnes Limited, London, Charles Scribner's Sons, New York, 1903.

Evelyn, John, *The Diary of John Evelyn*, ed. E.S. de Beer, Oxford University Press, London, 1959.

Falda, Giovanni Battista, *Il Nuovo Teatro delle Fabriche, et Edificii in prospettiva de Roma Moderna*, Rome, 1665.

Falda, Giovanni Battista, *Li Giardini di Roma*, Rome, 1670.

Falda, Giovanni Battista, *Le Fontane di Roma*, Rome, 1675.

Falda, Giovanni Battista, *Romanorum Fontinalia*, 1685.

Falda, Giovanni Battista, *Li Giardini di Roma*, Nuremberg, 1695.

Farber, Joseph C., and Henry Hope Reed, *Palladio's Architecture and its Influence*, Dover Publications Inc., New York, 1980.

Félibien des Avaux, J.-F., *Les Plans et les Déscriptions de deux des plus belles maisons de campagne de Pline le Consul*, Paris, 1699.

Fenwick, Hubert, *Architect Royal*, Roundwood Press, Kineton, 1970.

Fiennes, Celia, *The Journeys of Celia Fiennes*, ed. Christopher Morris, Cresset Press, London, 1948.

Fischer von Erlach, J.B., *Entwurf einer historischen Architektur*, London, 1730.

Fitz-Adam, Adam, *The World*, London, 1753-6.

Fleming, Laurence, and Alan Gore, *The English Garden*, Michael Joseph, London, 1979.

Fletcher, Banister, *A History of Architecture*, 11th ed., B.T. Batsford, London, 1943.

Ford, Boris, ed., *18th Century Britain*, Cambridge University Press, Cambridge, 1991.

Ford, Boris, ed., *17th Century Britain*, Cambridge University Press, 1992.

Francesco di Giorgio Martini, *Trattati di architettura ingegneria e arte militare*, Edizione il Polifilio, Milan, 1967.

Francini, Alessandro, *Livre d'Architecture*, Paris, 1631.

Ganay, Ernest de, *Bibliographie de l'Art des Jardins*, Bibliothèque des Arts Décoratifs, Paris, 1989.

Gautier, Théophile, *Voyage en Espagne*, Bibliothèque Charpentier, Paris, 1902.

Gibbs, James, *A Book of Architecture*, London, 1728.

Girouard, Mark, *Robert Smythson and the Elizabethan Country House*, Yale University Press, New Haven and London, 1983.

Grantham, A.E., *The Life and Times of Prince Henry of Prussia, 1726-1802*, The Bodley Head, London, 1938.

Halde, J.-B. du, *Déscription géographique, historique, chronologique, politique et physique de l'Empire de la Chine*, Paris, 1735.

Halfpenny, W., *New Designs for Chinese Temples*, London, 1750.

Halfpenny, W. and J., *Rural Architecture in the Chinese Taste*, London, 1750.

Halfpenny, W. and J., *Rural Architecture in the Gothick Taste*, London, 1752.

Halfpenny, W. and J., *Chinese and Gothic Architecture properly Ornamented*, London, 1752.

Harcourt, Duc d', *Traité de la Décoration des Dehors des Jardins et des Parcs*, Paris, 1919.

Harris, Eileen, *British Architectural Books and Writers, 1556-1785*, Cambridge University Press, Cambridge, 1990.

Harris, John, 'A pioneer in gardening: Dickie Bateman re-assessed', *Apollo*, October 1993, p.227.

Harris, John and Gordon Higgott, *Inigo Jones, Complete Architectural Drawings*, Philip Wilson Publishers, 1989.

Harris, Walter, *A Description of the King's Royal Palace and Gardens at Loo*, London, 1699.

Hazlehurst, F. Hamilton, *Gardens of Illusion: The Genuis of André le Nôtre*, Vanderbilt University Press, Nashville, 1982.

Headley, Gwyn, and Wim Meulenkamp, *Follies: A National Trust Guide*, Jonathan Cape, London, 1986.

Henderson, Paula, 'Sir Francis Bacon's Water Gardens at Gorhambury', *Garden History*, Vol. 20, No. 2.

Hentzner, Paul, *Travels in England during the Reign of Queen Elizabeth*, Cassell & Co., London, 1894.

Hibbert, Christopher, *The Rise and Fall of the House of Medici*, Penguin Books, Harmondsworth, 1979.

Hirschfeld, C.C.L., *Theorie der Gartenkunst*, Leipzig, 1779-85

Hobhouse, Penelope and Patrick Taylor, *The Gardens of Europe*, George Philip, London, 1990.

Hoog, Simone, ed. *Louis XIV, Manière de montrer les Jardins de Versailles*, Éditions de la Réunion des Musées Nationaux, Paris, 1982.

Holland, Elizabeth Lady, *The Spanish Journal of Elizabeth Lady Holland*, Longmans, Green & Co., London, 1910.

Honour, Hugh, and John Fleming, *A World History of Art*, Laurence King, London, 1991.

Hunt, John Dixon, *William Kent: Landscape Garden Designer*, A. Zwemmer, London, 1987.

Impey, Oliver, *Chinoiserie*, Oxford University Press, London, 1977.

Jackson, Catherine Charlotte, Lady, *Fair Lusitania*, Richard Bentley, London, 1874.

Jackson-Stops, Gervase, *An English Arcadia, 1600-1990*, The National Trust, London, 1992.

Jackson-Stops, Gervase, *Historic Houses and Collections Annual 1993*, The National Trust and *Apollo* Magazine.

Jacques, David, 'The Chief Ornament' of Gray's Inn: The Walks from Bacon to Brown', *Garden History*, Vol. 17, No.1.

Jellicoe, Geoffrey A., *Gardens of Europe*, Blackie & Son Ltd., London, 1937, Antique Collectors' Club, Woodbridge, 1995.

Jellicoe, Geoffrey A. and Susan, Patrick Goode and Michael Lancaster, *The Oxford Companion to Gardens*, Oxford University Press, Oxford and New York, 1986.

Jones, Roger and Nicholas Penny, *Raphael*, Yale University Press, New Haven and London, 1983.

Kielmansegge, Count Frederick, *Diary of a Journey to England in the Years 1761-62*, Longmans, Green & Co., London New York, 1902.

Kleiner, Salomon, *Schönbornschlösser*, Mainz, 1726.

Kleiner, Salomon, *Résidences Memorables de Monseigneur le Prince Eugène François de Savoie*, Augsburg, 1731.

Kip, Johannes, *Britannia Illustrata*, London, Vol. I, 1720, Vol. II, 1740.

Land Use Consultants, *Greenwich Park: Historical Survey*, 1986.

Langley, Batty and Thomas Langley, *Gothic Architecture Improved by Rules and Proportions*, London, 1742.

Lauro, Giacomo, *Antiquae Urbis Splendor*, Rome, 1612-14.

Leanti, Arcangiolo, *Lo Stato presente della Sicilia*, Palermo, 1761.

Le Rouge, George-Louis, *Curiosités de Londres et de l'Angleterre*, 2nd ed., Bordeaux, 1766.

Le Rouge, George-Louis, *Détails des nouveaux jardins à la mode: Jardins Anglo-Chinois*, 21 cahiers except 5, 20 and 21, Paris, 1776-87.

Levron, Jacques, *Royal Châteaux of the Ile de France*, George Allen & Unwin, London, 1965.

Lloyd, Robert, *The Poetical Works of Robert Lloyd*, Vol. I, London, 1774.

Louis XIV/Cabinet du Roy, *Les Plaisirs de L'Isle Enchantée*, Paris, 1664-1727.

Macartney, Mervyn, *English Houses and Gardens in the 17th and 18th Centuries*, Batsford, London, 1908.

Macdougall, Elisabeth, and F. Hamilton Hazlehurst, eds., *The French Formal Garden*, Dumbarton Oaks, Washington D.C., 1974.

Macky, John, *Journey through Scotland*, London, 1732.

Markham, Gervase, *A Way to get Wealth*, London, 1623.

Masson, Georgina, *Italian Gardens*, Thames & Hudson, London, 1961.

Merigot, *Promenade ou Itineraire des Jardins de Chantilly*, Paris, 1791.

Metzger, John, *The Castle of Heidelberg and its Gardens*, Heidelberg, 1830.

Meulenkamp, Wim, 'Turkish Tents in the Netherlands', *Follies*, Spring 1990.

Meusniers, L., *Veuë du Palais, Jardins et Fontaines d'Arangonesse*, Paris, 1665.

Mitford, Nancy, *The Sun King*, Hamish Hamilton, London, 1966.

Mollet, André, *Le Jardin de Plaisirs*, Stockholm, 1651.

Montagu, Lady Mary Wortley, *Letters written during her Travels in Europe, Asia and Africa*, 2 vols., London, 1763.

Montaigne, Michel de, *Montaigne's Journey to Italy in 1580 and 1581*, tr. E.J. Trechmann, Leonard and Virginia Woolf, London, 1929.

Morris, Robert, *The Architectural Remembrancer*, London, 1751.

Mosser, Monique, and Georges Teyssot, eds., *The History of Garden Design*, Thames & Hudson, London, 1991.

Murphy, James, *Travels in Portugal in 1789 and 1790*, London, 1795.

Nieuhoff, John, *An Embassy from the East India Company of the United Provinces to the Grand Tartar Cham, Emperor of China*, 3 vols., London, 1673.

Nolhac, Pierre de, *La Création de Versailles*, L. Bernard, Paris, 1901.

Nolhac, Pierre de, *Versailles*, Louis Conard, Paris, 1925.

Nyrerod, Anna-Lisa, *Lusthus*, Nordiska Museet, Uddevalla, 1979.

Over, Charles, *Ornamental Architecture in the Gothic, Chinese and Modern Taste*, London 1758.

Overton, Thomas Collins, *Original Designs of Temples*, London, 1766.

Paine, James, *Plans, Elevations and Sections of Noblemen and Gentlemen's Houses*, London, 1767.

Painshill Scenes (guidebook), Painshill Park Trust, 1991.

Palatine, Elizabeth Charlotte, Princess Palatine and Duchess of Orléans, *Letters from Liselotte*, ed. Maria Kroll, Victor Gollancz, London, 1970.

Palladio, Andrea, *I Quattro Libri dell' Architettura*, Venice, 1570.

Palladio, Andrea, *Architecture in Four Books*, Benjamin Cole, London, 1736.

Pennant, Thomas, *Journey from Chester to London*, B. White, London, 1782.

Pérac, Etienne du, *I Vestigi dell' Antichita di Roma*, Rome, 1575.

Pérac, Etienne du, *Topgraphical Study in Rome in 1581*, ed. Thomas Ashby, Roxburghe Club, London, 1916.

Perelle, Nicolas, *Vues des Belles Maisons de France*, 1685.

Perelle, Nicolas, *Suecia Antiqua et Hodierna*, 1723.

Pevsner, Nikolaus, *An Outline of European Architecture*, Penguin, Harmondsworth, 1990.

Piganiol de la Force, J.A., *Les Délices de Versailles, de Trianon et de Marly*, 2 vols., 2nd ed., Amsterdam, 1717.

Piganiol de la Force, J.A., *Description de Paris, de Versailles de Marly, de Meudon, de St. Cloud, de Fontainebleau*, 2 vols., Theodore le Gras, Paris, 1736.

Pococke, Dr Richard, *Travels through England during 1750, 1751 and later years*, The Camden Society, 1888.

Powell, Nicolas, *From Baroque to Rococo*, Faber & Faber, London, 1959.

Ramsey, Alex and Helena Attlee, *Italian Gardens*, Robertson McCarta, London, 1989.

Raymond, John, *An Itinerary Contayning a Voyage Made Through Italy*, London, 1648.

Rigaud, Jean, *Receuil de cent vingt-une des plus belles vues de palais, châteaux dessinés en 1780*, Paris, c. 1785.

Rigaud, Jean Antoine, *Bref Recueil des Choses rares, notables, antiques d'Italie*, Aix, 1601.

Ripa, Matteo, *Memoirs during Thirteen Years Residence at the Court of Peking*, John Murray, London, 1844.

Ripa, Matteo, *Views at the Summer Palace at Jehol*, Department of Oriental Antiquities, British Museum, London.

Rowan, Alastair, *Garden Buildings*, Country Life Books, London, 1968.

Rubio, N.M., *El Jardin Meridional*, Salvat Editores S.A., Barcelona, 1934.

Saint-Simon, Duc de, *Memoirs*, tr. K. Wormeley, 4 vols., William Heinemann, London, 1899.

Saudan, Michel, and Sylvia Saudan-Skira, *De Folie en Folies*, La Bibliothèque des Arts, Geneva, 1987.

Serres, Olivier de, *Le Théâtre d'Agriculture*, Paris, 1600.

Setterwall, Ake, Stig Fogelmarck, and Bo Gyllensvärd, *The Chinese Pavilion at Drottningholm*, Allhems Forlag, Malmo, 1974.

Sitwell, Sacheverell, *The Netherlands*, B.T. Batsford, London, 1948.

Smith, Robert C., *The Art of Portugal*, Weidenfeld & Nicolson, London, 1968.

Stein, Henri, *Les Jardins de France des origines à la fin du XVIII siècle*, Longuet, Paris, 1913.

Stoopendael, Daniel, *De Zegepraalende Vecht*, Amsterdam, 1719.

Strong, Roy, *The Renaissance Garden in England*, Thames & Hudson, London, 1979.

Swinburne, Henry, *Travels through Spain in the years 1775 and 1776*, London, 1779.

Switzer, Stephen, *Ichnographia, or The Nobleman, Gentleman and Gardener's Recreation*, 3 vols., London, 1718.

Symes, Michael, *The English Rococo Garden*, Shire Garden History, Princes Risborough, 1991.

Temple, Sir William, *Upon the Gardens of Epicurus*, Chatto & Windus, London, 1908.

Thacker, Christopher, *The History of Gardens*, Croom Helm, London, 1979.

Van der Groen, Jan, *Den Nederlantsen Hovenier*, Amsterdam, 1669, reprinted Stichting Matrijs, Utrecht, 1988.

Virgil, *Eclogues*, tr. C. Day-Lewis, *The Eclogues, Georgics and Aeneid of Virgil*, Oxford University Press, Oxford, 1972.

Visentini, Margherita Azzi, and Italo Zannier, eds., *Il giardino veneto: Storia e conservazione*, Electa Spa, Milan, 1988.

Voltaire, Francois-Marie Arouet, *Oeuvres complètes de Voltaire*, Vol. 53 of 70, Société Littéraire-Typographique, 1785.

Vries, H. Vredeman de, *Hortorum viridariorumque elegantes et multi plicis formae*, Antwerp, 1583.

Walton, Guy, *Louis XIV's Versailles*, Viking, Harmondsworth, 1986.

Wharton, Edith, *Italian Villas and Their Gardens*, The Century Co., New York, 1904, reprinted by The Classical American Series in Art and Architecture, Da Capo Press, New York, 1988.

Williams, Clare, *Thomas Platter's Travels in England*, Jonathan Cape, London, 1937.

Woodbridge, Kenneth, *Princely Gardens*, Thames & Hudson, London, 1986.

Woodward, Frank, *Oxfordshire Parks*, Oxfordshire Museum Services, 1982.

Woolfe and Gandon, *Vitruvius Britannicus*, London, Vol. IV, 1767 and Vol. V, 1771.

Worsley, Giles, 'The Lost Decade', *The Georgian Group: Report and Journal*, 1991.

Wright, Thomas, *Arbours and Grottos*, Scolar Press, London 1979.

Wrighte, William, *Grotesque Architecture, or Rural Amusement*, London, 1767.

Page numbers in *italic* refer to the illustrations and captions

Picture Acknowledgements

Bibliothèque National de France:	12, 40, 42
St. Mark's Library, Venice:	13
Photographs by May Woods:	15, 26, 27, 28, 29, 31, 35, 36, 37, 38, 39, 83, 91, 92, 93, 93, 94, 96, 97, 99, 110, 120, 125, 126, 133, 135, 136, 138, 139, 141, 146, 147, 154, 156, 157, 171, 173, 179, 191, 193, 195, 196, 197, 200, 201, 202, 204, 205, 206, 209, 211
By permission of the British Library:	16, 17, 18, 19, 20, 21, 24, 25, 30, 33, 34, 41, 43, 46, 47, 53, 55, 59, 60, 61, 62, 63, 64, 68, 69, 70, 72, 73, 74, 75, 77, 78, 79, 80, 81, 85, 87, 88, 90, 104, 107, 108, 109, 111, 112, 118, 119, 121, 124, 128, 132, 134, 142, 145, 148, 149, 160, 161, 162, 163, 165, 166, 168, 175, 176, 178, 180, 181, 182, 184, 185, 186, 191, 192, 194, endpapers
Scala/Firenze:	23
Photograph from Parco di Mostri, Bomarzo:	32
Louvre, Dept. des Arts Graphiques:	45
By courtesy of the Marquess of Salisbury:	49
The Royal Collections © 1996, Her Majesty Queen Elizabeth II:	50, 137
Ashmolean Museum, Oxford:	51
Photo Vatican Museums:	56
Kunstmuseum, Basel:	65
May Woods:	66, 129, 144, 189, 204
Copyright British Museum:	76, 122, 130, 177
British Architectural Library, RIBA, London:	84, 86, 127, 164, 170, 172
London Library:	98, 101
Réunion des Musées Nationaux, Copyright PHOTO R.N.M.	103, 114, 115
Editions Estel:	116
Photographs by Jonathan Maher:	150, 152
Copyright The Frick Collection, New York:	158
A private collection:	169
Royal Academy of Fine Arts, Stockholm:	174
Photo AKG London:	183, 199
Sir Francis Dashwood, Bt., photograph Courtauld Institute of Art:	187

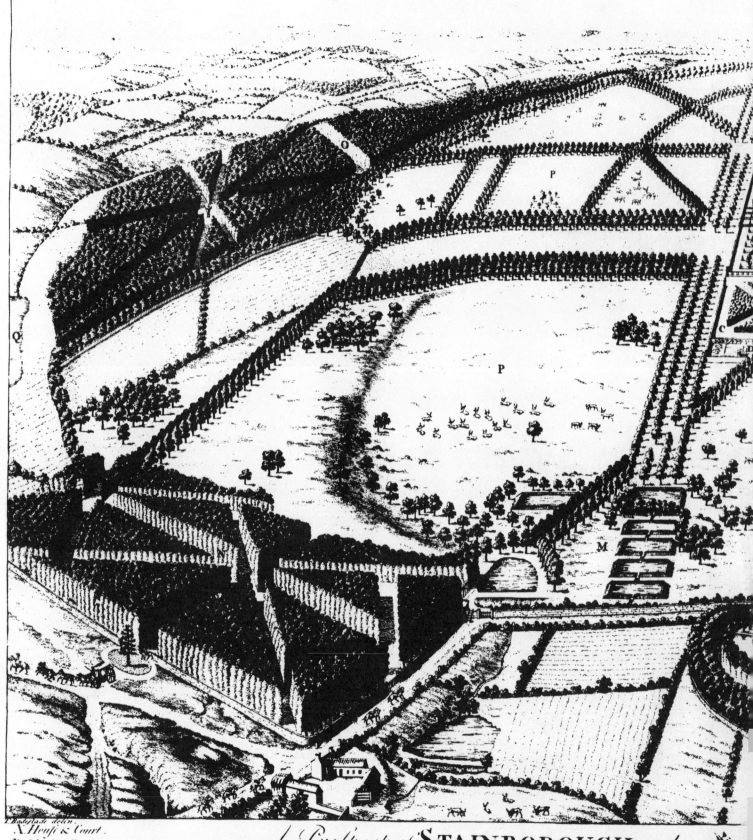

P. Boterscade delin.

A. House & Court.
B. Pleasure Gardens.
C. Fruit-Garden.
D. Ever-Green & Flower-Gardens.
E. Kitchen Gardens.
F. Orangerie & Gardens.
G. Wentworth Castle.
H. Law-Wood 100 Acres.

A Prospect of **STAINBOROUGH**, and of **YORK**, one of the Seats of the Right Viscount Wentworth of Wentworth; Raby, Newmarch, and Oversley, and Knight